The Federfuchser/*Penpusher*
from Lessing to Grillparzer
A Study Focused on Grillparzer's
Ein Bruderzwist in Habsburg

Concentrating on Klesel's role in Franz Grillparzer's *Ein Bruderzwist in Habsburg*, William Reeve argues that Klesel represents the culmination of a literary type – the *Federfuchser*, or pen-pushing secretary. Evolving out of the political and social conditions of the late eighteenth and early nineteenth centuries, the secretary is an intellectually gifted individual who acts as the agent of a less gifted, usually aristocratic, patron. In the secretary's hand, the pen proves mightier than the sword.

Reeve provides a detailed discussion of Klesel's importance in *Ein Bruderzwist in Habsburg* and examines possible predecessors for the *Federfuchser*: Wurm from Friedrich von Schiller's *Kabale und Liebe*, the *Sekretär* in Johann Wolfgang von Goethe's *Die natürliche Tochter*, and Leonhard in Friedrich Hebbel's *Maria Magdalene*. He focuses on the features they share, such as deep-seated resentment of social superiors who, by a mere accident of birth, have power over them and, above all, the cunning that they use to overcome their social disqualifications.

WILLIAM C. REEVE is professor of German literature, Queen's University.

The Federfuchser/ Penpusher from Lessing to Grillparzer

A Study Focused on Grillparzer's *Ein Bruderzwist in Habsburg*

WILLIAM C. REEVE

McGill-Queen's University Press
Montreal & Kingston • London • Buffalo

Legal deposit third quarter 1995
Bibliothèque nationale du Québec

Printed in the United States on acid-free paper

This book has been published with the help of
a grant from the Canadian Federation for the
Humanities, using funds provided by the Social
Sciences and Humanities Research Council of
Canada.

Canadian Cataloguing in Publication Data

Reeve, William C., 1943–
   The federfuchser, penpusher from Lessing to
Grillparzer : a study focused on Grillparzer's Ein
Bruderzwist in Habsburg
Includes bibliographical references and index.
ISBN 0-7735-1298-5
1. German drama – 18th century – History and
criticism. 2. German drama – 19th century –
History and criticism. 3. Secretaries in literature.
4. Grillparzer, Franz, 1791–1872. Ein Bruderzwist in
Habsburg. I. Title.
PT2259.B8R44 1995   832'.609'352   C95-900235-9

Typeset in Palatino 10/12
by Caractéra production graphique, Quebec City

Contents

Acknowledgments

Of the many people who have contributed to the realization of this monograph, I am especially grateful to Professor Friedrich Gaede and Professor Eckehard Catholy for their useful suggestions and to Professor G.W. Field for his careful proof-reading and constructive criticism of the manuscript. I should also like to recognize Brigitte and Bill McConnell for the much appreciated time and effort spent on the computer.

The Federfuchser/Penpusher
from Lessing to Grillparzer

CHAPTER ONE

Introduction

If one consults the extensive secondary literature dealing with Grill-parzer's *Ein Bruderzwist in Habsburg*, one is struck by the often contradictory interpretations it has inspired. At the beginning of the twentieth century, Volkelt faulted "starke Mängel" in the unravelling of its plot and the "dumpfen, drückenden Schluß"[1] and more recently Thompson registered a tendency to designate it as " theatrically his least effective play."[2] In direct contrast others have extolled *Ein Bruderzwist* as "die mächtigste geschichtliche Tragödie, die bis jetzt ein Deutscher geschaffen hat"[3] or "das gewaltigste Werk Grillparzers."[4] Fricke characterized it as "Summe und Ende von Grillparzers Dramatik,"[5] but then would seem to have retracted his praise when he also pronounced it the dramatist's "bühnenfremdestes Stück."[6] In its defence, Hering even goes so far as to blame an uneducated public for its lack of success upon the stage: "Der Zuschauer von heute ist leider nicht mehr im Besitze der Kenntnisse von Regeln eines normalen abendfüllenden fünfaktigen Stücks."[7]

The recognition of the central, unifying role assumed by Rudolf represents a rare example of unanimity amongst the commentators. Griesmayer makes the typical observation: "Eine Person, Kaiser Rudolf II, steht als Mittelpunkt, als Zentralfigur, da. Mit ihm ist alles Geschehen direkt oder indirekt verknüpft, alle Personen müssen sich zu ihm stellen, stehen zu ihm in engstem Bezug."[8] And yet when it is a question of assessing the emperor's personality, his attitudes and his actions, the note of contradiction surfaces again. On one side of the debate, Sternberger,[9] Wells,[10] or Naumann defend his policies and outlook: "Das Zögern des Kaisers ist gerechtfertigt,"[11] while on the other side Kleinstück,[12] Mason,[13] or David have mounted a serious challenge to this more positive evaluation: "Die Politik des Zögerns ist Ausdruck seiner [i.e., Rudolf's] Schwäche, nicht seiner Weisheit."[14]

Whereas there can be no doubt as to Rudolf's focal position in the tragedy – indeed Langvik-Johannessen has argued, "Die Personen sind mehr oder weniger Objektivierungen von verschiedenen Eigenschaften der Hauptperson"[15] – a consensus has yet to be reached on his main antagonist. At the most general level, the emperor and with him most critics see in the "Zeit" his "eigentliche[n] aktive[n] Gegenspieler,"[16] but this solution only begs the question as to who is the best dramatic, i.e., concrete embodiment of such an abstraction. Two major candidates[17] have emerged, Don Cäsar and Melchior Klesel: "Don Cäsar ist der eigentliche Gegenspieler des Kaisers";[18] "[Klesel] ist der eigentliche Gegenspieler Rudolfs."[19] After the emperor, his illegitimate son has attracted the most critical attention but as a particularly pernicious sign of the times and as an extension of the irrational side of his father.[20] Surprisingly enough, however, given the extent to which Klesel either directly or indirectly controls the turn of events within *Ein Bruderzwist*, the secondary literature, with one or two exceptions, has chosen to pass over the priest and his importance. One may attribute this omission to an overstatement of Mathias's function and thus a failure on the part of some to recognize his total reliance upon his servant, as for example in Naumann's analysis: "Mathias ist ein Rebell wie Wallenstein. Aber nicht wie bei Schiller wird gezeigt, wie die Rebellion sich im einzelnen Individuum als dem Träger der tragischen Einheit auswirkt. Vielmehr ist das Schicksal des Mathias die Einsicht in seine Verantwortung, in die Wirkung seines Tuns auf das Ganze."[21] The interdependence between puppet and puppeteer – "Mathias ist eine Marionette in [Klesel's] Händen"[22] – also tends to reflect adversely upon the handler since he loses his audience's interest once he forfeits his puppet. It follows from this line of reasoning that Klesel has no significance of his own: "Grillparzer has exaggerated his influence in order to accentuate his master's weakness."[23] Although acknowledging Klesel as the "Anstifter des Verrats," the one who "das Feuer schürt und den Konflikt weitertreibt," David dismisses him as a poorly conceived, stereotypical villain whose "Ruchlosigkeit … wirklich zu offensichtlich [ist]"[24] and who thus presumably deserves to be ignored. Such a view only encourages the neglect of Grillparzer's most intriguing intriguer, for no single individual, including the emperor himself, determines the course of the dramatic action and mirrors the changing values of the age in the political and social spheres more than does the "Priester," "Bischof," "Erzbischof," "Kardinal," "Sekretär," "Diener," and "Vizekaiser" Klesel.

Other critics have variously classified the Priest as "Mathias' 'Souffleur',"[25] "zugleich Zerrbild und Symbol der kaiserlichen Macht,"[26] "geballte, zielstrebige Energie am Werk,"[27] "der eigentliche Stifter und Drahtzieher des Bruderzwists,"[28] "der Bäckerssohn und Manager des Bruderzwists,"[29] [Mathias'] böser Geist,"[30] and "the *éminence grise* behind [Rudolf's] brother's treachery."[31] To date Thompson has offered by far the most extensive treatment of his role in the drama in an informative article entitled "Grillparzer's Political Villains," an examination of Zawisch von Rosenberg (*König Ottokars Glück und Ende*) and Klesel as practitioners of Machiavellian political strategies. "Of the two Klesel is the more professional politician, but Zawisch is the more obvious Machiavellian character."[32] Having a binary focus, Thompson's essay does not in my opinion do full justice to the priest, but it has paved the way for a greater appreciation of his function within *Ein Bruderzwist*, especially in its indebtedness to the Machiavellian mould.[33] The historical Klesel in a letter to Archduke Ferdinand may have even suggested this approach to the dramatist:

Merkwürdige Stelle wo Klesel von sich selbst sagt: ist es so gut, daß ich ein Pfaff und in keinem geheimen rath bin, ich würde sonst einigen *Machiavellisten* einen *Machiavelum* vor das Loch stellen und mit gleicher Münze bezalen wollen. In dem Calender saget es: gut ackern, gut säen, gut kriegen, sehe ich mit geschwindigkeit und guten Worten, gut Land und Leut einnehmen, so wollt ich einem mit guten Worten das Maul füllen [Klesel as Mathias's "Souffleur"] und danebens gewißlich nichts vergessen, was mir das leben oder die erfahrung in die Hand gäb.[34]

In this amazingly candid confession, one senses both the frustration and resentment of the "Pfaff" vis-à-vis those in a position of political authority, the desire for an opportunity to even accounts in the here and now, a scarcely repressed will to power over "gut Land und Leut," and finally a willingness to manipulate others and to exploit whatever means available, i.e., "was [ihm] das leben oder die erfahrung in die Hand gäb" to achieve his end. The historical model thus proffers an accurate summary of the motives prompting his dramatic equivalent.

Because of pronouncements by the author such as, "Rudolf soll in D[on] Cäsar nicht nur ein Bild seiner Zeit sondern auch ein Vorbild der künftigen, der *heutigen* [Grillparzer's emphasis] sehen,"[35] commentators have not hesitated to depict *Ein Bruderzwist* as owing a greater debt to the first half of the nineteenth century than to its historical setting two hundred years earlier. Accordingly, what has been perceived as a wholly negative portrayal of Klesel, van Stockum interprets as a symptom of mid nineteenth-century "Antiklerikalismus,"[36] while David explains the bishop's pejorative characterization as a vehicle to release Grillparzer's pent-up hostility towards the Church: "Als Kirchenfeind macht er einen Priester zum Motor des Dramas, wobei er ihn nach Belieben belasten kann."[37] This line of interpretation may stand up to scrutiny in view of Grillparzer's substantial social and professional set-back as a civil servant because of his "Geschichte mit dem Papst,"[38] but it does not take into account either Klesel's more positive presentation in the last act – his prophetic words and his dignified exit – or the social implications of his crucial but ignored capacity as the pen-pusher.

In order to impose a desirable limitation upon his creative fantasy, Grillparzer made extensive use of historical works dealing with the period up to the outbreak of the Thirty Years' War.[39] Josef von Hammer-Purgstall's *Khlesl's Leben* in four volumes supplied the major source for his depiction of Melchior Klesel, as indicated by his copious notes which Helmut Bachmaier has conveniently collected and arranged chronologically under the heading "Selbstaussagen des Autors zum Werk."[40] In reading through this material, one cannot help noticing the obvious fascination this priest, "einst lutherischer(?) Beckerjunge, zuletzt Erzbischof von Wien"[41] exerted upon the dramatist. These records contain a detailed account of Klesel's career – indeed, in terms of sheer volume, he ranks second only to Rudolf in the "Selbstaussagen" – and, as pointed out earlier in the reference to "Machiavellisten," already suggest possible motivation. In this regard one particular entry deserves special consideration: "Wenn man Klesels Religionseifer bei seinem Beginn und seine Lauheit im Verfolge betrachtet, so wird Einem klar, daß er nur einen Gegenstand für *Herrschbegierde* suchte und die entgegengesetztesten ihm gleich willkommen waren."[42] We shall later ascertain that the key word the play consistently associates with Klesel, his leitmotif, is "Macht": "Der Kirche *Macht* bekleidet mit dem Purpur, / Der mich den Königen zur Seite stellt."[43] This exploitation of the Roman Catholic Church as an instrument to obtain and exercise the power denied him by his lowly birth can be further confirmed in Grillparzer's judgment that Klesel's real interest lay in politics rather than in religion: "Klesel trotz seiner aufrichtig gemeinten Weigerung (da er vielmehr nach Theilnahme an den Staatsgeschäften trachtete) zum Bischof von Wien ernannt."[44] He is the only character whom *Ein Bruderzwist* links to the concept of "Politik."

Grillparzer's comments also underscore the often conflicting historical evaluation of Klesel, a feature which may account for the contradictory responses of unmitigated disdain but also grudging respect to his actions and utterances in the drama. Offsetting the ambitious, unscrupulous priest – in "Brief an die Erzherzogin Maria zeigt er sich als ein schändlicher angeberischer Pfaffe"[45] – the notes also present the image of a traditional, genuinely devout man of God who died in 1630 of dysentery "mit großer Seelenstärke, ja heldenmüthig": "Seine vorzüglichen Eigenschaften: Die Ehrfurcht gegen seine von ihm selbst bekehrte Mutter. Seine Enthaltsamkeit und Keuschheit. Seine Mäßigkeit. Sein Eifer in täglicher Lesung der vorgeschriebenen Gebete, so wie in Celebrirung oder Anhören der Messe."[46] Finally the "Selbstaussagen" leave the reader with the distinct impression that the archbishop was a prominent, if not the central, player at the beginning of the Thirty Years' War – "Klesel ist der Mittelpunkt des Ganzen [Mathias's decision to use the "akatholischen Stände" against the emperor]"[47] – an assumption on the part of the dramatist not shared by historians. Phrases such as "vornähmlich auf den Rath Klesels"[48] or "auf Anstiften Klesels"[49] in conjunction with Mathias as subject of the sentence already anticipate the puppet/puppeteer relationship in which paradoxically the servant/master roles are reversed.[50]

As part of a brief historical sketch, "Realgeschichtlicher Hintergrund des Dramas,"[51] Bachmaier puts forward the following comparison of the imaginary versus the real figure: "Kardinal Melchior Khlesl (1552–1630), dem in Grillparzers Drama der Part des pfäffisch durchtriebenen Intriganten in Purpur, des Kabinettstückchen – Lieferanten zugedacht ist, war in Wirklichkeit ein weitsichtiger, um den Ausgleich der Konfessionen und Stände bemühter Diplomat und Politiker. Jedoch hatte er sich durch sein oft taktloses und überhebliches Betragen Feindschaften zugezogen; als maßgeblicher Berater (im Volksmund galt er als der 'Vizekaiser') von Mathias war er im näheren Umkreis Rudolfs verhaßt."[52] If we juxtapose what Bachmaier calls "Wirklichkeit" with its dramatic recreation, are reality and fantasy really that far apart? Act five demonstrates that Klesel is more "weitsichtig" than any other person in the play with the possible exception of Rudolf, and the archbishop's plan includes reaching an "Ausgleich der Konfessionen und Stände":

KLESEL   Ihr irrt; ein fester Plan beherrscht das Ganze
           Und jeder Schritt führt näher an das Ziel.
FERDINAND Doch dieses Ziel, sag' ich, es ist verderblich.
           Ausgleichung heißts, Gleichgültigkeit für Jedes.   (2467–70)

If diplomacy means convincing people to do freely what one wants them to do without their being conscious of the manipulation involved, then the second act constitutes a diplomatic *tour de force* engineered by a mere secretary. There can be no doubt as to Klesel's credentials as a skilful politician, and what could be more tactless and arrogant than his appearance as an emissary of peace at the end of the third act?

> JULIUS   Und war kein Anderer als ihr zu finden
>   Zu solcher Botschaft, die fast klingt wie Hohn?
> KLESEL   Vielleicht weil ich allein kein Schranz' und Höfling,
>   Gewohnt zu sagen gradaus was gemeint.   (1766–9)

While he is clearly Mathias's "maßgeblicher Berater," the vernacular designation "Vizekaiser" describes more accurately the unusual relationship between "Herr" and "Diener," and the animosity between Rudolf's faction and the bishop's underlies the question and reply of the preceding dialogue. Hence Bachmaier may have only illustrated the old cliché that fiction can often be truer than fact.

In terms of actual historical precedents, Klesel has been likened to Cardinals Richelieu and Wolsey, especially the latter as he appears in Shakespeare's play *Henry VIII*.[53] Wassermann has submitted a possible contemporary model: "Der von Grillparzer zwar nicht geliebt, aber doch respektierte Metternich hat manche Züge zu diesem Bild geliehen. Er hat gerade Eigenschaften, die den Mitgliedern der Dynastie fehlen."[54] Grillparzer's *Selbstbiographie* fully substantiates Wassermann's assessment of the dramatist's attitude towards the man who virtually ruled the Danube Monarchy from 1815 till 1848 in the name of an ineffectual Habsburg regime: "Fürst Metternich ... stand geradezu an der Spitze der Verfolgung [the persecution suffered subsequent to the publication of the poem "Campo vaccino"], wenn nicht vielmehr seine elende Umgebung, die den *ausgezeichneten* Mann im Jahre 1848 zu so schmählichem Falle vorbereitete."[55] This ambivalent attitude – resentment toward the individual who nominally at least led the campaign to discredit Grillparzer and thus ruined his future career prospects in the civil service and admiration for the statesman/politician of proven administrative/leadership qualities – may add another reason for the inconsistent, contradictory reaction provoked by Klesel.

When Thompson considers likely literary prototypes, he proposes Goethe's Alba in *Egmont* and Schiller's Leicester in *Maria Stuart*, but, as he himself concedes, "Klesel has little in common with these figures."[56] The candidate he finally settles on and for whom he attempts to make a case is Schiller's Octavio Piccolomini from *Wallenstein*, "an equally skilful political operator" who like "Klesel ... is instrumental in securing the downfall of the hero, against whom he operates a treacherous and secret campaign."[57] Although this comparison does produce some striking parallels, there remain basic discrepancies other than those Thompson acknowledges in his article, the most significant of which is the fact that both Wallenstein and Octavio are born aristocrats. One could never say of the latter, "Der Bauer steckt noch ganz in seinem Leibe / Mit des Emporgekommnen Übermut"(2580–1). Thus the connection between Wallenstein and Octavio does not exhibit the same dialectic of master/servant or sword/pen so crucial to an understanding of *Ein Bruderzwist* and its implied sociological message.

It is possible to trace aspects of Klesel's literary pedigree as far back as the Roman comedies of Plautus and Terence in whose works slaves provide two crucial ingredients: humor and trickery. "The slaves most active in both capacities are the *serui callidi*, the cunning masters of intrigue ... Their schemes are ingenious and, despite moments of helplessness and despair, they carry their trickery through to a successful conclusion and boast of their achievements."[58] On the basis of our limited knowledge of Greek New Comedy, the "truly comic character, the deviser of ingenious schemes, the controller of events, the commanding officer of his young master and his friends ..., this greater than Ulysses and Agamemnon: he is a creation of Latin comedy, especially of Plautus."[59] The cunning slave owes a debt to the Greek original only to the extent that the Italian dramatists, having observed his independent spirit, recognized a potential for humorous exaggeration. The *seruus callidus* appearing, for example, in eight of twenty Plautine plays, acts on the basis of loyalty to his master, a fidelity often based on fear since he lives under the menace of physical abuse. However, as Duckworth points out, "such threats are primarily for humor and are seldom fulfilled; in general the cunning slave, even though he ridicules the love affair of his youthful master, does everything in his power to help him."[60] In contrast to the typical faithful servant, the *seruus callidus* tends to lack individuality and his relatively carefree existence does not reflect the harsh reality of a slave's life in ancient Rome.

From the sixteenth till the end of the eighteenth century, numerous comedies were composed in Latin and the vernacular with extensive borrowing from Plautus and Terence, a popular trend in which the intriguing servant continued to figure prominently. In the seventeenth century, the Harlequin of the *commedia dell'arte* and his many national adaptations (Pickelhering, Hans Wurst) enjoyed immense popularity: "the comic peasant or servant is the most constant figure in the European theatre and in a broad context we can view him in the seventeenth century as a descendant of the slaves of Greek and Roman comedy."[61] Moreover, "[a]s *meneur de jeu*, the servant is the *de facto* master, wiser and cleverer than his employer."[62] The *commedia dell'arte*, as an extemporaneous form of theater, could not, by definition, be preserved in written form, but Max Kommerell sees an indirect presence, a "Fortleben in der Opera buffa, die uns am herrlichsten durch den Barbier von Sevilla repräsentiert wird"[63] and in the works of Molière. The main character of Scarron's *Jodelet*, while tracing his roots to the clever slave of Roman comedy, also looks ahead to the many *valets* of later French comedy. In fact "the servant represents the most frequently portrayed profession"[64] of the eighteenth century.

As in the case of the Roman *seruus callidus*, it would be misleading to regard the servant figures of this later European variation as the authentic portrayal of a contemporary social reality or as a veiled form of political protest; they merely embody a theatrical convention. Even though they belong to the lower class and may be exploited and treated cruelly by current standards, their main attraction lay in their entertainment value.[65] The *Federfuchser*, however, illustrates a very specific historic phenomenon with a degree of nastiness and seriousness (tragedy rather than comedy) that goes beyond these literary antecedents.

When in the German-speaking countries of the eighteenth century the middle class grew increasingly impatient to participate actively in the determination of its political destiny, the figure of the "Diener-Sekretär" acquired particular prominence. Both the German states and the Austrian Empire, although experiencing the social and economic impact of the commercial revolution, still constituted monarchies on the basis of "Gottesgnadentum," with substantial feudal trappings still intact. The aristocracy, with its traditions based upon the sword and its glorification of the man of action, successfully excluded the growing commercial and industrial class from any meaningful sharing of power. The only way to get ahead, to achieve some measure of status in society, was through *Bildung*, one of the principal ideals of the bourgeois inspired *Aufklärung*. Bright young men of humble station could seek to exercise some indirect authority by going to court and serving as secretaries to the ruling nobility and, in large states such as Prussia or Austria, by entering the civil service. In the latter institution, the positions of any real influence remained the exclusive preserve of the upper class. It is not surprising then that the talented authors of the *Sturm und Drang* movement, thwarted in their desire to participate actively in the governance of their country and denied an outlet for their energy, vented their frustrations upon their "tintenklecksendes Säkulum"[66] by decrying the man of words, the subaltern *Federfuchser* who frequently reflected their own social and political limitations, and by glorifying the man of deeds.

Historical developments at the beginning of the nineteenth century only served to exacerbate this situation, especially after the Congress of Vienna in 1815 and the attempt to return to the absolutism of the previous century. The middle class continued to be the main loser during the Restoration years (1815–48). For an aspiring young writer living in the capital of the Danube Monarchy whose family fortune had been wiped out by the Napoleonic Wars and their economic aftermath, public service seemed the only viable alternative. As an attempt to rationalize the bourgeoisie's elimination from any significant power, the Austrian *Vormärz* in both Stifter and Grillparzer celebrated the virtue of service, i.e., they made a virtue out of a political necessity. Indeed, in two of Grillparzer's dramas, a servant becomes the central character, *Ein treuer Diener seines Herrn*[67] and *Weh dem, der lügt!*, and I shall subsequently try to prove that Klesel, – "Er [Mathias] ist der Herr und ich [Klesel] sein Diener nur" (2441) – deserves to be considered the second most important player in *Ein Bruderzwist*. Because this particular servant is unique in comparison to the other examples in the dramatist's works, he contradicts Baumann's general rule: "Die dienenden Figuren bei Grillparzer empfangen ihr Wesen aus Licht und Schatten ihrer Herrschaft; diese prägt nicht allein das Dienstverhältnis, sondern durchdringt auch den Charakter."[68] In the relationship between Klesel and Mathias, the latter is "Herr" in name only as it is the "Diener" in this case who dictates the tenor of the "Herrschaft."

The nature of the association between master and servant or master and slave has been a more or less consistent concern in philosophical writings since Aristotle. Because the Aristotelian master can find true self-fulfilment only in a mental state of contemplative independence, he needs a menial to attend to his material needs. The slave, not knowing the urge to deliberate, functions primarily as a tool: he produces while the master consumes. Work would only limit the intellectual freedom of the master. Within early Greek society slaves were frequently considered subhuman and thus no Greek citizen could ever be a slave. In words recalling Rudolf's apology for an autocratic world order, Judith Shklar summarizes the Aristotelian master/slave paradigm as "a manifestation of a universal principle of order. It would be difficult to exaggerate the importance of the image of master and slave in Aristotle's thought. It expresses the essential character not only of all relationships of superiority and inferiority, but of a pervasive dualism. Mind and body, spirit and matter, theory and practice, contemplation and action, all exhibit the necessity of ruling and subordination which originates in the very constitution of the universe,"[69] or as Rudolf puts it, "Und aus dem Wechselspiel von hoch und niedrig, / Von Frucht und Schutz erzeugt sich dieses Ganze, / Des Grund und Recht in dem liegt, daß es ist" (1612–14).

While Greek thought accepted as a given a natural inequality of men, Hobbes and Locke both posited an original natural state of equality, a view standing in marked opposition to the feudal hierarchical model of the pyramid. But at the same time they assumed a basic inequality attributable to human nature. For Hobbes, self-centered, animal passions bent on subjugating others and thus in need of domestication rule the human personality. In contrast to the Greeks, he viewed the *polis* as an organization designed to curb the worst aspects of human nature. Hobbes and Locke therefore formulated, to quote Horowitz and Horowitz, " a liberal theory of obligation which involved deducing from the state of nature principles which, when formulated as a social contract, would justify the domination of some men over others ... The state of nature was used as a basis for finding eternal principles of human nature which would justify political power."[70]

At the time the dramas under investigation were written, a period dominated historically by the French Revolution, several writers began to question the traditional justification of the master/slave dialectic, foremost among them Rousseau, especially in his *Discours sur l'origine et les fondements de l'inégalité parmi les hommes*. For him natural man is free in the paradoxical sense that he is one with nature and thus has no choice but to follow the promptings of his instincts. Because he is not conscious of any separation from the world about him and is not aware of the existence of another being like himself, he does not recognize the master/servant dichotomy. It is only with the fall of man, the temptation to be the master and not the servant, the desire to make one's own decisions and to establish one's own set of values, that social inequality enters the picture. As a result of the evolution of man's powers, he gains awareness of himself as distinct from the physical world, and nature then exists primarily as something to be controlled or subjected to his will. "The freedom aspired to in the rational state is the freedom of perfected power. Behind the desire for knowledge is the desire for power."[71] Moreover, in Rousseau's view, reason tends to engender vanity, while "amour-propre" originates with seeing oneself as superior to others on the basis of one's intelligence.[72] Here we have a philosophical explanation for the increasing importance of *Bildung* in the eighteenth century and the concurrent emergence of the pen-pusher. Rousseau was also one of the first thinkers to call into question the nature of the power relationship between master and slave. In anticipation of one of Hegel's arguments, the *Contrat social* maintains, "Tel se croit le maître des autres, qui ne laisse pas d'être plus esclave qu'eux"[73] and in the eighth of the "Lettres écrites de la Montagne" he wrote, "Quiconque est maître ne peut être libre, et régner c'est obéir."[74]

According to Rousseau, as long as obedience to God determines one's way of life, the master/slave polarity holds sway. He described this form of religious bondage in the "Profession de foi du Vicaire savoyard "from *Émile ou de l'Éducation.* The vicar views God not only as his benefactor but also as a master demanding absolute submission. Only when he senses God's presence and is confident in his compliance to His will does he feel at peace with himself, but unfortunately he experiences this state of mind all too rarely. Hence he longs for the spiritual tranquility which God alone can grant and which can only be fully realized in the life after death. "Until then he feels enslaved by his lower self, free only when he obeys the voice of God within him. ... At all times he desperately needs God for both moral and intellectual reassurance."[75] This all sounds like a psychological profile of Grillparzer's Rudolf, who constantly seeks God's support and who finally welcomes death as a release from evil times into the eternal realm: "Und [ich] eile dir entgegen, – nicht mehr deutsches,/Nein himmlisch Vaterland. – Willst du? – Ich will! –" (2425–6).

Like many of his contemporaries Hegel tried to come to terms with the French Revolution which, inspired in part by Rousseau, began as an attempt to secure freedom for all but concluded with its denial. His *Phänomenologie des Geistes* includes a section entitled "Herrschaft und Knechtschaft" in which Hegel speculates as to how the master/slave dialectic came into being. His solution is to see it as the first step in man's endeavor to gain self-consciousness or recognition of himself. At an early stage of human development, a self-conscious individual strives to affirm his identity through acknowledgment by a second self-conscious individual. In this respect he is already dependent upon another person whom he cannot control. Therefore, he must enter a life-and-death struggle with his opponent, "since it is only by risking one's life that one is aware of oneself as a free, autonomous individual."[76] If in the ensuing contest one combatant destroys the other, neither will achieve the desired result. One of them must yield to the other, thus creating the master/slave dichotomy. But since the desired recognition now comes from the defeated opponent transformed into a slave, the master relies heavily upon an unfree person to confirm his independent status and his identity, while the slave is in a position to discover self-fulfilment through the service he performs for his master. "Durch die Arbeit kommt [das Bewußtsein] aber zu sich selbst."[77] "By working on material objects not only does [the slave] learn skills, but he also develops an awareness that he dominates the matter that he moulds with his hands."[78] Since the slave has faced "die Furcht des Todes, des absoluten Herrn,"[79] he is familiar with fear for his life, and "through the experience of *service* [Norman's emphasis] this fear has spread itself over his whole life [cf. Klesel's "Niemand soll zittern!" (2573)]; and consequently he has experienced to the full that consciousness of his own existence which can be given objective expression in *work* [Norman's emphasis]."[80] It follows that the combination of work and fear transforms the slave into the self-sufficient person the master sought to be in the first place. Once the slave gains this awareness of himself as a human being, it is but a matter of time before he insists that his master acknowledge him as such (cf. "Mir [Klesel] bleibt der Vorrang, wär's in Ketten" [2700]). "Herrschaft und Knechtschaft" thus draws the paradoxical conclusion: "Aber wie die Herrschaft zeigte, daß ihr Wesen das Verkehrte dessen ist, was sie seyn will, so wird auch wohl die Knechtschaft vielmehr in ihrer Vollbringung zum Gegentheile dessen werden, was sie unmittelbar ist; sie wird als in sich *zurückgedrangtes* [Hegel's emphasis] Bewußtseyn in sich gehen, und zur wahren Selbstständigkeit sich umkehren"[81] The servant ultimately becomes the real master, a scenario amply confirmed in *Ein Bruderzwist* and its predecessors.[82]

Another of Klesel's unique features is his official status as a priest, a servant of God, who by the last act has risen in the Church hierarchy to the office of cardinal. In Stendhal's novel *Le Rouge et le Noir* (1830) the hero, Julien Sorel, also a social climber of modest background (the son of a carpenter), must decide whether to pursue a vocation in the military – "le rouge" – or in the Church – "le noir." Although Napoleon had instituted a policy of promotion founded on merit rather than birth within the French army, an unheard of and totally unacceptable innovation for the ruling Austrian and Prussian aristocracies, Julien was unfortunately born too late to be able to take advantage of these reforms. An army career thus holds little prospect of fulfilling his ambitious aspirations and, out of purely pragmatic considerations, not religious conviction, he opts for the priesthood as the better calling for getting ahead in nineteenth-century French society. As with Klesel we have an opportunist intent upon using the Church to improve his social position.

Klesel, "weil er bequem / Die Herrschaft auflöst in die Unterschrift" (2607–8), belongs to a line of pen-pushing secretaries from the lower class, intellectually gifted men who employ their talents to plot and conspire as an agent of a less gifted, usually aristocratic patron. The pen turns out to be mightier than the sword. The latter, traditionally the symbol of the ruling noble house, has become totally ineffective as signaled by its location: "Wo ist mein [Rudolf's] Degen? ... / Er lehnt am Tisch zunächst an meinem Bette" (1495–6). This play between pen and sword and the political lifestyles they imply, i.e., mental intrigue versus physical action, informs Ottokar's response to Rudolf I's herald: "Willst du mit Briefen mich und Worten meistern? / Noch hab ich Schwerter, noch ist mir ein Heer, / Das unbesiegt, du siegtest nur mit Ränken, / Und reißen will ich diese Ränke, wie ich / Den Brief zerreiße, den du dir erschlichst" (2:2376–80). According to Grillparzer's own testimony, Napoleon's "tatkräftig" career provided the inspiration for King Ottokar.[83] Literary examples of pen-pushers who come to mind and who could be regarded as fitting antecedents to Klesel are Wurm from Schiller's *Kabale und Liebe*, the Sekretär from Goethe's *Die natürliche Tochter*, "Schreiber" Licht from Kleist's *Der zerbrochne Krug*, or Leonhard from Hebbel's *Maria Magdalene*. Aside from Licht, they all come from a lower station than their master but use their brains in an attempt to overcome their social disqualifications. As a *Strebertyp* each one is ambitious and secretly resentful of his social superior who, by a mere accident of birth, has power over him. Of the five schemers, Klesel strikes me as being the most talented and most subtle – the stakes are higher – with the possible exception of Licht, to whom he is at least equal.[84] But for one fatal error, his underestimation of Ferdinand's religious fanaticism, he might possibly have averted the political calamity which ends the tragedy. At least the fifth act does not preclude this possibility. I shall examine Klesel's predecessors in greater detail later.

Since Klesel always appears in his function as advisor or secretary to Mathias, he would undoubtedly be dressed, not in the ceremonial robes of the bishop or archbishop, but in the simple black of the priest. This color conjures up satanic overtones, as in the dream servant Zanga from *Der Traum ein Leben*,[85] and allusions within the tragedy encourage the spectator to make this association: "Seht ihr den Schalk? er hats [i.e., the agreement] schon in der Tasche" (1035); "Das ist der Lohn der Schlauheit, daß sie fein / Den Faden spinnt, bis er, am feinsten, bricht" (2646–7). Of course, Mephistopheles best exemplifies the diabolical servant in German literature: "Ich bin dein Geselle, / Und mach' ich dir's recht, / Bin ich dein Diener, bin dein Knecht!"[86] and, as we shall see, the famous pact hinges to some degree upon the devil's insistence upon the written word: "Auch was Geschriebnes forderst du Pedant?"[87] In this same context, one of

Faust's speeches captures with astonishing fidelity the general disposition and the specific danger Klesel embodies in *Ein Bruderzwist*:

> Nein, nein! Der Teufel ist ein *Egoist*
> Und tut nicht leicht um Gottes willen,
> Was einem andern nützlich ist.
> Sprich die Bedingung deutlich aus;
> Ein solcher *Diener* bringt Gefahr ins Haus.[88]

Rudolf portrays self-interest as the greatest threat posed by the new age, and who better represents this evil in both domestic and external affairs than Klesel? Like Mephistopheles he must work for and through others to achieve his ends while maintaining the delicate balance between master and servant. The "Gefahr ins Haus" looks to Rudolf's designation of the priest's involvement as real "Gefahr" (1407) and Ferdinand's refusal to permit such a "Diener" (2441) to disturb "die Einigkeit von [ihrem] Hause" (2453).

One last outstanding feature which Klesel's enemies acknowledge: "Drum brauch' ihn [Klesel], er ist *klug*, doch hüte dich [Mathias]" (1058) and on which he himself insists: "Niemand soll zittern! / Vor allem der im Recht ist und der *klug*" (2573–4), is his superior intellect. It enables him to manipulate not only Mathias but also Ferdinand, Max, Leopold, and even Rudolf. If one reviews all the circumstances surrounding his rise to power and its implied incentive: "Mich hat umsonst aus meiner Niedrigkeit / Die Vorsicht nicht gestellt auf jene Stufe / Zu der sonst nur Geburt und Gunst erhebt. / Der Kirche *Macht* bekleidet mit dem Purpur, / Der mich den Königen zur Seite stellt" (2565–9), then Nietzsche's psychological diagnosis of resentment and its manifestation in the priest possesses a particularly unsettling relevance. "Die Priester sind, wie bekannt, die *bösesten Feinde* [Nietzsche's emphasis] – weshalb doch? Weil sie die ohnmächtigsten sind. Aus der Ohnmacht wächst bei ihnen der Haß ins Ungeheure und Unheimliche, ins *Geistigste* und Giftigste. Die ganz großen Hasser in der Weltgeschichte sind immer Priester gewesen, auch die *geistreichsten* Hasser – gegen den Geist der priesterlichen Rache kommt überhaupt aller übrige Geist kaum in Betracht."[89]

CHAPTER TWO

In His Servant's Footsteps

Grillparzer may have provided a sign as to the relative significance of the various players in *Ein Bruderzwist* by the manner in which he set up the *dramatis personae* (p.374). Rudolf I, as *"römisch deutscher Kaiser"* and the main protagonist, quite naturally heads the list. The next five characters are grouped according to their relationship to him, i.e., *"seine Brüder," "seine Neffen"* and *"des Kaisers natürlicher Sohn."* This arrangement suggests that family members exist primarily as reflections of the head of the household, the position put forward by Langvik-Johannessen: "Die Personen sind mehr oder weniger Objektivierungen von verschiedenen Eigenschaften der Hauptperson, sie sind Teilpersönlichkeiten der das Spiel beherrschenden Persönlichkeit."[1] Once Grillparzer has outlined the family players in the "Bruderzwist," the next one to appear is Melchior Klesel, a non-relative and a non-aristocrat. There is no mention of his social status as bishop – the next entry includes the title *Herzog* Julius von Braunschweig – nor of his role as advisor to Mathias. In contrast, Wolf Rumpf is designated *"des Kaisers Kämmerer."* Klesel stands alone, the only major character singled out by the stark simplicity of his name. By this disposition the dramatist could be indicating not only the priest's relative isolation in the play, the only commoner amongst the main protagonists, but also his importance as Rudolf's real antagonist. When Langvik-Johannessen speaks of "der das Spiel beherrschenden Persönlichkeit," he means Rudolf. Whereas the emperor may be said to dominate the tragedy's dramatic interest, it is Klesel who primarily controls its dramatic action.

The opening dialogue of *Ein Bruderzwist* conveys in a most dramatic and succinct fashion the major political, social, and psychological conflict of the tragedy:[2]

GERICHTSPERSON Im Namen kaiserlicher Majestät
             Ruf' ich euch zu: Laßt ab!
DON CÄSAR   Ich nicht, fürwahr!   (1–2)

The anonymous "Gerichtsperson" does not speak as an individual but as an agent of the law that he has sworn to uphold. The basis of that law and the community which it supports is a third-person authority, the imperial majesty. Since the bailiff, as an arm of the imperial force, does not act independently or arbitrarily ("Nach Recht und Urteil wie's der Richter sprach."[5]), he represents the civil servant who denies his identity to become an instrument of a larger principle designed to guarantee the welfare of the state. The "Laßt ab!" also anticipates in very concise form Rudolf's warning to those who would presume to shake the foundations of this system: "O prüfe nicht die Stützen, beßre nicht!" (1638). In other words, leave well enough alone.

Don Cäsar's response marks the new attitude of the times.[3] Far from denying himself, he places his "Ich" first and, in his next word, "nicht," emphatically ("fürwahr") refuses to submit to the authoritative rule of the old regime. He shall decide for himself. Later in the fourth act in the review of his own emotional and intellectual life before Lukrezia, he discloses the consequences of his upbringing – a pathological case of egocentricity: "Was ist es auch: ein Weib? Halb Spiel, halb Tücke, / Ein etwas, das ein etwas und ein nichts, / Je demnach *ich mirs* denke, *ich*, nur *ich*" (1898–1900). The mind, as the only reality, can determine the world according to its will. Don Cäsar's repudiation of the old order – "Ich nicht, fürwahr!" – when juxtaposed with the ideal principle of that order – "Nicht ich, nur Gott"(1221) – accentuates the incompatibility of the views espoused by father and son. Rudolf's motto, the negation of self in favor of service to the general good, here represented by the absolute ethical authority, amounts to the reverse of Don Cäsar's formulation and its affirmation of the self. Because the emperor casts himself in the humble role of God's servant in the world (1458–9), he persistently attributes the evils of the new age, such as the Reformation, to egotism: "Nein, *Eigen*dünkel war es, *Eigen*sucht, / Die nichts erkennt was nicht ihr *eignes* Werk"(336–7)[4] and sees the only hope for the future in his mythical,[5] medieval secret society of "Friedensritter," "Männ[er], die nicht dienstbar ihrem *Selbst*"(1209).

Don Cäsar embodies the most extreme and the most obvious illustration of egotism within the drama, and it is both ironic and revealing that he is the illegitimate offspring of the emperor, i.e., through irresponsible, self-indulgent behavior, Rudolf helped to create the problem in the first place.[6] However, this subplot remains on a more domestic, personal, and symbolic level and has no *direct* bearing on any of the fateful political events that transpire in the course of the dramatic action. It would appear that Rudolf himself recognizes this limitation when he concedes to Ferdinand, "Die Zeit kann ich nicht bänd'gen, aber ihn [Don Cäsar], / Ihn will ich bänd'gen, hilft der gnäd'ge Gott" (345–6). The more dangerous opponent, the one the list of characters introduces immediately after Don Cäsar, is Klesel, for he shows evidence of being both substantially more cunning and more capable of self-promotion, and hence on the wider political stage he proves to be more effective than Rudolf in deciding the actual turn of events.

As soon as the curtain rises on the second scene of the first act, the following visual image confronts the spectator: "*Ein Kämmerer kommt durch den Haupteingang, hinter ihm Klesel und Erzherzog Mathias*" (p.378). Klesel and Mathias enter together but significantly the former is mentioned first. Already the stage directions give an inkling of the archduke's dependency upon his adviser since one would expect the servant to follow his master. Klesel also has the opening line of the scene: "Ich bitt' euch, Herr!" (83) and as with Don Cäsar, the first word is the all-important "Ich." This initial utterance captures the priest's dilemma: while he may put himself first, at the same time his lack of proper credentials obliges him to assume the obsequious tone of the "Diener." He has to implore or request ("bitt'") as a subaltern to attain his goal, a particularly humiliating necessity in this instance, since he must demean himself before a mere chamberlain to obtain an audience with yet another chamberlain. The "Herr" at the end of his utterance expresses the power to which he secretly aspires but which he could never hold openly because of his social disqualifications. Whereas Rudolf genuinely regards himself as a servant of God, Klesel takes advantage of his master's shallowness and exploits the servant role to satisfy his own pride and thwarted political ambition.[7] Versed in the ways of the court, he knows how to appeal to both the chamberlain – "Des Kaisers Bruder selbst"(85) – and Mathias: "Den Kaiser? *Herr*, glaubt ihr, wir sind so weit? / Bei Wolfen Rumpf, geheimen Kämmerer, / *Sucht ihr nun Audienz*" (88– 90). Even as the supplicant seeking a benefit, Klesel still assigns the dominant, active role to his "Herr." The servant always takes care to preserve the illusion that the master, on whose behalf he does all the pleading, has charge, when in fact it is the former who pulls the strings, while attributing the string-pulling to the latter.[8] Already we have a demonstration of the shrewd interpersonal management of which this priest is capable.

When Mathias, in his flattering recollection of the past, refers to himself as "der geliebtre Sohn" (93), the sharpness of Klesel's response proves that he is not afraid to speak his mind and serves notice that the part of the sycophant does not sit well with him: "Je, der geliebtre Sohn! Da liegt es eben! / Hätt' euer Vater minder euch geliebt, / Was gilt es? euer Bruder liebt' euch wärmer" (94–6). This spark of independence in the disclosure of an unpleasant truth runs counter to the image called for by Grillparzer's early sketch dated "Frühjahr 1827": "Clesel Anfangs einschmeichelnd, speichellek-kerisch."[9] The priest divulges his psychological acumen in diagnosing the basis for the family conflict. Like his creator he knows human nature and its deceptive machinations and, briefly betraying his true colors, he cannot resist showing off his superior insight.

Mathias cuts quite a pathetic figure when he plays for sympathy. Klesel at first co-operates: "Hart, ich geb' es zu" (97), for he has to remain on his lord's good side, but he then proceeds to criticize Mathias for making bad decisions in his unsuccessful attempt to lead the rebellion in the Netherlands. While Klesel did not serve as the archduke's advisor at that time, his assessment of the incident tells us a great deal about his moral standards:"Und, was das schlimmste, kehrt dann endlich heim / Und habt nichts effektuiert" (103–4). By implication, as long as one achieves one's end, the means do not matter. Success is all that counts. Here we have our first intimation of the Machiavellian *Realpolitiker*. Klesel's reaction to Mathias's dream of independent glory – "Niemand darum verpflichtet als sich selbst" (110), a highly ironic aspiration given the dependent circumstances in which he voices it – contributes further to his image of the unscrupulous politician:

> Ich seh' es kommen. Weht der Wind von daher?
> Hab' was du hast, woher du's hast gilt gleich.
> Gekauft, ererbt, – nur nicht gestohlen, Herr.
> Zwar *Politik* nennt so was acquiriert
> Und find't sich wohl dabei.   (111–15)

Politics are presented as a convenient rationalization for unethical practices. Whereas the speaker has sufficient distance from this subterfuge to recognize it for what it really is, one does not sense any strong disapproval despite the sarcasm. For him the crucial consideration is clearly the preservation of appearances or a superficial respect for legality in obvious preparation for the paper-work of the second act. Also the line *"Hab'* was du *hast,* woher du's *hast* gilt gleich" evinces irony in retrospect: by engineering a conspiracy against the rightfully constituted head of state, Klesel will acquire the imperial sovereignty for his master: "Ihr *habt* die Schrift, / Die euch zum Herren macht in diesem Land" (1071–2).

Once Mathias, in another fit of self-pity, expresses his intent to renounce his right to succession, Klesel replies with another display of his mental discernment: "Nun allzuwenig, wie nur erst zu viel. / So treibt ihr euch denn stets im Äußersten / O Maximilians unweise Söhne!" (122–4). He seems to have made a thorough study of the ruling family. Providing such a valid description of a major character flaw, he is most likely the dramatist's own spokesman on this occasion, since the play does bear out the idea of emotional excess as a dominant feature of the Habsburg temperament: Mathias's frequent vacillations between highs and lows or Ferdinand's fanaticism. While Rudolf struggles to avoid imbalance as symbolized in the scale, he all too easily falls prey to the same propensity, cursing his capital city one moment (2263) and blessing it the next (2412). This perceptiveness suggests at an early stage that he knows the men he is dealing with, that he can anticipate their reactions, and that he can thus foresee what they will do in any given situation, important considerations to bear in mind in an analysis of the second act. If Klesel speaks for Grillparzer here and elsewhere, it would also seem to mitigate David's repudiation of the priest as "[d]iese wenig nuancierte Gestalt" whose main function is to act as a scapegoat for a surreptitious attack on the Church.[10]

In the midst of this dialogue between master and servant, the drama furnishes a second *visual* presentation of Klesel, this time cast unmistakably in the role of the intriguer: *"Nachdem er sich umgesehen, leise"* (p.379). What follows is clearly not meant for the ears of the court. "Eu'r Spiel steht gut, ihr habt die Trümpfe, Herr!" (125). Klesel depicts the power struggle as a game strategy, one in which Mathias holds the winning hand provided he plays his cards astutely and at the opportune moment: "Harrt aus! Harrt aus! Und nur nichts von Entsagung" (126). The conspiratorial context and the imploring tone in which the confidant couches his plea: "Begehrt mir ein Kommando / In Ungarn! Ein Kommando sag' ich Herr!" (127–8) intimate a willingness to resort to any stratagem to induce his interlocutor to comply with his scheme. Moreover, this is the third time in their conversation that "Herr" appears at the end of his utterance. The repetition and the emphatic location underline the delicate nature of the balancing act he must perform. He wants power through Mathias; however, to achieve this objective he must let the archduke think that he is in command. In this third example the "Herr" actually comes after an order made in a very emphatic voice as signalled by the reiteration of "ein Kommando" and the two exclamation marks. Once again the servant's dilemma becomes evident; he has devised a plan that ultimately leads to the attainment of power and works assiduously towards its fulfilment, but he must resort to flattery and cajolery to handle a master who lacks the intelligence to appreciate his political manoeuvres.

The verses: "Der Wagebalken steht, / Und kurze Frist, so schnellt ein Quentchen mehr / In eurer Schale, diese in die Höh'" (129–31), perhaps more than any other in the tragedy, establish Klesel as "der eigentliche Gegenspieler Rudolfs"[11] in the wider political arena, for whereas the servant wants to upset the precarious balance of power in favor of his master, the emperor has sought above all to preserve the internal equilibrium within the realm by uniting the conflicting religious factions in a war against a common foreign aggressor: "Nun wohl, ihr [Mathias/Klesel] habt das Zünglein an der Wage, / Das ich [Rudolf] mit Sorge hielt im Gleichgewicht, / Ihr habt es rohen Drängens angestoßen, / Es schwankt und blut'ge Todeslose fallen / Aus beiden Schalen auf die bange Welt" (1419–23). The identical metaphor returns once more in the last act, and although presented through the jaundiced eyes of the Roman Catholic zealot Ferdinand, the essential message remains the same: "denn Jener [Rudolf] war die Wage / Die beide Teile hielt im Gleichgewicht; / Ihr aber legt was euch noch bleibt an Schwere / Der einen Schale zu, und zwar der schlechten, / Der gottverhaßten, der verderblichen" (2481–5).

In a final effort to put Mathias in a conducive frame of mind to seize the proffered opportunity, Klesel has recourse to flattering hyperbole: "Auf euch ruht Habsburgs Heil, das Heil der Kirche, / Ruht unser Aller Heil" (132–3). Thompson cites these lines as one of "the earlier signs that Klesel is pursuing an altruistic policy in which he passionately believes. In Act One he feels that it is imperative for the good of all that Mathias should gain his command."[12] While I share Thompson's desire to rehabilitate Klesel's image in the eyes of his many negative critics, I would still counsel extreme caution when taking him at his word. Throughout the tragedy, whenever he has recourse to religion, there is always, as in this case, an implied *political* advantage to be accrued. Indeed, the fifth act leads to the unavoidable conclusion that what the archbishop perceives to be in the best interest, sacred or secular, of the whole would also do no harm to his own career. As he himself points out to the politically naive Ferdinand, "Auch ist der Seeleneifer und der Eigennutz / Nicht gar so unvereinbar als man glaubt" (2531–2). In addition, if one reflects upon the circumstances of Klesel's urgent "motherhood" appeal, an obvious contradiction arises. Only three speeches earlier Mathias gave ample evidence of his egotistical motivation: "Hineinzugreifen in den wilden Aufruhr / Und aus den Trümmern, schwimmend rechts und links, / Sich einen Thron erbaun, sein eigner Schöpfer, / Niemand darum verpflichtet als sich selbst" (107–10). "Der selbstische Wille zum Leben," comments Naumann, "äußert sich hier als das Streben nach Macht."[13] Now, suddenly, Mathias is supposed to renounce his self-indulgent personality and to act on behalf of family, Church, and nation. Taking into consideration the two previous illustrations of Klesel's verifiable insight into the Habsburg psyche, one has to assume some degree of conscious calculation, even if the ultimate end is a commendable one.

Mathias persists in his defeatist attitude: "Mit mir ists aus!" (133), prompting his adviser to retort, perhaps as a ploy to shame him into action, "Ich seh' es ist, und so geb' ich euch auf. / Hier kommt Herr Rumpf, *führt selber eure Sache*" (134–5). Nevertheless, when the chamberlain intentionally ignores Mathias, "*tritt ihm [Rumpf] Klesel in den Weg*" (p.379). Despite his resolution not to interfere, Klesel simply cannot deny himself. Having the determination, the will to act which his master lacks, he is prepared to confront the adversary. In the subsequent dialogue, he supplies the necessary cues – "*Leise zu Mathias:* Drängt ihn! Drängt ihn!" (141)[14] – and knows how to ingratiate himself with Rumpf: "Wer kennt nicht eure Macht an diesem Hof" (146).

In reply to Mathias's query, "Wer ist der junge Mann?" (171), at Don Cäsar's stormy entrance, Klesel answers with two essentially rhetorical questions of his own: "So wißt ihr nicht? / Ein Findelkind, im Schlosse hier gefunden. / Der Kaiser liebt ihn sehr. Begreift ihr nun?" (171–3). His greater knowledge again comes to the fore; he is privy to the court's secrets, including Rudolf's love for his bastard son. What is particularly striking in his response is the unmistakable tone of condescension the servant adopts, an attitude one would normally expect from the master, i.e., do I have to spell it out for you? The same impatient, arrogant flavor, as if he were dealing with a child, manifests itself in the following exchange:

KLESEL   Nun noch einmal
        Begehrt in Ungarn ein Kommando.
MATHIAS Wozu?
KLESEL   Ihr sollt noch hören. Doch verlangt es!   (174–6)

The schemer refuses to deviate from his scheme, persistently return-
ing to the command in Hungary. Mathias's "Wozu?" strongly suggests that this is the first time that he has heard of this plan and that
the servant, having chosen to keep his master in the dark, has not
even bothered to inform him beforehand. Therefore, one hears the
real leader speaking in the statement and admonition of the final line.

The secondary literature has ignored the serious implications of
this dialogue. Towards the end of the act the conversation between
Ferdinand and the emperor reveals the latter's awareness of the
intrigue to rehabilitate his brother: "Ich seh' es ist ein Plan. Was also
will man?" (442). But not once in this act does Rudolf ever mention
or even allude to Klesel and one cannot say with any degree of
certainty that the senile man he seems to be at first even acknowledges the priest's presence in the background. At the beginning of
the second act, Ramee informs Klesel, "Das Lager wird euch fürder
nicht mehr ärgern. / Ihr seid nach Prag berufen, wissen wir, / Der
Kaiser sieht euch hier nicht allzugern" (630–2). This constitutes the
first sign that Rudolf is in fact aware of Klesel's existence and, recognizing the threat he poses, he has him recalled to Prague. When
he learns from Prokop in the third act of "Bischof Klesel, / Der mit
der Gränze meuterisch verkehrt / … / Und … vor allen nahe dem
Erzherzog [steht]" (1396–7; 1402), Rudolf, at first incredulous, – "Wie
war das? Klesel? Ist er doch in Neustadt, / Wohin ich ihn gebannt,
in seinem Sprengel" (1398–9) – soon jumps to the correct conclusion:
"Das wäre schlimm. Wenn jener list'ge Priester / Das was dem
Andern fehlt, den Mut, die *Tatkraft*, / Ihm gösse in die unentschiedne
Seele" (1403–5). Rudolf does in fact fully appreciate that Klesel's
proximity to his brother may threaten his own policy of maintaining
the imperial status quo: "Das wäre schlimm, und denk' ich fort und
weiter, / Vergrößert sichs zu *wirklicher Gefahr*" (1406–7). In view of
the vehemence of his words and their accurate judgment of both
master and servant, may one assume that when he resolves to grant
his brother's request, he is aware of Klesel's involvement as many
critics seem to take for granted? "Mathias soll sein ungarisches Kommando haben; er wird ungefährlich sein – glaubt der Kaiser, den
Ehrgeiz des Klesel nicht ins Kalkül ziehend, also irrend."[15] He reaches
his decision reluctantly, but he does so confident in Mathias's defi-
ciency in "Tatkraft" (447) and his resultant malleability which will
allow General Mansfeld, not Klesel, to hold the effective reins of
command: "Er [Mathias] füge sich des Feldherrn beßrer Einsicht"
(461). In other words Rudolf counts on his brother's proven weakness, apparently ignorant of the fact that he is currently being molded
by the very capable hands of the bishop. Hence, I would contend,

Kleinstück's interpretation does a serious injustice to the emperor. "So gibt er [Rudolf], eben aus den Bereichen der Kontemplation zurückgekehrt ..., seinem Bruder Matthias das verlangte Kommando in Ungarn, ohne noch länger zu überlegen, ob Matthias auch seiner Aufgabe gewachsen sei."[16] On the contrary; Rudolf only agrees to the command on the negative assumption that his brother will *not* rise to the occasion. The fact that Ferdinand speaks on behalf of Mathias and the plan – the repetition of the phrase "In Ungarn ein Kommando" (455) appearing five times in the scene hints at the thoroughness of the campaign – indicates that Klesel has managed to get to the young archduke as well,[17] because, as we have observed, Mathias has no inkling of what is going on behind the scene on his alleged behalf. Since there has been no chance for Klesel to speak to Ferdinand in this act, he must have done so earlier and without consulting his master.

Several interpreters have maintained that the emperor's bad judgment on at least three occasions must bear part of the responsibility for having helped to create a situation leading to civil war. Thompson's analysis is typical: [It] is ... by no means true that Rudolf does nothing himself to affect the course of events for he takes several decisions which have important consequences. For example in Act I the main action is set in motion by Rudolf's decision to entrust Mathias with the command of the imperial army in Hungary."[18] First, Rudolf grants in name only, not in substance, what Ferdinand presents as Mathias's wish: "Zwar ist der Mansfeld dort, ein tücht'ger Degen, / Der gönnt ihm gern die Ehre des Befehls / Und tut die Pflichten selbst" (457–9), and, secondly, at the time he makes his decision, there is no indication that he believes Klesel to be in the picture. While Thompson and others rightly see in this decision the impetus setting the main action in motion and culminating in the Thirty Years' War, no one has recognized Klesel's very substantial, albeit indirect, part in the whole affair: he initiates the plan and then, to accomplish it, he programs two archdukes and deludes an emperor.

No sooner does a chamberlain announce Ferdinand's imminent arrival than Klesel takes advantage of the new situation to goad Mathias into action:

KLESEL   Seht ihr? Da kommt der künft'ge Kaiser an,
          Der Erb' von Österreich, wenn ihr nicht vorseht.
MATHIAS Ich will in Ungarn ein Kommando suchen.
          Dann – Hab' ich dich verstanden? – Klesel, dann,
          Die *Macht* in Händen –
KLESEL   Nur gemach, gemach!

Ihr habt die *Macht* noch nicht.
MATHIAS   Und ich soll betteln?
KLESEL   Um Gotteswillen, ihr verderbt noch alles.   (180–86)

Mindful of Mathias's desire for the throne ("sich einen Thron erbaun" [109]) despite all idyllic yearnings to the contrary, the bishop appeals to one of the lowest of human motivations, jealousy[19] and, of course, correctly reads his master as shown by his immediate and full compliance. However, when in keeping with Klesel's earlier character sketch Mathias jumps from the depths of abjection to the heights of pride, the servant must now caution patience and restrain his charge's arrogance. The success of his strategy to gain power – the dialogue leaves no doubt that "Macht" is what is really at stake – depends upon Mathias's willingness to demonstrate a subservient, repentant attitude. To insist upon his personal dignity at this crucial stage could only spell disaster.

The remainder of the episode serves to reinforce the message of the master's total dependency upon the servant who never moves far from Mathias's side: *"Klesel in seiner Nähe* (p.382), who tries to steel his courage: "Nur Mut, nur Mut!" (194) and who whispers the proper cues at the propitious moment: "Die Zeit ist günstig. Seine Majestät / Scheint frohgelaunt. Versuchts!" (202–3). Unfortunately for Klesel, his own effectiveness remains inexorably tied to a very unreliable master. As soon as Mathias has to face the emperor, he ignobly forfeits the resolve once displayed before the subordinate Rumpf (190), renounces his right of succession and takes refuge again in the "Schäferglück" (127) impatiently rejected by Klesel. At the same time, his obvious weakness, his tendency to fluctuate between pusillanimity and bravado, provides the servant with the opportunity to use him so easily and, for the most part, so effectively. Thus, when Rudolf rejects his brother with his repeated "Allein!," Klesel, preserving his usual presence of mind, reasserts his direct ascendancy over his master:

KLESEL   Kommt, kommt!
           Verloren geht sonst alles.
MATHIAS   Gott!
RUDOLF   *vor sich hin*:   Allein.
MATHIAS Führt mich ins Grab, da wird mir doch wohl Ruh.[20]
           Ab, von Klesel geführt.   (217–19)

With an eye to the future, he leads Mathias away, another evocative gesture visually summarizing for the spectator the inverted relationship between servant and master. Klesel may have lost this battle but not necessarily the war. To employ his own imagery, he has "an ace up his sleeve." His parting admonition implies that other chances may present themselves, and the ground-work he has laid for just such an opportunity will yield the desired result almost immediately, "In Ungarn ein Kommando" (455), in the subsequent dialogue between Rudolf and Ferdinand.

CHAPTER THREE

The Pen Triumphs

The first act demonstrates not only Klesel's complete control over Mathias but also the extension of his influence over others, notably Rumpf, Ferdinand, and indirectly the emperor. The second act, commencing with a vivid illustration of the chaos that erupts without an effective leader: "Ein Führer erst! – Dann folgen Alle" (566), portrays the priest's consummate skill in presiding indirectly over a meeting which he convened himself and at which he is ostensibly permitted to supply only clerical support. Even before the conference takes place, he discloses his independence of mind. When Ramee asks him when he proposes to leave the battle field in compliance with Rudolf's command, Klesel responds, "Wenns meine Pflicht erheischt, / Die keineswegs mir Prag bis jetzt bezeichnet. / Der Seelenhirt gehört in seinen Sprengel" (633–5). He is quite prepared to disobey an order from the head of state and rationalizes his insubordination by hypocritically invoking his sacred duty. We know this to be a mere pretext to remain close to his power base, Mathias, since, as Ramee points out, his diocese is Neustadt and Vienna, not a military camp, and he has been conducting secret negotiations in Mathias's name with the "protestant'schen Herrn aus Österreich" (594), i.e., the enemies of the Roman Catholic Church whose doctrine and supremacy he has sworn as a priest and bishop to defend.

The outspoken military man, Ramee, having no use for the schemer, bluntly outlines the true state of affairs: "Ihr [Klesel] seid hier Schuld an manchem Schief' und Argem, / Setzt eure Meinung durch und führt den Krieg / Als eine Wallfahrt nach 'nem Gnadenort, / Nebstdem daß wenig Gnad' in euerm Tun" (638–41). From the beginning Klesel's plan has had a political rather than sacred aim. According to the colonel's remarks, there are unmistakable signs that the priest has been using the war against the Turks as an opportunity to secure

Protestant support for his master in return for religious concessions, a very tricky maneuver, because at the same time he must not alienate the faithful Catholic faction. With Mathias lost, however, and assumed dead on the battlefield, "ist zur Zeit ein andres Regiment" (645). "Und die Erzherzoge, die ihr [Klesel] berieft / Aus Gräz und Wien, zu einem Ratschlag heißt es, / Sie sind im Lager, treten in sein [Mathias's] Amt / Und werden euerm *Flüstern* wenig horchen" (648–51). Ramee exposes Klesel's Achilles' heel: no matter how capable he is, he cannot stand politically on his own. He needs Mathias as a front. Ironically, in retrospect, the colonel feels confident that the intriguer – the "Flüstern" harks back to the prompter in the previous act – will not be able to use his devious devices as effectively with the other archdukes, an observation seemingly substantiated when they make their stage entrance and rebuff Klesel by ignoring his greeting. While his isolation *"im Mittelgrunde"* (p. 402) visually reinforces his vulnerability, his final reaction to the "put-down" underscores the source of his strength – his inordinate sense of self-worth: "Nein, lieber sterben, als den Einsichtslosen / Die Einsicht opfern und gerechten Stolz" (682–3). This resolve, shared with the audience, anticipates his last speeches in the drama when again he puts aside all pretence. Since he views himself as mentally superior to the archdukes, the "Einsichtslosen," and is willing to grovel only if it serves his greater purpose, he remains at heart convinced of his indispensability. He alone knows how to deal with the increasingly complex political situation and is blessed with the necessary insight and the will to put it to good use. Thus his pride is justified, i.e., "gerecht." Sure of himself he is not the man to vacillate when it comes to making a decision, for he has the "Tatkraft" noticeably absent in Mathias and Rudolf. As the latter himself concedes, "Wir beide [Mathias and Rudolf] haben / Von unserm Vater *Tatkraft* nicht geerbt, / – Allein ich weiß es, und er weiß es nicht" (446–8). Indirectly then, the emperor acknowledges Klesel's antagonistic role when he recognizes his opponent's "Mut" and "Tatkraft" (1404) and his own impotence: "Die Zeit kann ich nicht bänd'gen" (345). In contrast Klesel clearly believes in his ability to master the times through his preconceived strategy, the first stage of which was the "Kommando in Ungarn."

Because the servant's own personal career goes hand in hand with that of his master, the news of Mathias's survival elicits an ecstatic involuntary physical reaction: *"Klesel, der bei dem Worte Mathias zusammengefahren, stürzt jetzt auf den Hauptmann zu, ihm die Rechte mit beiden Händen drückend, dann eilt er nach der linken Seite ab"* (p. 402). Once he enters the tent in the next scene, both his gestures and words accentuate his dependence upon his master, creating the impression of a complete reversal of the relationship implied in the first act. This exhibition of explicit subservience, however, may be dictated by the sheer relief at seeing his puppet alive and well, and may be intended for public consumption:

KLESEL   *von rechts eintretend:*
          Gebt Raum! Gebt Raum! Ich muß zu meinem *Herrn*!
          Sich vor ihm auf die Kniee werfend und sein Hand fassend:
          Ihr seids, ihr lebt! O uns ist Allen *Heil*!
MATHIAS *Klesel emporhebend:*
          Habt Dank, mein Freund! Habt Dank für eure Liebe.   (698–700)

Not only the final word of each line but also the visual image readily lend themselves to a Christian interpretation: the Lord, our salvation, receiving the homage and love of his faithful servant and raising him from ignominy into grace. Mathias, who, so to speak, has been miraculously resurrected from the dead, holds the key to Klesel's "Heil," i.e., his political salvation, since on the basis of his repudiation by the archdukes, he is a lost soul in the political desert without the blessing of his lord. This episode thus comes across as a secularized parody. A priest for whom by another profanation "wenig Gnad" lies in his "Tun" (641) utilizes his faith as a ploy to obtain and retain power for himself. Grillparzer has recourse to religious concepts in a worldly context to decry the new self-serving idols of the age. The old, genuine sacred values still have meaning for Rudolf, but significantly he feels obliged to live in isolation from the evils of the world: "Damit ich lebe muß ich mich begraben, / Ich wäre tot, lebt' ich mit dieser Welt" (1160– 1).

As the next step in his campaign to secure the imperial throne for Mathias, Klesel must convince his master to sue for peace with the Turks. "[P]eace would be to Mathias's advantage, for it would gain him popular support, particularly amongst the Protestants with whom Klesel has been secretly negotiating … Mathias could then offer a credible and powerful alternative to the authority of the Emperor Rudolf himself …"[1] Although Klesel's reasoning makes perfect sense, Mathias, true to form, thinks only of himself and wants to win the glory of victory at any price, an attitude that reminds us of his disastrous, selfish involvement in the Dutch struggle for independence. Throughout this dialogue the spectator becomes increasingly conscious of Klesel's duplicity in his efforts to dissuade Mathias. He points out that the archdukes "von euch [i.e., Mathias] berufen" (737) have arrived to discuss the treaty while in reality Klesel did the summoning himself (648), but gives his master credit in order to cater to Mathias's gigantic ego. Then, in the next argument, he resorts to scare tactics: "Und wenn der Kaiser nun erfährt, daß man / Hier Rat gehalten gegen seinen Willen" (743–4). One can safely surmise that the bishop has already foreseen this scenario since the meeting takes place at his behest. Because he has ignored Rudolf's order to return to Prague, we already realize that he does not lay much store in obeying the emperor. Later he will seek to justify the illegality of the conference on the grounds that the archdukes have convened with the best interest of the throne at heart, but at the same time he does not hesitate to profit from the conspiracy angle to compel them to authorize Mathias to act on behalf of the family. Other grounds include the Machiavellian end-justifies-the-means approach: "Doch schützte der Erfolg vor seinem [Rudolf's] Zorn" (746), the desirability of being perceived as a peacemaker, thus assuring public support and finally the acquisition of power and influence:

Halbleise:
Vergaßt ihr denn, daß Sultan Amurat
Der Frieden braucht, dem Geber dieser Ruh
In Ungarn *Macht* und *Einfluß* gerne gönnt;
So wie, daß Östreichs Stände beiden Glaubens
Dem Retter in der Not sich in die Arme
Die doch auch Hände haben – freudig stürzen.   (754–9)

This speech proves both Klesel's grasp of the total situation and his intent to take advantage of it wherever possible. By negotiating peace he can assure political good will not only with the foreign enemy – he has no qualms of conscience in dealing with an infidel if it serves his purpose – but also with the internal warring factions. These, he strongly implies, could in turn become instruments, "Hände," enabling Mathias to seize the reins of imperial authority. Adroitly weighing the pros and cons, he has already decided what would be in the best political interest of his master and, by inference, of his servant. Nonetheless, despite the compelling cogency of Klesel's political pragmatism, Mathias cannot see beyond his short-sighted arrogance and conceit: "*Ich* hab's gesagt. Die Schmach ertrüg' *ich* nicht" (760).

At this crucial point a servant announces, "Die Herrn Erzherzoge" (761). Having been unsuccessful in his attempt to convince Mathias, Klesel's reaction to their imminent arrival is particularly noteworthy:

> Um Gotteswillen!
> Erkennt doch, daß es Wahnsinn was ihr wollt.
> Und doch – kommts wie ein Lichtstrahl nicht von Oben?
> Es ist zu spät. Bleibt, Herr, bei eurer Weigrung.
> *Sich nach dem Vorgrunde entfernend:*
> Vielleicht reift unsern Anschlag grade dies.
> *Die Erzherzoge werden eingeführt.*   (761–5)

Grillparzer gives us a dramatized demonstration of how the schemer's mind works, how the association of ideas proceeds. First, in his extreme frustration over his master's ignorant obstinacy, he throws caution to the wind and tells him his true opinion. If the occasion so demands, Klesel can be brutally blunt. The "Und doch" followed by a pause signals time to reassess the situation, to consider whether or not he can translate a disadvantage into an advantage. Suddenly, in a flash of insight,[2] he realizes that Mathias's stubbornness, his determination to continue hostilities, could serve his ultimate aim in the subsequent meeting with the archdukes, and he therefore orders him – "Bleibt" – to remain firm in his resolve, however impractical it may be. This little incident illustrates how Klesel's quick and subtle mind derives inspiration on the spur of the moment and reacts instantly. He has the foresight to look ahead and transform an apparent hindrance into a possible benefit. Moreover, the first act has shown that he understands the mentality of his opponents and since he has summoned them to this conference, one may infer that he knows their positions on the various issues in advance. He may even unwittingly tip his hand by the ambiguous choice of "Anschlag." In its present context he no doubt intends Mathias to see it as calculation or plan, but it also has the more common meaning of an attempted assassination. Given the conspiracy about to transpire, it turns out to be a very apt choice indeed.

"Der zweite Akt," observes David, "ist eine der eindruckvollsten Szenen politischen Theaters. Melchior Klesel, der spätere Kardinal von Wien, zieht mit Bauernschläue die Fäden so geschickt und zugleich so offensichtlich, daß es weder den Zuschauern noch den Beteiligten entgeht."[3] The majority of critics has recognized Klesel's oblique but all the more effective domination in the second act, particularly the conference scene[4], and some, most notably Thompson, have listed the general tactics adopted by the master politician: "Klesel's achievement represents a remarkable piece of political manipulation. It depends on an astute strategy of personal reticence and of allowing the Archdukes to interact with each other in the manner that he anticipates."[5] However, "this remarkable piece of political manipulation" deserves a more detailed examination than it has received to date, largely, I suspect, because of the reluctance to pay the servant his due.

Max's opening greeting, while giving the official excuse for bringing the archdukes together, already contains its share of dramatic irony: "Man rief uns her, / Als Zeugen dachten wir von einem Sieg, / Um zu bewundern eure *Strategie*" (768–70). While Mathias is the butt of the humor, the tables are about to be turned on Max and his family who become the unsuspecting victims of a real strategist in diplomatic and political maneuvers. In fact their very presence in the camp stems from his strategy. Grillparzer, using Klesel as stagemanager – *Klesel zieht an einer Schnur, der Vorhang des Zeltes öffnet sich und zeigt einen grünbehangenen Tisch und Armsessel* (p.407) – clearly shows us who really pulls the strings at this meeting, who is the true master of ceremonies.

A review of the stage directions in this scene indicates that almost all the gestures belong to Klesel. The other players may have relegated him to a minor role, but the opening and closing of the curtains – "*Er tritt ins Innere des Zeltes, dessen Vorhänge er herabläßt*" (p.416) – visually confirm his theatrical function as director, one which he fulfils despite the imposed linguistic limitations. Of the nineteen major stage directions depicting the actions from the outset of the conference to its conclusion, thirteen describe Klesel's interventions, two contain responses by others to his stratagems, two involve Leopold, Rudolf's only loyal supporter, and the last two portray Mathias's puzzlement over his servant's contradictory words and behavior. Moreover, most of the non-active, referential directions allude either indirectly ("*Leise zu Mathias*" [p.467], i.e., the subject of the conversation will be Klesel) or directly to the bishop; five instances of "*Zu Klesel*" and three of "*Auf Klesel*" offer further evidence of his almost total domination through circuitous psychological tactics.

The following dialogue typically exhibits how, through knowledge of the adversary, presence of mind and anticipation, one can fulfil one's secret intent:

MAX   *Leise zu Mathias*:   Doch hier ist Einer,
Der überlei mir dünkt in unserm Rat.

KLESEL *zu Mathias*:
Befehlt ihr irgend noch, erlauchter Herr,
Sonst, mit Erlaubnis, zieh' ich mich zurück.

MAX   Bleibt immer denn, und führt das Protokoll!
Man spricht sonst her und hin und weiß zuletzt
Nicht ja, noch nein und wer und was gesprochen.   (808–14)

Klesel's instant response to the whispered conversation between Max and Mathias, one which he realizes is not meant for his ears but the content of which he can easily guess, is to present himself in the part of the self-effacing, disinterested, obedient servant and to offer to withdraw of his own accord. If he were to give the slightest hint of his true desire to remain and influence the proceedings, he would arouse the opposition of the archdukes, whom, from his brief encounter with them earlier in the act, he knows to be hostile to his involvement. This proposal also has the double benefit of making his presence appear less of a threat than it really is, and of embarrassing Max for having correctly suspected Klesel's ulterior motives. Under the circumstances, to insist upon his removal would be tantamount to overreacting, and the command to remain and record the minutes, by its very tone, suggests a means to save face. This exchange has additional wide-spread implications: it establishes Klesel's permanent official role throughout this scene. As Thompson has observed, "When he actually gets the conference going he functions as a civil servant with his ministers, taking the minutes and offering devious advice of doubtful logic where required ..."[6] By assigning Klesel to this subaltern, secretarial position: "Hier euer Platz! / Doch mir zulieb, sprecht erst wenn man euch fragt" (815–6), Max unconsciously exposes his fear of the priest in attempting to gag him, but what is more important, he inadvertently plays into his hands, because Klesel will gradually gain ascendancy over the meeting and its outcome by his mastery of the written word. One may not recall what one has said, "Nicht ja, noch nein," in the heat of the debate; however, once it has been committed to paper, it can return to haunt its speaker. Without perceiving the full implications, Max himself points out, "Tunkt ihr die *Feder* ein? Ihr werdet doch nicht / Das alles [Leopold's nocturnal escapades] setzen schon ins Protokoll? / Seht nur, er mahnt uns Klügeres zu sprechen / Und er hat Recht, nun also denn: zur Sache" (824–7). Even in a state of imposed silence, Klesel still has sufficient presence to get the proceedings underway and to make Max feel guilty by a simple gesture. The secretary wields a potent weapon, "die Feder."

After Leopold raises the issue of the legitimacy of their convening, an embarrassed *"Pause"* (p.408) follows, which Mathias breaks, no doubt speaking for the rest with his order, "Sagt etwas, Klesel!" (831). Almost from the outset they defer to his superior intelligence.

KLESEL   Wenn ich also darf:
   Es will gewiß der Mensch sein eignes Bestes.

> Wird nun des Kaisers Bestes hier beraten,
> Kann man noch zweifeln, ob es auch *sein Wille*?   (831–4)

As a sign of respect for his audience Klesel begins by putting himself down as the humble servant. Not wishing to appear as a threat in any way, he only offers his counsel at their insistence. A mere nine lines later, challenging the altruism of Leopold's loyalty to Rudolf, Mathias, without realizing it, unmasks the very deceptive technique turned to account so adroitly by his servant: "Doch hängt ein Nebenvorteil manchmal noch / Der *Demut* an, die nur *Gehorsam* schien" (839–40). The advice Klesel offers amounts to the worst kind of sophistry, which, however, only the spectator can fully appreciate. What Klesel here characterizes as "[Rudolf's] Wille" (834), in his earlier exchange with Mathias he presented as "gegen seinen [Rudolf's] Willen" (744) in an effort to coerce his master. Ever the opportunist, he can take the same example and interpret it in a diametrically opposed sense to meet the exigencies of a new situation. Also, at this stage, the spectator has little, if any, confidence in his claim that the current deliberations will promote the interest of the emperor since all the signs to date point to Klesel's pursuing what benefits his master. Leopold underlines the fallacy of this argument as well: "Ich aber will nur was ich selber will, / Und Herrscher heißt wer herrscht nach eignem Willen" (835–6). Only the individual can determine what he/she wishes; no one else can make this decision, and in the political arena the true autocratic ruler is neither dependent nor obligated to anyone other than himself. While Leopold advocates an absolute, egocentric assertion of self as the basis of power, in direct contrast, Rudolf, acknowledging a will higher than his own, purports to reign according to "Gottesgnadentum": "Doch was mein eignes Amt, daß diese Welt / Ein Spiegel sei, ein Abbild deiner Ordnung, / Daß Fried' und Eintracht wohnen brüderlich / Vom Unrecht ungestört und von Verrat, / Das will ich üben, stehst du, Gott, mir bei" (1465–9).[7]

Once Klesel has rationalized a conspiracy to the apparent satisfaction of all save for Leopold, he turns his subtle mind to the realization of the first aim of the conference:

MAX   Nun also denn: was solls?
>   *Da Klesel nach einer Schrift in seinem Busen greift*:
>   Laßt stecken, Herr, wir wissen was ihr bringt:
>   Ein künstlich ausgefeilt Elaborat
>   Das uns den Frieden mit den Türken soll

Als rätlich, nötig, unerläßlich schildern.
Ihr seid der Widerhall von euerm Herrn,
Wenn nicht vielmehr das Echo er von euch.   (846–52)

Again Klesel raises the issue by a gesture[8] without having to utter a single word, and secretly determines the agenda through his role as secretary, the fabricator or bearer of a "Schrift." (His visual leitmotifs are the "Feder" and the "Schrift.") Whereas Max stresses quite accurately the interdependence between "Herr" and "Diener," implying the predominance of the latter, Klesel is already several steps ahead of the archdukes in that he knows that they know, he can predict their reactions and he has an important piece of information in reserve, i.e., his knowledge that Mathias favors war and thus will not be "das Echo" of his servant. Aware that they recognize and resent his influence over Mathias, he is counting on their pent-up hostility, the perversity of human nature, to gain his objective, and as Max's conditional clause later reveals: "Vor allem aber wisse: / Warst Eines Sinnes du [Mathias] mit diesem Mann / *Auf Klesel zeigend*: / Ich hätte die Gewalt dir nicht gegeben" (1055–7), he has calculated correctly.

It really is quite amazing how Klesel's Machiavellian manipulations manage to get three out of four archdukes on side. First, he works on Max. Once the difference of opinion between master and servant emerges, the untenable nature of Mathias's "kindisch" (881) position becomes painfully evident to all, especially Max: "Hoffst du, geschlagen mit dem ganzen Heer, / Nun, mit dem halben, Sieg dir zu erringen?" (882–3), a logical reaction Klesel could presumably anticipate.[9]

KLESEL *die Feder eintauchend, eifrig*:
         So seid ihr für den Frieden?
MAX   Ich? Bewahr!
KLESEL Doch spracht entgegen ihr dem Krieg.
MAX   Ei, laßt mich!   (888–9)

The telling gesture resurfaces to stress the source of Klesel's power as he uses his pen to intimidate the archduke. He also speaks out before he is asked to do so; gradually and inconspicuously he is taking more overt control of the meeting, directing it as he wishes. In this particular instance he tries to get Max's support in writing and when he resists, the "Federfuchser" indicates the illogic of his interlocutor's stance. Unable to deny the weakness of his position, Max can only admit defeat by childishly ordering to be left in peace.

Klesel has succeeded in backing Max into a corner, in reducing the senior spokesman of the Habsburgs to a rather pathetic figure subdued by the realization of having been outmaneuvered by a servant.

Since Max has been reduced to silence – from this point on he makes only three short statements of a line or less, one of which closes the segment: "Wir sind zu Ende" (946) – Klesel can turn his attention to Ferdinand whose narrow-minded Roman Catholicism renders him a predictable adversary. After prompting his master: "*zu Mathias*: / Beliebts euch hoher Herr?" (898) to give a summary of the religious situation in Hungary and the army (no doubt the product of the servant's schooling), Klesel attempts inconspicuously to drop a hint: "*auf sein Papier herabgebeugt, wie vor sich*: / Der Krieg ist dieser Spaltung Keim und Wurzel" (906). "Der Protestantenhaß Ferdinands wird von dem Bischof geschickt benützt."[10] As part of Klesel's usual pattern we have a gesture associated with his secretarial function and a statement, both of which are intended to convey the impression of an off-the-cuff observation meant for his ears only, but which are clearly calculated to appeal to Ferdinand's prejudice. The tactic immediately has the desired result: "Da spracht ihr wahr, wenn irgend jemals sonst!" (907). Peace enabled him to deal decisively with the Protestant menace in Steiermark.

When Ferdinand wishes to know the Turks' conditions for peace, Klesel almost gives himself away in his eagerness to supply the requested information: "*Den Stuhl rückend*: / Das ist zu wissen leicht aus erster Quelle. / Des Ofner Bassa Sekretär und Dolmetsch / Ist hier im Lager; wenn ihr es gestattet, / Führ' ich ihn her, hört selbst dann was er bringt" (928–31). Despite the deferential conditional clause designed to sustain the illusion that the archdukes are still in command, this speech again demonstrates that Klesel has a good overall view of the situation – indeed, he already knows the enemy's favorable terms which he outlines four lines later: "Der Stand wie vor dem Krieg" (935). He makes it his business to be well informed of what is going on at home and abroad (cf. act five), and it is this knowledge which helps him orchestrate this conference.

Now that Ferdinand has been brought on side, partly, one suspects, out of his fear of Leopold's ambitions, the servant can again concentrate upon his master; his obstinacy has outlived its usefulness.

KLESEL   *ruhig zu Mathias*:
           Ihr seid für Krieg?
MATHIAS   Wenn man mich überstimmt!
LEOPOLD Hier ist noch Einer. Ohm, wir sind zu Zwei.
MATHIAS Gerade deshalb Frieden auch.   (944–6)

One has to assume that again Klesel could count on this reaction. Mathias would not wish to be perceived as standing with the bellicose Leopold (937–40) whom he views as a competitor for the imperial throne: "Man merkt es wohl, ihr sucht des Kaisers Gunst" (837). Thus not "Das Wohl des Lands" (892), as Ferdinand would have it, but rather aspirations for "Macht und Einfluß" (756) cunningly exploited by Klesel dictate the final decision for peace against the emperor's will.

Having achieved his first conference objective, Klesel then pushes for a speedy settlement and announcement of the peace treaty on the grounds the enemy may choose to take advantage of their current strong position. "Wir haben dann was ihr / In eurer Weisheit wünschenswert erachtet" (950–1). He gives exclusive credit for the agreement to the archdukes, making them appear wise in the process, while all along he planted the seed, nourished it and brought it to fruition. "Klesel has clearly anticipated his success," observes Thompson, "for he had the Turkish negotiator waiting in the wings to sign the peace treaty and the document empowering them to ratify it ready to hand."[11] The real reasons behind the urgency, however, are Klesel's justified fears that given time to reconsider, the archdukes could easily go back on their decision: "In mir [Ferdinand] ringts wirren Zweifels. / Was gäb' ich nicht wär' mir der Schritt erspart" (957–8), and the need for the treaty to be in place before he can proceed to his second goal. Hence, with the archdukes' reluctant compliance and without further delay, he takes decisive action: "*Klesel den gefalteten Zettel übergebend*: / Des Ofner Bassa Sekretär. Sogleich!" (964). Significantly a folded paper and a foreign secretary as its recipient mark the conclusion of the second stage in Klesel's overall campaign which originated with the "Kommando in Ungarn."

"Klesel now takes complete charge of the meeting and moves to his main objective, the conferment upon Mathias of full power to act in the Emperor's name."[12] To mark this auspicious occasion he rises to his feet to contradict Max for the second time: "Nicht ganz, erlauchte Herrn!" (966) and delivers his first long speech of this scene:

> Wenn ich bisher
> Nur auf Erlaubnis sprach und wider Willen,
> Tret' ich nun auf in meinem eignen Amt,
> Als Seelenhirt, als Redner für ein Volk
> Und als Vertreter unsers heil'gen Glaubens.   (966–70)

He begins with a lie. Because the dramatist has made us privy to the priest's duplicity, we immediately identify his opening clause as a fabrication. He has often spoken without permission and far from denying himself, he has succeeded in achieving *his* will which he has consistently portrayed as *their* will: "was ihr / In eurer Weisheit wünschenswert erachtet" (950–1), a tactic prescribed by his subordinate status. The mask he now adopts, that of the "Seelenhirt," is also rendered suspect, if not ludicrous, by his known dealings with the Protestants as reported by Ramee (638–44) and Max (862–9), i.e., what he earlier disclaimed as "Verleumdung" (872) turns out to be valid. Religion is merely the means to an end, the nature of which he unwittingly divulges in the next section of his speech: "Dieselbe Stimme, die in Wien und Neustadt / Zu Tausenden bekehrt mit ihrer *Macht* / Erheb' ich nun mit gleichem Feuereifer / Im Angesicht der Gegenwart und Zukunft" (971–4). As we noted earlier, now and then Klesel, the man of peasant stock, proud of his achievements and resentful of those in authority, asserts itself; he cannot resist boasting of the influence he once exerted over the masses. Here, for a brief moment, seemingly forgetting himself and reverting to his former calling as a fiery folk preacher, he both celebrates and demonstrates the power of his language in an oration intended to convert those present to his lord rather than his Lord. "Ihr schloßt den Frieden edle Herrn, allein / Wenn ihn, gesetzt, der Kaiser nun verwirft?" (975–6) As a skilled speaker he has been "setting up" his audience for a climactic conclusion couched in the form of a question. The timing of this revelation, both within the speech and in terms of the dramatic sequence of events, is crucial and renders Klesel's motive for the hasty ratification of the treaty patently obvious, so obvious, in fact, that even Ferdinand sees through it: "Das sagt ihr uns, nachdem der Bote fort, / Der unser Wort verpfändet an den Türken?" (979–80). The treaty will act as the perfect lever compelling the archdukes to engage in the more direct conspiracy of electing Mathias as Rudolf's defacto successor.

A minor incident worthy of consideration occurs once Leopold confirms that Rudolf will reject the peace they have just concluded. "Klesel *zu Leopold höhnisch*: Ihr habts getroffen / Und kennt, so scheints, des Kaisers tiefste Meinung. / *Mathias will auffahren, Klesel hält ihn mit einer Handbewegung zurück*" (977–9). Klesel feels so secure and confident under the current conditions that he treats an archduke with open scorn without fear of being reprimanded. This stands in marked contrast to his earlier status: "Ich [Max] will euch [Klesel] schelten, Herr, drum hieß ich euch / Hier sitzen unter uns" (858–9). Furthermore, he even impugns Leopold's intentions, craftily insinuating that he is seeking to curry favour with the emperor to further his own career, an allegation which not surprisingly raises Mathias's hackles. Because Leopold as a minority of one presents an easy target and because Klesel now presides openly over the meeting – he silences his master with a simple wave of his hand – he can get away with discrediting the young archduke.

When Max proposes Pontius Pilate's recourse (984) if the emperor were to reopen the war, Klesel delivers his longest political speech of the act, attacking Rudolf's regime as ineffective, moody and remote (actually a fair assessment!), appealing to the archdukes' patriotic sentiment and insisting they assume responsibility for their actions. "Am heut'gen Tag, vertragend mit dem Feind, / – Obgleich vorläufig nur, auf spätern Abschluß – / Erkanntet in euch selber *ihr die Macht* / Zu sorgen für des Vaterlandes Beste" (991–4). Realizing that the thought of having negotiated with the Turks may not sit well with his listeners, he minimizes the damage done in an aside, maintaining the peace treaty has only postponed the day of reckoning. He is at obvious pains to put the best face on what amounts to treachery and conspiracy: (1) to have met against the emperor's will and without his knowledge; (2) to have entered an agreement contrary to the expressed wishes of the emperor; and (3) to have made a treaty with a heathen enemy. The key verse is so arranged that the "ihr," i.e., the archdukes and "die Macht" are juxtaposed as if the tempter were dangling the bait, their potential power, before their eyes. Naumann's analysis of this line focuses upon the far-reaching implications of Klesel's apt formulation: "Aus *eigenem* [Naumann's emphasis] Urteil über das Wohl des Gemeinwesens zu entscheiden, da liegt der Kern der Bewegung, die an der höchsten Stelle, bei den Erzherzögen, anfängt, sich aber unaufhaltsam fortsetzt, die Prager Stände befähigt, zu ihrem Nutzen zu regieren, und schließlich dem liederlichen Türsteher das Recht gibt, sich gegen den Kaiser selbst zu empören."[13]

> Doch *nicht* der Kaiser *nur* ist wankelmütig,
> Der Türk' ist treulos, als ein Heide schon,
> Im ganzen Reich der fernen Möglichkeiten
> Ist nichts als Zweifel, Arglist und Gefahr.   (995–8)

Although this part of Klesel's discourse is superficially designed to reflect a reality external to the current deliberations, Grillparzer may have wished to suggest an ironic relevance to the dramatic situation at hand. The first line harks back to Mathias's own pronouncement seventy-four lines earlier: "Das ist der Fluch von unserm edeln Haus: / Auf halben Wegen und zu halber Tat / Mit halben Mitteln zauderhaft zu streben" (921–3).[14] While the Turk cannot be trusted – what can you expect from a heathen after all? – the Catholic archdukes have just broken faith with their liege lord. And finally, the last three nouns, "Zweifel, Arglist und Gefahr," describe the times epitomized by Klesel. He has cast serious doubt on the reliability of Rudolf's regime, has substantially helped to undermine it, and has thus promoted the new self-centered order founded on "Zweifel" set opposite the old regime established on the basis of "Ehrfurcht." To no avail the emperor warns, "Der Zweifel zeugt den Zweifel an sich selbst, / Und einmal Ehrfurcht in sich selbst gespalten, / Lebt sie als Ehrsucht nur noch und als Furcht. / Maßt euch nicht an zu deuteln Gottes Wahrheit" (1647–50). As for the last two categories, cunning and danger, as soon as Rudolf learns of the bishop's presence at Mathias's side, he sees the involvement of that "list'ge[n] Priester" (1403) as "wirklich[e] Gefahr" (1407). Hence, the very features Klesel singles out, the emperor categorizes as symptomatic of the orator.

> Ihr könnt nicht immer hier zu Rate sitzen,
> Deshalb ist nötig, das für Alle Einer
> Mit *Macht* bekleidet, *wenns die Not erheischt,*
> Zu handeln als des Hauses Hort und Säule.   (999–1002)

"Macht" as the audible leitmotif that persistently crops up in Klesel's utterances denotes his obsession. Sultan Amurat will concede "Macht und Einfluß" (756) in Hungary to the man who makes peace; the bishop has converted thousands "mit [seiner Stimme] Macht" (972); the archdukes should recognize in themselves "die Macht" (993) to act in the best interest of the country; and "bei anvertrauter Macht" (1013) a regent should be faultless. The person Klesel has in mind, of course, is his master, a front behind which he can exercise the real authority. Therefore, in the conditional clause lies the real danger, for who will make this judgment call if not the bishop? The third act will detail the consequences of granting him *carte blanche,* i.e., giving him their written authorization and support before the deed.

As the next strategic step he once more outfoxes the archdukes who naturally assume he will propose Mathias.[15] Klesel must create in their minds the impression that he does not view his master as a suitable candidate: "Allein zu solchem Amt fehlt ihm die Festigkeit, / Nicht Kraft, doch das Beharren im Entschluß" (1008–9). We have the novel situation where the Machiavellian schemer even exploits the truth to achieve his illicit aim, i.e., he only seems to be working against his own best interests. To state what has become almost a cliché and what Mathias himself has conceded (921–3) has the advantage of increasing Klesel's credibility on this one issue with those who openly fear and despise him. In a subtle sense he is lying by telling the truth, namely he appears to be speaking against Mathias ("Herr, wider euch?" [1071]) when in reality he is speaking for him ("für euch!" [1071]) by using reverse psychology. If he tells them not to vote for Mathias, they will do the opposite just to prove him wrong and to assert their own independence. Mathias's spontaneous, angry outburst – "Ich will euch zeigen, ob ich fest, ob nicht" (1010) – only serves to buttress Klesel's strategy, proving that master and servant are not in collusion.

Never one to miss an opportunity, Klesel now turns to advantage the accusation (862–9) he earlier repudiated as "Verleumdung" (872): "Auch hat man uns geheimes Einverständnis / Mit Ketzern, Unzufriednen Schuld gegeben, / Das darf nicht sein bei anvertrauter Macht. / Erzherzog Maximilian wäre rein" (1011–14). From what we have witnessed of and heard from Max throughout this scene, we have fashioned the image of an easy-going, unambitious older man who wants nothing better than to return as quickly as possible to his creature comforts in Vienna. "Auch will ich keine Lorbeern hier erwerben; / … / Ich bin von Blei, das zwar aus der Muskete / Ein rasches Ding, sonst aber träg und schwer" (794; 801–2). In short he has neither the energy nor the will to rule. It would therefore seem reasonable to assume that Klesel recognizes Max's limitations as readily as the audience and that he only makes this nomination confident that the nominee will decline, as is the case. Thus with one down, he returns to the next in line with an equally predictable outcome: "ein Muster hier der Festigkeit, / Der Herr der Steiermark, der, rascher Tat, / die Ketzerei getilgt in seinem Land" (1017–19). As this portrait reveals, Klesel is equally aware of Ferdinand's vulnerability – his religious rectitude which will not permit him "Übertretung, förmliche Verletzung / … gält' es eine Krone" (1028–9). Hence, when the archdukes "come to realize that alternative candidates are either unacceptable or unwilling, the choice reverts to Mathias as 'des Hauses Ältester (l.1030).'"[16] Now that Klesel has achieved his major objective, the spectator can only concur with Leopold's general observation: "Ihr [Klesel] habt uns hier am Narrenseil geleitet" (1039).

Resorting to the same telling gesture for the second time in this meeting: *"ein Papier aus dem Busen ziehend,"* Klesel declares, "Da braucht es nur noch eure Unterschrift" to which Leopold, the most perceptive of the archdukes, retorts, "Seht ihr den Schalk? er hats schon in der Tasche" (1034–5). The "Schalk" has traditionally been one of the designations bestowed upon the devil and in this particular context where the scoundrel, a priest in black, asks for signatures, Goethe's Mephistopheles comes to mind. The paper produced from the breast pocket verifies that Klesel has planned all along every step down to the last detail, and had the foresight to omit the name of the authorized person. In fact, since he has maneuvered the archdukes into a position where his strategy seems the only viable alternative, he can boldly issue the following challenge: "Sie [die Vollmacht] liegt noch hier; es braucht nur sie zerreißen, / So stehen wir auf gleichem Platz wie vor " (1049–50).

Once the archdukes have made their exit under a heavy cloud, Klesel, left momentarily alone, exclaims, "Nun rasch ans Werk! Vor allem die *Depeschen. / Er setzt sich und schreibt*" (1068), and without hesitation he recommences his correspondence with the various factions to win further endorsements for his master. The visual image with which the dramatist leaves us again reinforces the figure of the "Federfuchser," the man who rules by his pen, his "Klugheit" translated into written form which will eventually be transformed into action. In direct opposition Rudolf has little use for papers of state: "*die auf dem Tische liegenden Papiere unter einander schiebend*: / Es ist hier wohl Verwirrung oft mit *Schriften*" (481). He ignores them, even detests them: "*Depeschen* auch von Eurer Majestät / Gesandten an dem Hofe zu Madrid. / *Rudolf schiebt die auf dem Tische liegenden Briefschaften verächtlich zurück. Er setzt sich und liest, das aufgeschlagene Buch in der Hand*" (197–8). "Schriften" only appeal to him in the form of *belles lettres* – "Divino autor / Fenix de España" (203–4) – as they offer an escape from the unpleasant demands of political life: "'Ring des Vergessens' – Ja, wer den besäße!" (207). Whereas Klesel pursues a policy of being informed of all events, Rudolf would seem to have adopted a plan of essentially doing nothing, ignoring the problems in the vain hope they will go away in time, and ruling in name only. "Mein Name herrscht, das ist zur Zeit genug. / … / Zudem gibts Lagen wo ein Schritt voraus / Und einer rückwärts gleichweis verderblich. / Da hält man sich denn *ruhig* und erwartet / Bis frei der Weg, den Gott dem Rechten ebnet" (1166; 1175–8). But as Julius points out, such inaction has a serious potential flaw: "Doch wenn ihr ruht, ruhn deshalb auch die Andern?" (1179).[17] Far from resting ("Nun rasch ans Werk!"), Klesel has been very busy with his pen.

MATHIAS *zurückkommend*:
    Wie, du noch hier? Du trittst vor meine Augen,
    Nachdem du erst gesprochen wider mich?
KLESEL   *aufstehend*:
    Herr, wider euch? für euch! *Ihr habt die Schrift*
    Die euch zum Herren macht in diesem Land.   (1069–72)

After a further embarrassing illustration of Mathias's dim-witted, naive nature, Klesel triumphantly claims absolute power through the "Schrift" and makes no mention whatsoever of the condition outlined in the presence of the archdukes, i.e., "wenns die Not erheischt" (1001). Mathias, by virtue of the signed document, is now ruler in Hungary even though there has been no time for Rudolf to rescind the illegally negotiated peace treaty. This episode bears comparison with the scene in the next act where Rudolf faces the representatives from the Bohemian estates of the realm; both incidents hinge on the identical focal point: "Ich seh's an jener *Schrift*. Es ist das gleiche, / Wie sie seit Monden liegt in meinem Zimmer, / Gleichstellung fordernd für den *neuen* Glauben" (1546–8). The "Schrift" has become here an instrument to blackmail the emperor, to force him into compliance. When Rudolf offers his word, [f]rei zu bewilligen" (1554) what they demand, not wishing to base his relationship to his subjects upon a piece of paper, he meets only with distrust: "Gebt her die *Schrift*! Sie ist wohl gleichen Inhalts / Mit jener frühern; doch da ihr mißtraut, / Ziemt Mißtraun wohl auch mir. Gebt eure *Schrift*!" (1571–3). According to Rudolf, the old, idealized feudal order has good cause to fear the pen:

> Denn was Entschlossenheit den Männern heißt des Staats
> Ist meisten Falls *Gewissenlosigkeit*
> *Hochmut* und Leichtsinn, der allein *nur sich*
> Und nicht das Schicksal hat im Aug der Andern;
> Indes der gute Mann auf hoher Stelle
> Erzittert vor den Folgen seiner Tat,
> Die als die Wirkung Eines *Federstrichs*
> Glück oder Unglück forterbt späten Enkeln.   (1695–1702)

What Rudolf has in fact drawn is a reasonably accurate portrait of his antagonist Klesel, his determination, unscrupulousness, arrogance and rashness. He is clearly toying with the fate of others to serve his own purpose by organizing an insurrection against Rudolf. (The Bohemian delegation would not have thus presumed to confront their emperor without the threatening circumstances created by the bishop's machinations.) While Rudolf fears to commit himself to paper since it would result in a deed bringing in its wake misfortune for the nation, Klesel feels no such qualms since he is only anxious to gratify his own lust for power.

ABGEORDNETER   Wir baun auf festen Boden, auf die *Schrift*.
RUDOLF   Die *Schrift?*
                   Rasch unterschreibend:

> Hier meine *Unterschrift*. Da ihr
> Den toten Zügen einer toten Hand
> Mehr traut als dem lebendig warmen *Wort*,
> Das von dem Mund der Liebe fortgepflanzt,
> Empfangen wird vom liebedurst'gem Ohr,
> Hier schwarz auf weiß. – Und nun noch Blut als Siegel.
>
> (1651–57)

The "Schrift" drawn up by the hand of an indifferent, anonymous functionary symbolizes a new diabolical age in which impersonal formalities replace the person-to-person relationship based on love and trust of the old order.[18]

Just as Leopold's reference to the "Schalk" in the context of an "Unterschrift" (1034) may have sought to associate Klesel with Mephistopheles, the echoes from *Faust* are unmistakably audible in this dialogue as well. The "schwarz auf weiß" recalls the Schüler's proverbial lines: "Denn, was man schwarz auf weiß besitzt, / Kann man getrost nach Hause tragen"[19] a post-factum description of Mephistopheles' grounds for insisting that Faust sign an agreement.

> FAUST. Auch was Geschriebnes forderst du Pedant?
>> Hast du noch keinen Mann, nicht Manneswort gekannt?
>> Ist's nicht genug, daß mein gesprochnes Wort
>> Auf ewig soll mit meinen Tagen schalten?
>
>> Allein ein Pergament, beschrieben and beprägt,
>> Ist ein Gespenst, vor dem sich alle scheuen.
>> Das Wort stirbt schon in der *Feder*,
>> Die *Herrschaft* führen Wachs und Leder.
>> Was willst du böser Geist von mir?[20]

The parallels are striking: the pen-pusher as the evil spirit, the written document as lifeless, and, in contrast, the human word as vibrantly alive. The paper becomes more important than the person it is designed to serve and leads to and is a significant sign of distrust. Rudolf's sarcastic offer to seal the agreement in blood also harks back, of course, to the terms of the pact:

> MEPHISTOPHELES. Ist doch ein jedes Blättchen gut.
>> Du unterzeichnest dich mit einem Tröpfchen Blut.
> FAUST.　　　Wenn dies dir völlig G'nüge tut,
>> So mag es bei der Fratze bleiben.
> MEPHISTOPHELES. Blut ist ein ganz besondrer Saft.[21]

The devil is intent upon blood, for red represents his element: violence, passion, destruction and death.[22] Rudolf intends the same symbolic value: "Blut ist das rote Wachs, das jede Lüge / Zur Wahrheit stempelt; wenn von Volk zu Volk, / Warum nicht auch von Fürst zu Untertan?" (1658–60). Since the blood of war – might is right – has been viewed as a justifiable measure to settle disputes between nations, why not between sovereign and subject? By simply putting one's signature to a paper, "[ist] Mord und Brand geschleudert in die Welt" (1665). These corresponding episodes, therefore, point indirectly to Klesel, the "Pedant" who thrives on "Schriften":

> Es gilt zu schreiben, schreiben, rasch und viel.
> Und diese *Schrift*, ihr sollt mir sie noch küssen,
> Wie ich sie küsse jetzt.
> > Wir sind geborgen.   (1074–6)

Whereas Rudolf speaks of "Mund der Liebe" (1655) and "liebedurst'gem Ohr" (1656), one loving human being directly meeting the need for affection of another human being, Klesel's utterance and gesture of kissing the "toten Züg[e] einer toten Hand" (1653) demonstrate a self-serving perversion of this caring relationship. He passionately kisses the "Schrift" since it has become the most expedient means to gain, to hold and to exercise power.

Grillparzer has directed his reader's attention to the importance of the half verse, "Wir sind geborgen" by setting it off on a separate line. In the past, during his discussions with Mathias, Klesel has always taken great care to portray his master as the sole beneficiary of his various intrigues: *"Eu'r* Spiel steht gut, *ihr* habt die Trümpfe, *Herr*!"* (125). On only one previous occasion did he employ the first-person plural to acknowledge the allegation of a "geheimes Einverständnis / Mit Ketzern, Unzufriednen" (1011–12), an assignment of censure which he diplomatically deflected in part from his lord by using "uns." Now, for the second time in the play, he has recourse to the inclusive "Wir" – *"Ihr* seid geborgen" would also have fit the metric needs – to designate a shared bounty. The pretence of working exclusively for Mathias's advantage breaks down momentarily in this spontaneous boast born of overweening confidence in the strength of his position. Indeed, he feels so sure of himself that he adopts the tone of the master: "Wenn ihr mich stört such' anderwärts ich Ruh" (1073) and ignores his call: "Er [Klesel] gibt nicht Antwort. Lass' ich ihn denn jetzt! / Ein Meer von Bildern schwimmt vor meiner Seele. / *Auf die Seitentüre zugehend bleibt er stehen, als ob er umkehren wollte, geht aber nach einigem Besinnen ab*" (1080–1). The dramatist leaves his audience with one further visual confirmation[23] of the indecision, the susceptibility to intimidation of the man who would be emperor.

The only character who was not completely duped by Klesel's manipulative tactics but who, nonetheless, was their victim, Leopold, has the last word of the act: "Voraussicht ist ja Vorsicht, oder nicht? / Die *Klugheit* gibt nur Rat, die Tat entscheidet. / Es soll sich alles noch zum Guten wenden" (1136–8). The proverb turns out to be particularly ironic because of what has just happened. Klesel, not the archdukes, had the necessary foresight (the two "Schriften" prepared in advance) to anticipate the moves of his opponents. Although they wanted to exercise caution, they only succeeded in playing into the hands of the master intriguer, the "Permanent Secretary" as Thompson so aptly describes him.[24] By "Klugheit" Leopold most likely has Klesel in mind, for the archdukes readily admitted his shrewdness and continually sought his advice throughout the meeting. While the all-important deed may decide the final outcome, what Leopold, his fellow archdukes and the emperor fail to comprehend is that intelligence or cunning, combined with a repressed will to power, brings about almost all the decisive action and developments within *Ein Bruderzwist*. The pen proves mightier than the sword.

CHAPTER FOUR

Role Reversals

Although Klesel does not appear in person again until the end of the third act, his indirect influence becomes evident as soon as Julius attempts to convince the emperor of the urgency to act demanded by the political situation. Accurately diagnosing Mathias's limitations:[1] "Ihm fehlt der Mut. Ich kenne diesen Menschen: / Zum Anfang rasch, doch zögernd kommts zur Tat" (1391–2), Rudolf portrays the archduke essentially as a child: "Mein Bruder ist nicht schlimm, obgleich nicht *klug*. / Ich geb' ihm *Spielraum*, er begehrt zu *spielen*" (1286–7). Childish immaturity would seem to be a consistent feature projected initially, at any rate, by Mathias. Klesel frequently treats him as a child. Mathias's political adventure in Holland comes across as an adolescent prank for which he was made to sit in the corner ("seinen Bann in Linz" [443],) while in his audience with his brother to plead for rehabilitation, he creates the impression of a naughty schoolboy afraid to present himself before an annoyed teacher. His determination to continue the war with the Turks solely in order to redeem his own reputation discloses puerile obdurateness and selfishness bordering on sheer stupidity and prompts Max to admonish him: "Nun Bruder sei nicht kindisch," (881). The spoilt "brat" of the family, "der geliebtre Sohn" (94), he has become accustomed to getting his own way; the choice of "Spielraum" suggests that even the emperor indulges his whims. However, as Julius warns Rudolf, infantile games can easily have deadly consequences, especially if the playpen is the political arena: "Wars Spiel? daß eigner Macht er schloß den Frieden, / Ists Spiel? daß er den Herren spielt im Land?" (1288–9). Of course, at this point in their dialogue, Julius and Rudolf do not share the audience's awareness of the other key person's involvement. We know that it was Klesel who concluded peace with the enemy, not Mathias, and that if the archduke is playing the master, we can be reasonably confident in guessing who is pulling the strings. Interestingly enough, no sooner does Rudolf learn of the "wirklich[e] Gefahr" through Prokop's eye-witness report than he immediately orders Rumpf, "Bringt die Berichte dieser letzten Tage, / Und was an Briefen, in mein Kabinett" (1411–12). Now, suddenly mindful of the threat posed by Klesel, he shows a willingness to read the reports which he formerly chose to ignore. In other words, fear of the bishop forces the emperor to confront unpleasant political developments and to realize that the balance he had hoped to maintain (1419–23) has been forfeited. Whereas Rudolf has been paralyzed by his own insight into the destructive potential of the deed, Klesel, as we have noted, shows no hesitation to disturb the status quo (129–131) to create internal strife as long as he comes out on top. It is surely one of the peculiar ironies of *Ein Bruderzwist* that the protagonist who consistently expresses his ideal world view in theologically inspired terms,[2] who, for instance, takes upon himself the suffering of the world (2411), is a secular political ruler while his antagonist, who actively promotes and engages in various forms of morally suspect political intrigue and who never once gives any evidence of genuine religious conviction, is a Roman Catholic bishop/archbishop/cardinal.

As the second example "to affect the course of events," Thompson singles out Rudolf's yielding "to the demands of the Bohemian Protestants when he signs the 'Majestätsbrief' which may be held to be a direct cause of the Thirty Years' War."[3] But who in the first place created the political pressure enabling the "bömischen Stände" to blackmail the emperor into compliance with their demands? For the second time Klesel is the indirect force behind one of Rudolf's ill-fated decisions, however reluctantly taken. Even more ironic in this particular case is that, by agreeing to sign a "Schrift," he unwittingly succumbs to the tempter, the "Pedant," and therefore goes against his better judgment: "Scheint es nicht, als verführte das Dokument zur Signatur?"[4] "But the most crucial of his [Rudolf's] decisions is yet to come, namely that taken at the end of Act III to allow Archduke Leopold to bring an army from Passau to relieve Prague. As a result Rudolf loses altogether the loyalty of the Bohemians who unite with Mathias's troops against the invading Passau army."[5] Fülleborn suitably calls this incident "die Herzpause des Stücks."[6] Once again, I would argue that the deciding factor behind this fateful example of bad judgment, the person who, to use the play's imagery, tips the scales in favor of war, is Klesel. In view of the dramatic situation Grillparzer has created at this momentous juncture with its culmination of internal and external pressures, all does in fact seem to hang in the balance. Rudolf confesses to Julius, "In diesen Adern sträubt sich noch der Herrscher / Und Zorn und Rachsucht glüht in meiner Brust" (1704–5), and, as if on cue, Leopold, "der Versucher" (1718) makes his entrance, thus providing the opportunity to satisfy this thirst for revenge. At first, Rudolf flees from the temptation embodied by his nephew and refuses to see him; however, Leopold, making a plea before the closed door in an effort to persuade his surrogate father to accept his help "zum Schutz der Majestät" (1737), finally gains admittance: "Die Türe wird bewegt – sie öffnet sich – Mein Vater!" (1742). Frequently the tragedy's *raisonneur*, Julius recognizes that the next few minutes will decide whether or not cool, collected deliberation will prevail over outraged personal sentiment:

> O daß nun nicht der Groll, gekränkte Würde,
> Und die Empfindung, die, wenn aufgeregt,
> Gern übergeht in jegliches Empfinden:
> Von hart zu weich, von Innigkeit zu Zorn,
> Ihn hinreißt einzuwill'gen in das Schlimmste:
> Zu handeln, da's zu spät.   (1743–48)

At this precise moment in the climactic buildup, Rumpf, *"zur Türe hereinsprechend,"* announces, "Herr Bischof Klesel" (1748) completing Julius's verse "Zu handeln, da's zu spät" and thus emphasizing the crucial nature of the timing involved:

> JULIUS *Nicht* jetzt, nur jetzo *nicht!*
> RUMPF   Sie lassen sich
>   Abweisen nicht.
> KLESEL *eintretend*:   *Nein* wahrlich, in der Tat.   (1749–50)

The vehemence of Julius's reaction to the news – he seeks to deny it twice – indicates the danger Klesel's arrival represents to the equilibrium Rudolf has tried to preserve both in himself and in his realm.

The dramatist has constructed this sequence as an antithesis to an earlier episode in act one. Whereas in the latter Klesel was obliged to play the humble, deferential servant, here his arrogant self-confidence manifests itself in the first line. Indeed, his initial word "Nein" is a contradiction reinforced by "wahrlich" and "in der Tat" and recalls another negation, the second line of *Ein Bruderzwist*:"Ich *nicht*, führwahr!" Klesel may seek to hide behind his subaltern function: "Ich komme her im Auftrag meines Herrn" (1753), but his blunt language, brutal tone and provocative actions are those of a man who feels himself to be very much in control of the situation:

JULIUS   Wollt Ihr [sic] den Kaiser zwingen euch zu sprechen?
KLESEL   Da sei Gott für! Gemeldet will ich werden,
         So heißt mein Auftrag und, wenn abgewiesen,
         Kehr'ich zurück. Doch melden *muß* man mich.
         Er setzt sich links im Vorgrunde.   (1754–7)

This response may be seen as an ironic inversion of the earlier situation where Klesel had to plead to a chamberlain for the mere privilege of being presented to Rumpf, while now he can insist that he be announced to the emperor. His positioning himself in the foreground, and the very act of sitting in the presence of his social superior, visually confirm his own sense of self-importance. Also, if we take into consideration our previous knowledge of the relationship between master and servant, especially as revealed the last time we observed the two together at the end of the second act, there can be little doubt as to who devised the message and who decided on the messenger.

JULIUS   *Ich bitt' euch, Herr, sprecht leise.*
KLESEL   Und warum?
JULIUS   Glaubt ihr denn nicht die Stimme schon des Mannes,
         Der ihm, er glaubts, so Schlimmes zugefügt,
         Muß in des Kaisers Brust, jetzt, wo Entschlüsse
         Hart mit Entschlüssen kämpfen, Scham und Zorn -
KLESEL   Jetzt ist nicht von Entschlüssen mehr die Rede,
         Notwendigkeit ist da und sie schließt ab.
         In des Kaisers Kabinett wird geklingelt.
JULIUS   Es ist geschehn! Nun wahre Gott der Folgen!   (1758–65)

To make the reversal complete, Julius repeats verbatim Klesel's opening words of the drama, i.e., "Ich bitt' euch, Herr!" (83). The duke, the emperor's confidant, is now compelled to assume the subservient role, to adopt the pleading tone while Klesel, the "Diener" of low origins, has become the "Herr" (Rumpf also announces him as *"Herr* Bischof Klesel"). Julius's request "sprecht leise" further underscores Klesel's current dominant status since in the first two acts circumstances required that as the prompter behind the scene he whisper the requisite cues to his master: *"Nachdem er sich umgesehen, leise"* (p. 379); *"Halbleise"* (p.405). Because the schemer is now more openly in charge, he can interrupt his high-born interlocutor to expound his own brand of political pragmatism and he can express himself in a voice loud enough for the emperor to hear through a closed door. (Rumpf responds to a signal from Rudolf's private room and there is no direct evidence that the chamberlain has to apprise his lord of Klesel's arrival.) The fact that Rudolf would seem to deduce the bishop's presence from his voice alone is but one of several signs that he now has a greater appreciation of Klesel's part as the principal instigator of the present unfavorable turn of events and hence as his main antagonist. Moreover, Julius, who has the emperor's ear, speaks of "denselben Räumen / Die … [Klesel's] Rat mit Zwietracht angefüllt – " (1751–2) and of "die Stimme schon des Mannes, / Der ihm [Rudolf], er glaubts, so Schlimmes zugefügt" (1759–60).

In clear recognition of the importance of Klesel's presence as the deciding factor for Rudolf to revoke his original resolve not to sue for personal vengeance – "Ich darf nicht, will nicht" (1724) – Julius asks, "Und war kein Anderer als ihr zu finden / Zu solcher Botschaft, die fast klingt wie *Hohn*?" (1766–7). To have been deceived, manipulated and outmaneuvered by "jene[m] list'ge[n] Priester" (1403) and then to have to deny one's aristocratic pride to negotiate the terms of a peace agreement and ultimately to share one's power with that same priest would indeed be "a difficult pill to swallow," however beneficial it might be to the state. While we the spectator must inevitably fault Rudolf for surrendering to his worst emotions, we can understand the provocation leading up to the most far-reaching and politically ill-advised decision of the play.[7] "Man erkennt einen psychologischen Meistergriff Grillparzers darin, daß mit dem Eintreffen des von Rudolf verachteten Klesels ein Augenblick zorniger Betäubung dem Kaiser die Besinnung raubt und er in unbedachtem Entschluß die Vollmacht unterzeichnet."[8] I am reminded of Elisabeth's decision in Schiller's *Maria Stuart* to sign Maria's death warrant: in the final analysis personal motives such as envy of her rival's sex life and the desire for revenge gain the upper hand over the wider political advantages that may or may not accrue.[9]

Klesel's haughty answer to Julius's question bears further evidence of the former's pride in himself and confidence in his relative position of strength enabling him to speak the unembellished truth as he perceives it: "Vielleicht weil ich allein kein Schranz' und Höfling, / Gewohnt zu sagen gradaus was gemeint" (1768–9). However, what we have observed in the first two acts gives little credence to this flattering self-evaluation. In his attempts to obtain an audience for his master, he displayed all the sycophantic skills of the born courtier, and when he used his knowledge and cunning to secure Mathias's election as the family's representative, he rarely said what he really meant, and if he did, his words were intended to deceive the archdukes.

If we were to investigate the role in which Klesel, no longer responding to the need to conceal his own complicity, now casts himself, we could presumably gain some insight into the real person behind the mask. He sees himself as a physician administering distasteful but nonetheless salutary medicine to a sick nation: "Und Heilung war gemeint mit diesem Umschwung" (1773). As a benefactor of society, he assumes credit for this "Umschwung" which he prescribes as a cure for the current social, political and religious ailments. While stating his faith in himself and his plan for the future – "Man wirds zuletzt erkennen" (1774) – he unintentionally divulges his major weakness, i.e., "hört man mich" (1774). His authority depends upon his talent to persuade people to follow his advice. He cannot act directly, much as he would like to, but must always work indirectly through others less intellectually endowed than he. The last image of his speech: "Wer den Ertrinkenden erfaßt am Haar, / Er hat gerettet ihn und nicht beleidigt" (1775–6) once more reinforces his self-portrayal as the nation's potential savior and begs the questions as to whether or not Klesel could have saved the day and prevented the Thirty Years' War if he had continued to exercise influence through Mathias. We shall return to the issue in the analysis of the fifth act.

When Rudolf orders Klesel's immediate withdrawal from court and threatens him with further punishment, the bishop is not in the least perturbed:

> *Ich* gehe denn. Den Frieden wollt' *ich* bringen,
> Wählt man den Haß, so suche man nach *Macht*.
> Die Strafe die man droht, sie liegt so fern,
> *Wir* freuen uns indessen an dem Lohn.   (1780–3)

For the second time in the tragedy Klesel depicts himself as the peacemaker: while he first sought peace with the Turks and then with Rudolf, the latter has always opted for war. One senses in this instance as well that Klesel's mission was more *pro forma* than genuine, for as Julius commented earlier, why, of all people, was the bishop chosen to deliver the message? Was not the outcome self-evident and perhaps even consciously engineered? Renouncing all pretence, he presents himself, not Mathias, as the instigator with the "Ich" emphatically placed at the beginning and near the end of his first line. Then he reverts to the impersonal "man" partly out of defence to the emperor but also, one suspects, partly as a means to disguise his own drive for "Macht," that key word which almost inevitably crops up in his utterances. By implication, he would prefer not to have recourse to the violence of a power struggle but his opponent leaves him no choice. This is hypocrisy at its worst given that he stagemanaged this whole "Umschwung" (for which he earlier took credit) by exploiting the underlying rivalries, jealousies and resentment in the house of Habsburg. Rightly designating Rudolf's threat as a hollow one, Klesel then resorts to the encompassing first-person plural, the royal "we," to associate himself with the ruling aristocratic party, as he did in his telling final words of the second act: "Wir sind geborgen" (1076). Only in this way can the politically impotent "Ich" be effective and acquire its just reward ("Lohn"), an allusion to his materialistic bent of which the fifth act will provide additional proof.

As soon as Klesel departs, Julius immediately draws our attention to the commotion in the emperor's private chamber. Leopold subsequently emerges, *"einen Zettel in die Höhe haltend,"* declaring, "Ich hab's, ich hab's!" (1787). Later, in the context of Julius's thwarted attempt to undo the damage, the young archduke enlarges upon the "'s" of his triumphant exclamation: "Ich habe *schriftlich* seinen hohen Willen" (1816). Rudolf, together with the archdukes of act two, has again made the fatal error of signing his name to what in actual fact runs counter to his better moral self. Even though he would like to retract his word, he no longer has that option. His signature affixed to a document, which does not represent his true will as the holder claims, sets in motion a political chain reaction over which he has in effect relinquished control, for, to paraphrase Klesel, "Leopold hat die Schrift" and the paper, not the person, rules. "Das Wort erstirbt schon in der Feder, / Die Herrschaft führen Wachs und Leder."[10] Hence, not only does Klesel directly supply the final deciding momentum for Rudolf's third bad decision, but he is also indirectly present in the diabolical manner by which the emperor yields to the "Versucher" (1718) to become a repentant (1794) captive of his own "Unterschrift."

Klesel does not make an appearance, nor is he even mentioned in the fourth act. And yet, throughout, we witness the consequences of his machinations for the "Bürger" (Prokop), the Bohemian leaders (Turm and Schlick) and the Habsburgs, particularly Rudolf. One can see why critics have tended to overlook the pen-pusher's significance just as the emperor elects, perhaps out of class prejudice, to ignore his real antagonist and to censure only the figurehead, his brother:

> Nur Einen tadl' ich, den ich hier nicht nenne;
> Den ich verachtet einst, alsdann gehaßt,
> Und nun bedaure als des Jammers Erben.

> Er hat nur seiner Eitelkeit gefrönt,
> Und dacht' er an die Welt, so wars als Bühne,
> Als Schauplatz für sein leeres Heldenspiel.   (2306–11)

"Tatsächlich spielt Mathias auf barocke Manier," remarks Politzer, "die Rollen der Machtgier, des Ruhmes und der Zerknirschung; sein Spiel ist voraussehbar und daher ohne Geheimnis, er selbst nichts als der Schatten des Schattens, den das geistesstille Licht des Kaisers auf das dramatische Geschehen wirft."[11] While not contesting this sketch of Mathias who comes across as a simple-minded, predictable child, I would assign the part of the shadow's shadow to Klesel and go one step further. In reviewing his own life, Rudolf acknowledges, "Ich selber war ein Mann der Dunkelheit" (2361), intimating his preference for seclusion. The tragedy also exposes an irrational, darker side of his personality and, as already ascertained, on at least three occasions, when outside pressures induce him to react to this aspect of his psychological makeup, Klesel, the black-robed priest, sets the stage. Finally, when Rudolf has no alternative other than to resign his office and proclaim, "Mathias herrsche denn" (2329), he only confirms his opponent's earlier triumphant pronouncement: "Ihr [Mathias] habt die Schrift, / Die euch zum Herren macht in diesem Land" (1071–2). The last act will illustrate how Rudolf might more appropriately have declared, "Klesel herrsche denn."

CHAPTER FIVE

He Who Lives by the Pen ...

"Der fünfte Aufzug lebt wesentlich aus dem Widerschein, wie im zweiten fehlt die Mittelfigur [i.e., Rudolf], und sie beherrscht dennoch stärker als dort das Ganze. Sie und zugleich das Geschehene werden durch das Medium der beteiligten Figuren reflektiert."[1] Baumann's view offers an accurate summation of the critical reaction to the last act: despite his absence Rudolf remains the central character and the catastrophe that comes in the wake of his death vindicates his policy.[2] The new emperor warrants only passing mention, as for example in Yates's synopsis: "The last act shows Mathias achieving the power that has been his goal, but doing so only against a background of disaster for which he himself is responsible ..."[3] This is the truth, but certainly not the whole truth, for he is only accountable to the extent that he made himself the willing instrument and beneficiary of his servant's intrigues. The character of Rudolf has cast such an all-pervasive shadow over *Ein Bruderzwist* that the critics have largely overlooked Klesel's masterly but necessarily indirect control of both the second and, more importantly, the last act: "Die Diskussion politischer Möglichkeiten zwischen Ferdinand und Klesel gibt der besonderen Lage der dargestellten Zeit einen zu weiten Raum und läßt den Zuschauer unbeteiligt."[4] Whereas Baumann argues for Rudolf's presence in his absence as evidence of "Wie kaum ein zweiter ... Grillparzer die Dramatik des Mittelbaren [beherrscht],"[5] I would propose that Klesel represents an even better illustration of this "Dramatik des Mittelbaren," since the priest's social status obliges him to work deviously through others.

"The significance of Klesel's role in Act Five of the *Bruderzwist* has been largely ignored by commentators ...,"[6] Thompson has observed and his excellent article has gone a long way to encourage a greater awareness of the priest's overall crucial participation in the plot, providing a useful summary of his policy's strengths and weaknesses.[7] While I shall return on occasion to Thompson's interpretation to buttress my own, his essay, because it still does not provide a detailed analysis of the revealing dialogue between Klesel and Ferdinand at the outset of the act, fails to rectify fully the situation it correctly diagnoses. Thompson and others have not recognized, and hence have not taken into account, Klesel's dominant image, that of the "Federfuchser." To paraphrase an old proverb, he who lives by the pen, dies by the pen, i.e., runs the risk of forfeiting his political status.

As yet another instance of the extent to which the critics have underestimated Klesel, David notes the "Parallelismus zwischen dem ersten und fünften Akt – Mathias schließt sich in seinem Kabinett ein und will niemanden, nicht einmal seine Vertrauten, sehen, ganz wie am Anfang Rudolf jedem Besucher seine Tür verschloß ...'[8] but omits to mention the ironic reversal whereby Ferdinand, who in act one gained immediate access to Rudolf, must now appeal to Klesel for permission to see the emperor designate, Mathias. The priest's strategy becomes quite clear. Having encouraged his master to rely totally upon his advice, he makes it a point never to allow Mathias to be in a one-on-one situation with another person who would conceivably come between "Herr" and "Diener." In order to retain his influence Klesel must remain in Mathias's immediate proximity:

KLESEL   Die Tür steht euch offen jederzeit,
            Ihr seht ihn [Mathias] täglich, stündlich, wenn ihr wollt.
FERDINAND   O ja, im Schwall des Hofs, bei Spiel, beim Tanz.
            Wohl auch im Kabinett, *in eurem Beisein.*
KLESEL   Er ist der Herr und ich sein Diener nur.
            Befiehlt er mir zu gehen, geh' ich; bleibe,
            Wenn er mein Bleiben förderlich ermißt.   (2437–43)

The last quoted speech contains Klesel's general justification for his office and attitude – he is only an obedient subaltern – but the play has shown on numerous occasions that this is a mere pretense, for the one who really issues the crucial orders is the servant: "Drängt ihn [Rumpf]! Drängt ihn!"(141); "Begehrt mir ein Kommando / In Ungarn!"(127–8); "Kommt, kommt! / Verloren geht sonst alles"(217–18); and "Bleibt, Herr, bei eurer Weigrung"(764). When Ferdinand recounts an anecdote describing how he tried to speak to his uncle in private but noted his constant glances towards a "Tapentür"(2446), Klesel, not denying the allegation, says in his defence, "Wär' es geschehn, geschah es auf Befehl: / Gehorchen schließt das

Horchen selbst nicht aus"(2449–50); he was just following orders. Klesel's position would appear to be unassailable. For public consumption he goes to great lengths to paint a picture of himself as wholly dependent upon the will or whims of his lord; however, since we, the audience, have been witness to their relationship, we know who really holds the reins of power. Because of his intellectual limitations, Mathias is content with the trappings, the prestige of the office, while he is quite willing, indeed compelled, to leave the decision-making and the long-term planning to his secretary.

At the conclusion of the fateful meeting in act two, Leopold appeared to be the only archduke not to be completely taken in by Klesel's clever machinations. As Ferdinand's final counsel to Mathias made evident: "Vielmehr begehr' ich, daß ihr ihn [Klesel] gebraucht, / Er ist ein Eifrer für die fromme Sach"(1060–1), Klesel successfully exploited Ferdinand's religious bigotry on that occasion to win his support. Now, however, the priest's strategy has begun to have obvious political and religious consequences, so obvious that even Ferdinand cannot ignore them: "Wir aber wollens länger nicht mehr dulden, / Daß sich ein Fremder eindrängt zwischen uns / Und stört die Einigkeit von unserm Hause"(2451–3). Klesel has been able to take advantage of the underlying rivalry and resentment within the family (2307). Because the unity to which Ferdinand alludes never really existed, the resultant discord allowed Klesel to divide and rule in the name of his master.

The original justification for granting Mathias the "Vollmacht" was to ensure decisive action, but now, in Ferdinand's judgment, the new regime has only reverted to Rudolf's policy of inaction: "Doch kaum erreicht das langersehnte Ziel, / Gestillt die Gier des Herren und – des Dieners, / Wankt man auf gleichem Irrweg durch den Wald, / Und meint: sich regen sei schon weiter gehn"(2463–6). While the archduke confirms the central importance of the will to power, the dramatist also prepares the spectator for another consideration by the inclusion of a pause as signaled by the dash. However repulsive we may find Ferdinand's narrow-minded religious stance, the drama has convinced us of his need, at the conscious level at least, to be honest, no matter how unpalatable the truth may be: "Auch, habt gerühmt ihr meine Festigkeit, / Vergaßt ihr ihre Wurzel: das Gewissen"(1024–5). He has a conscience that would never allow him to tell a lie. The dash thus suggests some reluctance to mention Klesel, a reluctance which only his moral rectitude enables him to conquer. What here is only implicit in the punctuation will become explicit later.

Ferdinand's open attack forces Klesel to admit what the audience has long known: "ein fester Plan beherrscht das Ganze / Und jeder Schritt führt näher an das Ziel" (2467–8), a plan that began with the "Kommando in Ungarn" and includes compromising and granting religious equality to the Protestant factions.[9] In the midst of this exchange, Klesel manages to elicit an indirect admission of his continuing influence from Ferdinand:

FERDINAND Sagt selbst ob euer Herr –
KLESEL   Nur meiner?
FERDINAND   Meiner auch.   (2472)

Since the archduke must concede, out of loyalty to the family and according to the document he signed in the second act, his obedience to Mathias, and since the latter is essentially the priest's puppet, Klesel has power over his interlocutor and, as a demonstration, interrupts the dialogue briefly to make this point surreptitiously. He clearly believes that he is debating from a position of strength and wants his opponent to know it.

To meet Ferdinand's criticism: "Die hohe Schule, deren Rektor ihr,[10] / Ertönt von Worten frecher Kirchenleugner"(2488–9), Klesel retorts, "Wir suchen Wissen bei der Wissenschaft, / Der Glaube wird gelehrt von gläub'gen Meistern"(2490–1). A Roman Catholic archbishop/cardinal arguing for the separation of knowledge and faith announces and condones the growing schism between science and religion which will ultimately undermine the socio-political power base of the Church. In direct opposition Rudolf pleads for a unified view of life and warns against questioning the foundations of traditional belief: "Daß deine Väter glaubten was du selbst, / Und deine Kinder künftig treten gleiche Pfade / Das ist die Brücke die aus Menschenherzen / Den unerforschten Abgrund überbaut / Von dem kein Senkblei noch erforscht die Tiefe. / O prüfe nicht die Stützen, beßre nicht!"(1633–8). The debate continues:

FERDINAND Fluch jedem Wissen, das nicht aufwärts geht
                   Zu aller Wesen Herrn und einz'gem Ursprung.
KLESEL   Von oben rinnt der Quell, doch rinnt er nicht zurück,
                   Wo er das Licht betritt ist er schon Lauf, nicht Quelle. (2492–5)

While Ferdinand sees God as the only acceptable source of knowledge, Klesel, picking up on his interlocutor's metaphor, points out that in pragmatic, scientific terms, a spring must obey the law of gravity and thus runs down from a height but never in the reverse order as this would contradict natural law. In other words he is using science or reason – the reference to "Licht" – to refute his opponent's religious argument. In addition, once the spring leaves the ground and enters the light, it no longer constitutes a source but rather a flow or current, perhaps an allusion to Heraclitus' thesis "πάντα ρεῖ," i.e., all things flow, from which several implications may be drawn. Since all of life is caught up in flux, there are no permanent, eternally valid human truths, no being, only becoming. Also, whereas wisdom comes from God above, once it leaves this source, it is, so to speak, contaminated and by implication lesser mortals are constrained to compromise and to make do with something less than the divine.[11]

A similar debasement or profanation of a sacred gift occurs in Mephistopheles' famous opening speech from the "Prolog im Himmel" which exploits the image of light to criticize the *Aufklärung*: "Ein wenig besser würd' er leben, / Hättst du ihm nicht den Schein des Himmelslichts gegeben; / Er nennt's Vernunft und braucht's allein, / Nur tierischer als jedes Tier zu sein."[12] Later in the same scene "Der Herr" describes his strange relationship to his servant Faust ("Fürwahr! er [Faust] *dient* Euch [dem Herrn] auf besondre Weise"[13]) by having recourse to the same metaphor: "Zieh diesen Geist von seinem *Urquell* ab, / Und führ' ihn, kannst du ihn erfassen, / Auf deinem Wege mit herab..."[14] The Lord associates the descending thrust with Mephistopheles: the water must flow downward into the complexities, contradictions and uncertainties of earthly existence, the Devil's domain: "Solang' er [Faust] auf der Erde lebt, / Solange sei dir's [Mephistopheles] nicht verboten. / Es irrt der Mensch, solang' er strebt."[15]

No match for Klesel on an intellectual level, Ferdinand resorts to a personal attack and accuses his adversary of being an opportunist who has exploited the Roman Catholic Church as a means to further his own political ambitions – "Kirchenfürst" (2496) being the first allusion to his promotion between acts three and five from bishop to archbishop/cardinal – and to provide for his own material security by setting in a good store of the "Schätz[e] dieser ird'schen Welt" (2502). The fact that Klesel does not deny the latter allegation: "Man sieht sich vor; die Zeiten schlagen um" (2504) gives it credence and would seem to remove all doubt as to whether one should put any faith in what Thompson calls "the early signs that Klesel is pursuing an *altruistic* policy in which he passionately believes."[16] Moreover, when Ferdinand proposes an altruistic model for the state: "So mag der Einzelne vielleicht sich trösten, / Doch für den Staat gibt es kein Einzelnes, / Für ihn hängt alles an derselben Kette" (2505–7), he really exposes his own self-interest since the common chain he has in mind is the Roman Catholic faith, the instrument to which he has recourse to impose his own will. This has really been a pretext to attack the apparent "Lauheit" (2510) of Klesel's policy of making concessions to the Protestants which have alienated the Catholic party, i.e., Spain, the Papacy, and Bavaria.

This censure goads the priest into stating his own view of human nature, some of the most unembellished, cynical observations contained in a Grillparzer drama but nonetheless possessing a disturbing ring of truth. "Es sorgt ein Jeder doch zunächst für sich, / Der Freund ist mehr als meiner noch sein eigner" (2514–15). While Rudolf, to counteract the growing egotism of the new age, has established an ideal order of knights "die nicht dienstbar ihrem Selbst" (1209), Klesel, the pragmatist, maintains that we are all at heart egoists and serve our own interests first. Since he couches his statement in universal, proverbial terms admitting no exception, he must also recognize the implications for himself: he may be a friend to Mathias but only because of the advantage that will inevitably accrue to himself. Hence he has shown that his own self-effacing pose – "Er [Mathias] ist der Herr und ich sein Diener *nur*" (2441) – is a sham. He goes on to give some specific political examples: Spain wants to use the Empire to acquire Holland and as for Rome, "Der Papst ist der Kompaß, des sichre Nadel / Die Richtung anzeigt uns zum fernen Pol; / Allein die Segel stellen und das Ruder brauchen, / Das überläßt er uns; wir hoffen so" (2518–21). In these four verses expressed in diplomatic language or, more bluntly put, in political double-talk, Klesel proclaims the separation of Church and State, of religion and politics just as earlier in the scene he endeavored to make a case for a strict division between religion and science. (The text later designates "Klügeln" as an instrument of "Trennen.") Whereas the Church may indicate the ideal orientation the ship of state should follow, the politician must set its actual course, i.e., deal with the political practicalities of real life without interference from the clergy. This, of course, represents a radically modern, anachronistic view for the seventeenth century, especially in the mouth of the Archbishop of Vienna, but at the same time it offers a good illustration of Klesel's talent to rationalize his own stance.

Having effectively demolished the religious pretexts of Ferdinand's first two allies, Klesel then turns his attention to the third, Bavaria. "So seht ihr nicht wohin sein [Baiern] Streben geht? / Ist Östreich erst verworren und geschwächt, / Steht nichts in Weg ihm zu der Kaiserkrone" (2523–5). The *Realpolitiker* readily perceives how a state will not hesitate to exploit a rival's weakness to expand its power base. This priest knows the nature of power and its corrupting influence, for he himself is a prime example: his overweening confidence in the strength of his current office surfaces in his condescending manner of addressing an archduke: "Arglos frommer Herr" (2522).

As an unwitting confirmation of this assessment of naive piety and of the extent to which religious narrow-mindedness blinds the archduke to the intrigues of others, Ferdinand retaliates in defence of his ally, "Der Baierfürst hegt gottesfürcht'gen Sinn, / Das Wohl der Kirche sucht er, nicht sein eignes "(2526–7). This brings the discussion back to the issue of altruism versus egoism. "Will Einer erst die Herrschaft Gott verschaffen, / Sieht er in sich gar leicht des Herren Werkzeug / Und strebt zu herrschen, damit Jener herrsche. / Auch ist der Seeleneifer und der Eigennutz / Nicht gar so unvereinbar als man glaubt" (2528–32). *Libussa* offers supporting evidence that Klesel most likely articulates the dramatist's own unflattering analysis of the mind's subterfuges, for the titular heroine's prophetic vision warns against the identical process of self-deception: "Da du [the equivalent of "man"] so lange dich in Gott gedacht, / Denkst du zuletzt den Gott nur noch in dir. / Der eigne Nutzen wird dir zum Altar / Und Eigenliebe deines Wesens Ausdruck" (2371–4). And, as another one of *Ein Bruderzwist's* retrospective ironies, Rudolf attributes essentially the same underlying inducements, self-interest and the will to power, to the Protestant factions: "Nein, *Eigendünkel* war es, *Eigensucht*, / Die nichts erkennt was nicht ihr *eignes* Werk" (336–7); "Die *Macht* ists was sie wollen" (1231). Klesel's, Libussa's or Rudolf's more realistic, pessimistic view of human motivation parallels La Rochefoucauld's association of even the most unselfish, philanthropic actions with "l'intérêt"[17] and reflects a growing cynicism vis-à-vis the humanistic, idealistic image of man and the belief in human goodness and perfectibility. Dramatists such as Kleist or Büchner,[18] whose works ran counter to the standards of Weimar Classicism in form and content, and who were obliged, to quote Kleist, "auf die Zukunft hinaus[zu]sehen"[19] shared the same scepticism expressed here by Grillparzer's priest. The presentation of religion as a sublimation of the will to power is particularly ironic in this context for two reasons. First, Klesel, pretending to evaluate the King of Bavaria's motives, boldly presents a valid description of Ferdinand's own psychological makeup: "So werde nie mir [Ferdinand] Heil, / Als je mein Sinn ein andres Trachten kannte, / Als Östreichs Wohl und Jesu Christi Ruhm" (373–5). The first act bore testimony to this fanaticism as he boasted to Rudolf of the forced conversion of sixty thousand subjects and the banishment of twenty thousand Protestants in the middle of winter (474–8), while in the fifth act Ferdinand will counsel Wallenstein: "laßt uns ihn [Rudolf] rächen. / Zwar Rache ziemt dem echten Christen nicht, / Doch seine Feinde strafen die auch unsre; / Und strafend sie, wär's mit dem Äußersten, / Zugleich erretten von dem ew'gen Tod" (2841–5). In this speech, his initial, spontaneous impulse is to exact bloody revenge on the Protestants but then, suddenly realizing that Christianity does not permit such a response, he nonetheless exploits his faith by rationalizing his desire for revenge as punishment against the enemies of God. His "Seeleneifer" even goes to the ludicrous extreme of imitating the logic of the Spanish Inquisition: it is far better that the Protestants lose their mortal lives rather than their eternal souls; he is only doing them a favor. Grillparzer is indulging in black humor, especially when one bears in mind that Ferdinand is abusing the emperor's name to sanctify the civil war which Rudolf's policy sought above all to avoid: "Da stehts vor mir [Rudolf]! Der Mord, der Bürgerkrieg. / Was ich vermieden all mein Leben lang, / Es tritt vor mich am Ende meiner Tage. / Es soll, es darf nicht. Steckt die Schwerter ein, / Vertragt euch mit dem Feind!" (1673–7). Secondly, Klesel's cynical speech applies equally well to himself, but on the *secular* level; whenever he portrays himself as "des Herren Werkzeug," he always means Mathias's servant: "Ich bin meines Herrn. / Er ist mein uns, mein euch, mein ich, mein alles" (2541–2). His arrest, however, calls this self-effacing posture into serious question: he only mentions his master to criticize him (2659–61) and shows concern solely for his own survival. Klesel rules through Mathias just as Ferdinand has the ambition to rule the empire through God: "Und ich, ich bin berufen, / Im Sinn der Schrift. Berufen und – erwählt, / In Böhmen *wenigstens* als künft'ger König" (2576–8). By including the qualifying adverb he unconsciously unmasks his own more far-reaching political aspiration.[20] Of the two men the religious fanatic poses the greater threat because of his self-delusion and the subsequent, narrowly defined, violent pursuit of his objective, whereas the priest is more apt to compromise because he has the awareness to recognize, make allowances for and turn to account the less commendable motives behind human activity, including his own: he does admit to his materialism for example.

Klesel's speech now moves from irony to sarcasm: "Die Überspannung läßt zuweilen nach, / Und wie der Adler, der der Sonne nächst, / Holt er sich Kräftigung durch ird'sche Beute. / Man meints selbst von der Kurie in Rom" (2533–6). One suspects that Grillparzer is using an archbishop to get back at the Roman Catholic Church for having stigmatized the dramatist as an irreverent, disloyal freethinker because of a poem he wrote. With tongue in cheek Klesel suggests that the Church's mission to deal exclusively with spiritual matters, a psychologically taxing task, parallels the flight of the eagle which despite its proximity to the sun/ideal still obtains its real sustenance "durch ird'sche Beute," a sardonic allusion to the Church's vast wealth, material power and worldly desires from which even its executive body is not exempt.[21] As Mephistopheles jeeringly points out, "Die Kirche hat einen guten Magen, / Hat ganze Länder aufgefressen, / Und doch nie sich übergessen."[22] Klesel may well embody the more misanthropic, down-to-earth side of Grillparzer's own personality, the mercilessly censoring mind of the "Tagebücher," essentially the same function Mephistopheles fulfils for Goethe.

Since this line of reasoning strikes "too close to home," Ferdinand betrays his understandable unease by attempting to shift the focus of the dialogue to the main issue at hand. "Ob ihr nun sprecht, was euch und mir nicht ziemt, / – Ihr nennt, ich weiß es, derlei *Politik* – / Doch Eins tut not in allen ernsten Dingen: / Entschiedenheit; ob unser ihr, ob nicht" (2537–40). For the second time *Ein Bruderzwist* associates politics in the pejorative sense with Klesel. This reference recalls his observation to Mathias in the first act: "Zwar *Politik* nennt so was aquiriert / Und find't sich wohl dabei" (114–15), i.e., a process whereby, having performed an unethical deed, one tries to disguise it with a euphemism. But Ferdinand himself has been and will be guilty of adopting an equally accommodating and not unrelated standard of moral behavior – the notion that the end justifies the means. In seeking to excuse his betrayal of Rudolf he vaunted his "Gewissen; / Das eine *Beugung* [i.e., bending the rules] etwa [ihm] erlaubt / Zu gutem *Zweck*" (1025–7) and, using the same argument to defend his abduction of Klesel, he will maintain, "Das böse Beispiel das ich etwa gebe, / Es findet sich geheiliget im *Zweck*: / Der Ehre Gottes und dem Sieg der Kirche" (2616). In addition, at the very moment he repudiates politics as a "dirty word," he is in the very process of playing the questionable strategic game of forcing his interlocutor to declare sides – you are either for us or against us – and, in the event of an inappropriate response, is prepared to eliminate him as a political force.

The question of decisiveness provokes the following telling reaction from Klesel: "Er [Mathias] ist entschieden und ich bin es auch. / Doch wenn die Macht nicht einig wie der Wille, / Wer trägt die Schuld als Jene, die im Dunkeln / Am Hofe selbst sich bilden zur Partei / Und die Parteiung in den Ländern nähren?" (2543–7). He prevaricates in the initial half of the first quoted line and tells the truth only in the second half. Later, in the same scene, under the duress of fighting for his political survival, he will blurt out what has become patently obvious throughout *Ein Bruderzwist*, namely that his master exhibits the worst possible flaws in a ruler – "Unsicherheit und Mangel an Entschluß" (2661). The balancing act whereby he always puts his master ostensibly first dictates in part the earlier misrepresentation and reinforces his dilemma as it emerges in the next lines. Klesel has the will to act – we have observed irrefutable proof of his decisiveness – but having always to work through his weak intermediary, he lacks the power to thwart effectively the strong opposition mounted by the Catholic party against his conciliatory policy. In direct contrast Rudolf has the power but not the will to act since he fears the consequences: "Dazu noch das Bewußtsein, daß im Handeln, / Ob so nun oder so, der Zündstoff liegt, / Der diese Mine donnernd sprengt gen Himmel" (1446–8).[23]

Up to this point in the dialogue Klesel has strictly avoided any allusion to himself other than in the guise of the faithful, subservient "Diener." Universal or impersonal subjects dominate his speeches, giving his *realpolitisch* pronouncements a proverbial flavor: "Gehorchen schließt das Horchen selbst nicht aus" (2450); "Man sieht sich vor; die Zeiten schlagen um" (2504); "Will Einer erst die Herrschaft Gott verschaffen" (2528); "Der Schwächere gibt nach" (2558), etc. It is only when Ferdinand goads him out of his self-effacing posture over an issue crucial to his plan that he leaves the relative safety of the impersonal for the personal mode in the one speech where he momentarily throws caution to the winds:

KLESEL   Sie [die Utraquisten] sollen Kirchen baun, so wills ihr König.
FERDINAND Sagt doch vielmehr nur: Ihr.
KLESEL   Nun also: *Ich*,
    Sofern mein Rat ein Teil von seinem Willen.
    Mich hat umsonst aus meiner Niedrigkeit
    Die Vorsicht nicht gestellt auf jene Stufe
    Zu der sonst nur Geburt und Gunst erhebt.
    Der Kirche Macht bekleidet mit dem Purpur,
    Der *mich den Königen* zur Seite stellt.
    Ich werde nicht vor Menschen feig erzittern,
    Und wärens Könige – im Land der Zukunft;
    Die nämlich kommen kann, nicht kommen muß.   (2562–72)

The emphatic positioning of the first-person pronouns at either the beginning or the end of the lines allows the dramatist to highlight the implied cult of self and the confidence or pride it engenders to view one's career as the workings of Providence. The resentment of a system based on birth and favoritism rather than on personal merit

or talent has driven this son of a Protestant baker to exploit the
Roman Catholic Church as the one available avenue by which to gain
"Macht," his obsession, and to achieve equality with the hereditary
ruling class – in his very formulation he places himself side by side
with kings. Frustrated by Ferdinand's interference with his sacred
mission, he falls prey to "Unvorsichtigkeit im Reden," one of the
"Fehler des heftigen [historic] Klesel"[24] according to Grillparzer's
notes, exposes his true colors in the heat of the dispute and confirms
Ferdinand's earlier diagnosis of a "Kirchenfürst, / ... / Der sie
[Dogma] verteidigt auch, ... / So lang der Kirche Gold und Rang
und Ansehn / [Ihm] noch ein Lohn schien, der des Strebens wert"
(2496–2500). But in fairness to Klesel, he never denied this charge,
maintaining that the changing times demanded such an attitude. The
dash marks the point at which he recognizes that he may have gone
too far in his vehement defence of his own personal career; hence he
softens his statement by maintaining that the new age (the revolution) is not necessarily imminent and may not even materialize.
Despite this attempt to backtrack, he has actually destroyed himself
with this bold display of independence, his claim to equality with
the ruling family. Since he has left no doubt that he is his own man
and not "unser," i.e., not one to be intimidated by the likes of Ferdinand, the archduke can have no illusions about the type of person
he is dealing with: "Der Bauer steckt noch ganz in seinem Leibe /
Mit des Emporgekommnen Übermut" (2580–1). Feeling too secure in
his current position at court, Klesel has made two fatal errors: revealing his true feelings and underestimating his enemy. Ferdinand is the
only other person in the tragedy who has both the will and the
opportunity to act decisively[25] provided he can convince himself that
he is following his conscience and thus acting as "des Herren
Werkzeug" (2529).

Earlier in this chapter, I analyzed the significance of the dash before
"des Dieners" (2464) in Ferdinand's speech in which he displayed
some resistance to mentioning "Herr" and "Diener" in the same
breath. A common, underlying consciousness emerges in Herzog
Julius von Braunschweig's question: "Und war kein Anderer als ihr
[Klesel] zu finden / Zu solcher Botschaft, die fast klingt wie *Hohn*?"
(1766–7) What, however, may only be insinuated in these two
instances becomes more explicit once Ferdinand tries to put Klesel
down as a mere peasant without any claim to refinement. The realization that a servant of lowly origins has outwitted no less than one
emperor and four archdukes: "Wars darum daß wir [the archdukes]
uns euch [Klesel/Mathias] angeschlossen / Und gegen ihn den
rechten güt'gen Herrn?" (2454–5) must be particularly galling and

come as a damaging blow to an aristocracy that proclaimed its superiority both in mind and body.[26] There are some grounds for the view that Ferdinand reacts partly out of damaged pride. While "Eminenz" (2582) gains immediate admittance to Mathias and confidently *"geht mit starkem Schritt ins Kabinett"* (p. 470), the archduke, obliged to "cool his heels," bitterly confirms his inferior status: "Ich bins gewohnt den *Dienern* nachzustehn" (2586).

The same scenario seen from Klesel's point of view reflects the growing resentment on the part of a prosperous and intelligent middle class unable to have a say in the fate of the nation. Grillparzer's own experiences at the hands of the aristocracy were not on the whole positive. As a tutor he almost died when a wealthy count's family left him for dead at their country estate;[27] as a civil servant, with the exception of his patron Count Stadion, he was compelled to serve under incompetent, intellectually inferior appointees from the upper class[28] (It was the general practice that all senior posts within the Austrian bureaucracy went to members of the nobility); and as a dramatist, he suffered continually under a repressive, narrow-minded censorship supported and administered by an aristocracy eager to preserve its privileged position.[29]

He put it most succinctly in his "Erinnerungen aus dem Revolutionsjahre 1848": "Der Depotismus hat mein Leben, wenigstens mein literarisches zerstört, ich werde daher wohl Sinn für die Freiheit haben."[30] I suspect that Grillparzer may have indeed been seditiously sympathetic towards part of what Klesel represents. "Wenn ihm nicht diese in Grillparzers Augen höchst unvorteilhaften sozialen und geistigen Eigenschaften [a reference to Ferdinand's disparagement, "Der Bauer steckt" etc. (2580–1)] anhingen, so hätte gerade Klesel die eigentliche tragische Gestalt des Stückes werden können."[31] Although I concur with Sternberger who attributes greater importance to Klesel's role, I would exercise extreme caution in taking Ferdinand's assessment of the archbishop as synonymous with that of the author, for the speaker in this instance is hardly an unbiased observer but rather a victim of the very "Übermut" he decries. While Klesel is beyond a doubt a "schlauer Ränkeschmied,"[32] what other option does he really have if he wishes to get ahead given the circumstances of his background and the autocratic society in which he moves? Hence our attitude towards him may well be an ambiguous mixture of esteem and disdain.

FERDINAND Da wär' zu zittern denn an mir?
KLESEL   Niemand soll zittern!
         Vor allem der im Recht ist und der klug.   (2573–4)

Meeting his opponent's veiled threats head-on, Klesel appears to be advocating a more democratic form of government, one which would not tolerate intimidation but would function on the basis of his own strengths. He has distinguished himself throughout *Ein Bruderzwist* by his cleverness, a feature which even his opponents must acknowledge. To realize that one has mental abilities superior to that of one's master and yet, for reasons of birth, to have to play the deferential subaltern must rankle and cause a deep-seated sense of frustration. For example, in response to Hero's insolent treatment in *Des Meeres and der Liebe Wellen*, the Tempelhüter, in an effort to salvage some self-respect, asks rhetorically, "Und nennst du mich nicht *klug*? / Weil ich ein *Diener* nur, ihr hohen Stamms? / Meinst du, die Klugheit erbe eben fort[33] / Vom Vater auf den Sohn, wie Geld und Gut?" (3:1283–5). On the positive side of the ledger, Klesel does win some support for standing up to the more dangerous autocrat Ferdinand, and if the priest had been permitted to continue in his office as "Vize-Kaiser," his intelligence with its practical grasp of political realities might conceivably have averted the impending catastrophe. On the negative side, Klesel's qualities lend themselves equally well to a less favorable interpretation. He insists upon "Recht," implying complex legal arguments, skillful analysis of legal precedent and dependence upon "Schriften" leading to hair-splitting, quibbling sophistry – in short "Klügeln." Grillparzer, who had a very low opinion of the justice system in general, employs Julius in the fourth act to present the Hobbesian position, i.e., society created laws essentially to protect its interests from the ravages of its own selfishness (2118–30), while in *Libussa* he paints a very depressing picture of what happens when people begin to insist upon their rights: "Und Recht ist nur der ausgeschmückte Name / Für alles Unrecht das die Erde hegt" (3:907–8).

Once again *Ein Bruderzwist* sets up a contrast between protagonist and antagonist. While Klesel stands for "Recht," "Klügeln," and "Trennen," the tools of the majority for dissolving the existing system, Rudolf advocates "Geburt," "Glauben," and "Verknüpfen" as the means to promote minority rule and preserve the feudal order. The priest appeals to justice as a proper recourse to shield himself against arbitrary abuses of power ("Niemand soll zittern!") and ultimately to achieve social and political equity; in contrast, the emperor views it as the path leading to the self-centered tyranny of the majority: "Der ruft: Auch mir mein Teil, vielmehr das Ganze! / Sind wir die Mehrzahl doch, die Stärkern doch, / Sind Menschen so wie ihr, uns unser Recht!" (1252–4). The one position effectively cancels out the other.

As soon as Klesel has exited, Ferdinand, left alone, reviews the political situation and comes to the conclusion: "Vor allem jetzt muß dieser Priester fort, / Des schlimme Schmeichelei, gehüllt in Derbheit, / Ihn ehrlich nennt wo *listig* er zumeist" (2603–5). Although the text provides several specific examples of "Schmeichelei," but none "gehüllt in Derbheit" – Ferdinand himself has been the unsuspecting victim of subtle flattery in act two – a combination of bluntness and honesty is how Klesel wishes to be perceived: "Vielleicht weil ich allein kein Schranz' und Höfling, / Gewohnt zu sagen gradaus was gemeint" (1768–9). Since his appearance at the end of the third act, he has exhibited the conceit and arrogance of a man who, once he has reached the top, no longer feels the need to keep up the deceptive appearance that rendered his ascendancy possible. The cunning that facilitated his rise to power, having become obvious, has turned into a liability as even Ferdinand now sees through him.

The archduke's soliloquy also includes a valid summary of Klesel's strengths and, in the process, outlines one of the drama's main underlying themes: "Des Leichtigkeit in *Schrift* und *Wort* und *Tat*, / Ihn unentbehrlich macht, weil er bequem / Die *Herrschaft* auflöst in die *Unterschrift*" (2606–8). First comes the written word, for Klesel dominates by virtue of his outstanding intellect as manifested through the pen. The spoken word points to his rhetorical skills, his ability to convince others by his verbal logic and rationalizations (act two). And, lastly, he is quite willing, indeed anxious, to transform what his mind conceives to be the best plan of action into deeds. Quite correctly Ferdinand sees in the "Unterschrift" as affixed to the "Vollmacht," to the "Majestätsbrief," or to Leopold's "Zettel" (p.441) the key to power in a new bureaucratic age. "Da braucht es nur noch [the archdukes'] Unterschrift" (1034) for the servant to rule through the master. Whereas in the old order, hegemony depended upon the sword, "Geburt und Gunst" (2567) or the sacred trust of one's given word ("*noblesse oblige*"), the new regime will function on the basis of legal rights, concomitant formalities and impersonal officialdom. Writing from first-hand experience, Grillparzer, himself a bureaucrat, had to contend with the petty, suspicious and ambitious nature of civil servants in the pay of an autocratic government. "Wenn nur dort [Vienna] der schändliche Geistesdruck nicht wäre und die Erniedrigung des Nebenmenschen. Was mit mir selbt geschähe, sollte mich wenig anfechten. Mich erniedrigen sie nicht. Und wenn sie tausend Jahre dran versuchten."[34]

While at the beginning of the nineteenth century Goethe's Faust declared his preference for "die Tat" over "das Wort,"[35] in the second half of the century Nietzsche announced the triumph of the herd's re-evaluation of values, a move away from activity (sword) to intellectualism (pen). As a symbol of a great past age, he glorified "die Vornehmen, Mächtigen, Höhergestellten und Hochgesinnten, welche sich selbst und ihr *Tun* als gut, nämlich als ersten Ranges empfanden und ansetzten."[36] In his ideal aristocrat, the "Herr," he saw the man of action, full of vitality and confident self-affirmation, seeking out conflicts to confirm his supremacy and living without fear before his own conscience. The herd system of morality devised by a physically inferior but intellectually superior majority of servants advocates passivity, equality, asceticism and self-denial, values born out of a deep-seated resentment and envy of the masters and designed to promote the transfer of power from the lord to his slave. According to Nietzsche, this pernicious development whereby the last became first began historically with the rise of the priestly caste. The following passage from the *Genealogie*, outlining the consequences of this moral evolution, also furnishes a surprisingly apt description of several characteristics *Ein Bruderzwist* associates with "jen[em] list'g[en] Priester" (1403): "Bei den Priestern wird eben *alles* [Nietzsche's emphasis] gefährlicher, nicht nur Kurmittel und Heilkünste, sondern auch Hochmut, Rache, Scharfsinn, Ausschweifung, Liebe, Herrschsucht, Tugend, Krankheit- mit einiger Billigkeit ließe sich allerdings auch hinzufügen, daß erst auf dem Boden dieser *wesentlich gefährlichen* [Nietzsche's emphasis] Daseinsform des Menschen, der priesterlichen, der Mensch überhaupt *ein interessantes Tier* [Nietzsche's emphasis] geworden ist, daß erst hier die menschliche Seele in einem höheren Sinn *Tiefe* [Nietzsche's emphasis] bekommen hat und *böse* [Nietzsche's emphasis] geworden ist – und das sind ja die beiden Grundformen des bisherigen Überlegenheit des Menschen über sonstiges Getier!"[37] No one, not even the dramatic characters, can doubt the "Tiefe" of Klesel's intellect, and as Nietzsche observed in *Jenseits von Gut und Böse*, "Alles, was Tiefe ist, liebt die Maske."[38]

An essential part of the scheme to eliminate the priest entails the confiscation of his papers: "Merk wohl, er darf zurück nicht in sein Haus, / Denn seine *Schriften* sind vor allem wichtig" (2635–6). It is one of the many ironies of this drama that just as "Schriften" made possible Klesel's rise to prominence, they will now contribute to his fall, a scenario confirmed later when Klesel attempts to bribe Seyfried: "Nur gönnt mir Aufschub, eine Viertelstunde. / Laßt mich zu Hause ordnen noch *Papiere*, / Man hat so Viel was nicht für Jeden taugt" (2682–4). His correspondence will obviously incriminate him. The pen thus shares with the sword a figurative double edge: what exists in writing may confer authority but, falling into the wrong hands, it may also ruin its author.

The details leading up to the archbishop's overthrow contain further examples of retrospective humor. "Zuletzt aber verfängt sich der Berechende in eignen Kalkül."[39] In seeking to prevent his opponent Ferdinand from seeing Mathias, Klesel sends his master to chapel, but in doing so he commits a tactical error: he robs himself of the very protection he needs to avoid arrest. He also exploits religion – "Die Andacht bindet sich an keine Zeit" (2642) – as an excuse to ensure his own domination: he really wants to distance his malleable master from the other politically strongest influence of the tragedy, the man who normally does not hesitate to act. I say normally, because Ferdinand does show some reluctance to take this particular step: "Und der ich Festigkeit von Andern fordre, / Mir ringen Zweifel selber in der Brust" (2610–11). But ironically he also derives support and resolve for his questionable tactical move from papers in a gesture reminiscent of Klesel: *Aus der Tasche seines Mantels Briefe hervorziehend*" (p.471) and from a letter of authorization: "Bin ich gewappnet nicht mit aller *Vollmacht* / Von Rom, von Spanien, dem kathol'schen Deutschland?" (2612–13). A "Vollmachtsbrief" once enabled the priest to appropriate the reins of power; another now topples him. And as the final irony Ferdinand interprets the situation created by Klesel's tactics as the requested "Zeichen … vom Himmel" (2644). Both speakers thus use a religious pretext to justify what they know to be a questionable act ("Das böse Beispiel" [2614]).

Once Klesel realizes that he has outsmarted himself, far from being the least cowed by his arrest, his true self comes even more to the fore. Assuming a prophetic voice, he sketches a grim picture of future events in the midst of which he will reappear to play a major part:

> Doch später, wenn der Samen aufgegangen,
> Den man gesät in den entzweiten Landen,
> Verwirrung und Empörung, ja der Krieg
> In blutigroter Blüte wuchernd sprossen,
> Dann wird man pilgern hin zu Kufsteins Toren,
> Dann kehr' ich heim in siegendem Triumph.   (2662–7)

Since both audience and dramatist share the wisdom of hindsight and know these prophecies to be valid, this speech does allow us to view Klesel more sympathetically. Announcing his ultimate vindication, his return to power as the savior of his country, Klesel may alienate his listeners through his arrogance, but Grillparzer's notes indicate the dramatist's awareness that even this part of the prediction would materialize and, ironically, at the behest of the very man responsible in the tragedy for sending the archbishop into exile in

the first place. "Letztlich begehrt ihn Ferdinand II vom Papst zurück
… Der Papst gibt nach anfänglicher Weigerung endlich seine Einwil-
ligung und Klesel kehrt im höchsten Alter … nach Östreich zurück.
Am Pauli Bekehrungstag … 1628 hält er seinen Einzug in Wien unter
Geläute und dem Entgegenströmen unzähliger Menschen."[40] Interestingly enough, Klesel's apocalyptic warning echoes his antagonist's[41]: "Und ist das Tor dem Unheil nun geöffnet, / Ist Mord und
Brand geschleudert in die Welt, / Dann denkt einst spät, wenn längst
ich modre: / Wir [Standesherren] waren auch dabei und haben es
gewollt" (1664–7). Both seers foretell the impending disaster, blame
others for its sudden, violent eruption into the world [Klesel's "man"
refers to his opponents, the radical Catholic party], and see history
as providing their subsequent ("später"; "erst spät") justification, i.e.,
I told you so. The only real distinction between the two speeches is
that Klesel, ever keen to be a mover of events, plans to be around
and still politically active on the day of reckoning, while the older
Rudolf, ever anxious to avoid contact with this arena ("Damit ich
lebe muß ich mich begraben" [1161]), takes for granted his absence.

In Ferdinand's last speech in this segment, he again exposes his
petty but dangerously vindictive personality:

> Es ziemt nicht meiner Würde
> Den Schergen hier zu spielen nebst dem Richter.
> Obwohls mich freut, erquickt in meinem Sinn,
> – Nicht meinetwillen, nein um Gottes wegen -
> Im Staub zu sehn den Mann, der ihm getrotzt.   (2671–5)

As an aristocrat conscious of his station, he is anxious to avoid
placing himself in a situation beneath his dignity, i.e., his "Übermut"
is socially justified, but not that of a presumptuous commoner. The
concessional clause then interjects what amounts to a spontaneous,
uninhibited utterance of the truth: Ferdinand finds sadistic pleasure
in the fall of his enemy. The following dash signals the intrusion of
greater conscious control over his words; now he seeks to deny any
personal benefit and as usual resorts to his sustaining illusion: he is
only defending God against a man who defied His will. Without
realizing it Ferdinand convincingly substantiates Klesel's previous
analysis of the rationalizations operative in the religious zealot: "Will
Einer erst die Herrschaft Gott verschaffen, / Sieht er in sich gar leicht
des Herren Werkzeug / Und strebt zu herrschen, damit Jener herrsche" (2528–30). Through an ironic turn of events, partly engineered
by himself, the archbishop has become the victim of the very same
twisted motivation.

When Klesel's attempts to suborn Seyfried prove fruitless, he falls back on his pride: "Ihr [Seyfried] mahnt mich recht. Ich habe hier geboten / Und will nicht betteln um der Bettler Gnade" (2688–9) and, for a final time, becomes the tragedy's prophet:

KLESEL   Vollführt denn die Befehle eures *Herrn,*
                Der sich von Eisen fühlt, wie euer Harnisch
                So oft ihn Glaubenseifer vorwärts treibt,
                Doch kommts einmal zu menschlicher Zerwürfnis
                Vor Jedem zittern wird, der, starken Sinns
                Sich *dienend* aufgedrungen ihm zum *Herrn.*
                Er wird mein Rächer sein. Ich ahn' ihn schon
                Und höre seine Tritte aus der Ferne.
EIN DIENER *der die Mitteltüre öffnet, anmeldend*:
                Herr Oberst Wallenstein.
KLESEL   Hört ihr den Namen?   (2690–8)

The underlying theme of this speech is the relationship between master and servant introduced by the first quoted line: a servant orders a servant to fulfill the commands of his "Herrn." Seyfried embodies the typical soldier, a "treuer Diener seines Herrn," impervious to bribes and unquestioningly obedient, in keeping with his military mentality: "Ich bin vom selben Stoff wie meine Waffen: / Die Faust von Eisen und die Brust von Erz" (2685–6). This type of servant Ferdinand can use effectively to consolidate his power and reinforce his oversimplified, black and white approach to political or moral issues. If, however, he were to face social upheaval where circumstances compelled him to engage the services of a more independently minded agent, the roles could just as easily be reversed. The knowledgeable spectator realizes that Klesel will in fact have the last laugh: the Thirty Years' War will reduce Ferdinand essentially to Mathias's impotent status vis-à-vis his more autonomous servant. As a convenient fulfillment of this prediction, another "Diener" announces Wallenstein whom Klesel hails as his instrument of revenge.[42] Although one may feel somewhat uncomfortable with the contrived nature of the general's fortuitous appearance, the too obvious effort to present *Ein Bruderzwist* as an introduction to Schiller's *Wallenstein*, one should not lose sight of the fact that Grillparzer selected Klesel, the alleged villain of the tale, to foretell Ferdinand's fate which history, as any German-speaking theater-goer knows, will confirm. Such a "sweet" vindication has to suggest some affinity between the author and his spokesman and to prejudice the audience in Klesel's favor, especially since this is the penultimate impression with which the secretary leaves the spectator.

The priest's parting words and gestures leave no doubt as to his frame of mind in his downfall: "*zu Seyfried, der vorausgehen will:* / Zurück! Mir bleibt der Vorrang, wär's in Ketten. / *Er geht mitten durch die Trabanten ab. Seyfried folgt*" (2700). "Klesel departs in *anger* [Thompson's emphasis] at his disposition, still convinced of his own rectitude."[43] There is no sign of remorse or submission, only defiance born out of the certainty of his own worth. Indeed, with his prophetic words still ringing in our ears and an awareness of his eventual triumphant return, his exit from the stage bears all the marks of a victory in defeat.[44] Now, when there is no longer any need for dissimulation, he places himself, "Mir," first – even his syntax puts this ranking into effect – and not a man to speak in vain, he walks out ahead showing deference to no one. Since his arrest, he never once alludes to Mathias and thinks only of himself. He may mention the nation but solely as an instrument to glorify himself, for he remains unrepentantly convinced of his indispensability. Hence his choice of "Vorrang," balancing the "mir," suitably captures his ambition, the striving of the "Streber" to advance himself politically. In a sense we have come full circle from Klesel's opening line of the play: what was only implicit in his words, "*Ich bitt' euch, Herr!*" (83) has become explicit in his last line, "*Mir* bleibt der Vorrang, wär's in Ketten" (2700).

Just as Rudolf remains very much in evidence despite his physical absence from the last act, the same claim holds true for his antagonist after his forced withdrawal. At the beginning of the dialogue between general and archduke, the following exchange takes place:

WALLENSTEIN Allein im Land bedarf es unsre Sorge,
              Da ist der *Unterste* zu *oberst*, Herr.
FERDINAND   Vielleicht das *Oberste* zu *unterst* bald.   (2706–8)

This play on the contrast between high and low only confirms Rudolf's worst fears:

Aus eignem Schoß ringt los sich der Barbar,
Der, wenn erst ohne Zügel, alles Große,
Die Kunst, die Wissenschaft, den Staat, die Kirche
Herabstürzt von der Höhe, die sie schützt,
Zur Oberfläche eigener Gemeinheit,
Bis alles gleich, ei ja, weil alles niedrig.   (1269–74)

Appalled by the "Albernheiten und Schlechtigkeiten Frankreichs und des übrigen Deutschlands"[45] and their Austrian imitations,[46] Grillparzer shared Goethe's or Nietzsche's low opinion of the masses, seeing in majority rule a threat to the cultural achievements seemingly guaranteed by a civilization based on hierarchical distinction. Rudolf finds further support for this autocratic social order when reflecting on the natural, overall productive relationship between mountain and valley: "Und aus dem Wechselspiel von hoch und niedrig, / Von Frucht und Schutz erzeugt sich dieses Ganze, / Des Grund und Recht in dem liegt, daß es ist" (1612–14). Two typical features of aristocratic thought form the basis of this metaphor used to describe the relationship between "Herr" and "Diener": first the legitimate, self-evident role of the nobleman as warrior/protector vis-à-vis the lower classes – indeed, one measures one's power, according to Hobbes, in terms of one's ability to protect –[47] and second, the non-utilitarian, unproductive aspect of this function mirroring the aristocratic prejudice against work.[48] It is within this same tradition that Rudolf characterizes himself as "das Band, das diese Garbe hält, / *Unfruchtbar* selbst, doch nötig, weil es *bindet*" (1163–4).[49] Of course, Klesel is clearly the best candidate for the indigenous barbarian who has risen from the depths ("Der Bauer steckt noch ganz in seinem Leibe" [2580]) to the heights of real political influence. His debate with Ferdinand brings the traditional ideal views, especially those espoused by his own Church, down to a very low common denominator, he promotes those values supportive of his own equality with the mighty, and his thoughts and actions, his "Klügeln," have encouraged separation, if not disintegration, within the realm.

Ferdinand's reformulation of Wallenstein's original antithesis – "das Oberste zu unterst" – while voicing the future emperor's desire to turn back the clock and annul the concessions made to the Protestant leaders, harks back to what has just transpired on stage, his toppling of Klesel: "Obwohls mich [Ferdinand] freut, erquickt in meinem Sinn, / ... / Im Staub zu sehn den Mann, der ihm [God] getrotzt" (2673;2675) and may thus insinuate his exalting in his recent exercise of power. But it also looks ahead to his problematic relationship with "*Herr Oberst* Wallenstein" (2698) with pun intended. "Und wie im Feld der Heeresfürst gebeut, / Nicht fremde Meinung oder Tadel scheut, / So sei auch in des Landes Regiment / Ein Gott, Ein Herr, Ein Wollen ungetrennt" (2731–4). By implication Wallenstein, in his self-sufficient, self-serving attitude, will eventually take vengeance for Klesel's fall at Ferdinand's hands, i.e., a servant will avenge a servant by seeking to become the master in his own right. On his own initiative the general has already written and sent off the orders to the garrisons, a minor act of insubordination, but one which nonetheless prompts Ferdinand to retaliate, "Ich dank' euch, *Herr*; und denk' euch wohl zu brauchen, / Wenn mich einst Gott auf diesen

Thron gesetzt. / Doch will ich mich auch hüten, nehmts nicht übel, / Daß ihr nicht mehr mir *dient*, als lieb mir selbst" (2749–50). Ferdinand resolves not to make the same mistake as his uncle and become overly dependent upon his servant: when Mathias learns of the troops' departure to counteract the rebellion in Prague, he commands predictably, "Schickt nach dem Kardinal!" (2776). Even though Ferdinand intends to keep a tight rein on Wallenstein, the latter's response: "Wer kann wohl sagen, meint ein altes Sprichwort: / Aus diesem Brunnen will ich niemals trinken! / Die Zeit entscheidet da, *Herr* – und der Durst" (2753–5) leaves considerable doubt as to who is the genuine "Herr" since each confers the coveted title upon the other.

Continuing the polarity between high and low, the report of the incident which ignited the Thirty Years' War, the *Prager Fenstersturz*, includes an ironic prefiguration of the social transformation Klesel embodies with a possible allusion to the biblical verse "Viele Erste aber werden Letzte sein und die Letzten Erste."[50] "Sie [the faithful Catholic faction] haben noch gar höflich sich entschuldigt / Weil nach dem Rang sie nicht zu liegen kamen, / Zu *oberst*, weil *zuletzt*, der Sekretär" (2724–6). Because of the social fluidity of the times, a secretary, the least significant in terms of social rank – "Rang" recalls Klesel's defiant parting declaration: "Mir bleibt der *Vorrang*, wär's in Ketten" (2700) – comes out on top. In the approaching new order, the pen of the politician, not the sword of the warrior, will determine status. As if in recognition of this eventuality, Ferdinand, who up to this point with only one or two exceptions,[51] has stood as "ein Muster … der Festigkeit, / … der, rascher *Tat*, / Die Ketzerei getilgt in seinem Land" (1017–19), informs Wallenstein, "Denn gleich der Tat ehr' ich *die kluge Schrift*; / Die Feder schlägt oft sicherer als die Waffe" (2864–5). Only the audience can fully appreciate the humorous suitability of his uncharacteristic choice of words and image. The changing values have left their mark on the archduke as well; he even adopts Klesel's own tactics, including the conspiratorial whisper to blackmail Mathias into accepting his servant's removal: "Ferdinand *Schriften aus dem Mantel ziehend, halblaut*: / Die Briefe hier von Baiern, Spanien, Rom / Den einz'gen Stützen unsrer guten Sache, / Die nur auf die Entfernung dieses Manns / Den Beistand uns verheißen, den wir brauchen" (2783–6). There is also a measure of irony in the fact that a member of the upper nobility acknowledges the new priorities, since the "Federfuchser," normally viewed with disdain and distrust, could never be reconciled with the traditional aristocratic ethos and its values.

CHAPTER SIX

Summation

When the walls of the feudal empire begin to crumble and the most devastating war in the history of the German-speaking people breaks out, Mathias, "des Jammers Erben" (2308), maintains, in his desperation to find a way to avert the now inevitable disaster, "Wär Klesel hier, er wüßte des [i.e., what to do] wohl Rat" (2795). The claim begs the question as to whether or not the priest could have in fact prevented the bloodshed of the Thirty Years' War. No one, including Thompson who more than anyone else has paid Klesel his due, has grasped the full extent of his control over the plot. As I have attempted to demonstrate in my analysis of Klesel's role, he is either directly or indirectly responsible for the three politically far-reaching decisions Rudolf makes, all of which involve the signing of a document against the promptings of his better judgment: the "Kommando in Ungarn," the "Majestätsbrief," and the authorization to relieve Prague. The second act illustrates how Klesel craftily maneuvers the four archdukes into making, once again, three portentous decisions which he engineered from the outset: to convene an unauthorized meeting, to affix their names to the peace treaty, and then to the "Vollmacht," "Die [Mathias/Klesel] zum Herren macht in diesem Land" (1072). While Politzer interprets Klesel's political demise in general terms: "Aber auch er fällt einer Geschichte zum Opfer, die sich nicht einmal von ihm machen läßt, sondern mit Elementargewalt selbst über ihn hereinbricht,"[1] the tragedy offers sufficient specific detail to make him at least in part responsible for his own fall. As a stage in his overall plan he honors "Kaiser Rudolfs Brief" (2554), since it coincides with his own policy of making concessions to the Protestants, but this step disabuses the politically naive Ferdinand of the second act: "Er [Klesel] ist ein Eifrer für die fromme Sach" (1061), and fully justifies the priest's removal in the eyes of the Catholic faction. Even when Ferdinand hesitates to make use of the warrant for Klesel's arrest, the archbishop himself furnishes the impetus, the "Zeichen … vom Himmel" (2644), and the circumstances rendering it feasible: "Ihr habt ja *selbt* des Schutzes euch beraubt. / Der König ist von seinen Zimmern fern, / Gesendet habt ihr ihn nach der Kapelle / Und seid gegeben nun in unsre Macht" (2651–4). Klesel therefore makes the fatal error of underestimating the lengths to which Ferdinand is prepared to go to satisfy his drive for power sublimated as obedience to a religious authority. The secretary simply outsmarts himself: "Das ist der Lohn der Schlauheit, daß sie fein / Den Faden spinnt, bis er, am feinsten, bricht" (2646–7).

"Auf solche enge Verbindungen zwischen Individuellem, Privatem und Universal-Geschichtlichem haben wir auch sonst in Grillparzers historischen Dramen zu achten. Sie sind es, die der Weltgeschichte ein menschliches Maß aufprägen und dem Individuellen zugleich überindividuelle Bedeutung verleihen."[2] Fülleborn has, of course, Rudolf and the conflict with his relatives in mind, but the same could be said of Klesel and what he typifies in the total historical picture, whether it be the seventeenth or nineteenth century, specifically "das Emporsteigen eines neuen Standes."[3] Critics have called the author of *Ein Bruderzwist* a "skeptischen und *aristokratischen* Dichter,"[4] a "Reaktionär."[5] "[Die] Perspektive des Stücks läßt den angedeuteten Niedergang des Feudalstaats als einen tragischen Prozeß erscheinen, als eine negative Emanzipation von einer positiv entworfenen Ordnung."[6] It follows from this apology for the old order that Rudolf's political and social outlook becomes synonymous with the dramatist's own, and that the tragedy as a whole vindicates the emperor's policy of inaction: "Er selbt, der Dichter, gibt dieses Urteil ab, es ist das Ziel seines Weges. Hier im *Bruderzwist* zeigt er es als die weitertreibende Zeit, die Auflösung die kommt, Wallenstein, den Dreißigjährigen Krieg, die Rudolf rechtfertigen und das Tun seiner Feinde verurteilen."[7] However, one can detect a revisionist trend in Grillparzer, scholarship, one which quite rightly has cast considerable doubt upon any absolute justification of Rudolf, both as a person and political leader. For instance, Mason has proposed, "The ethical rift is not between confidence in heaven and despair over mankind, not between order above and muddle below, but in the bewilderment of the hero in the face of God's will as expressed in the religious differences of Catholics and Protestants. Because he cannot resolve the question why God permitted this to happen, Rudolf is unable to take any decisive action at all."[8] Kleinstück has further argued, "Rudolf trägt durch seine Inaktivität Schuld an der Rebellion, die sich gegen ihn vorbereitet. Und er selbt hat ihr in Mathias ein Haupt gegeben."[9]

While almost all the critics have stressed the parallels between Rudolf's views and those of the dramatist, no one has dared to suggest that Klesel may also embody aspects of his creator. One should never forget that Grillparzer, throughout his life, was subject to the surveillance of one of the most severe and often most arbitrary censorships of nineteenth-century Europe. In his *Selbstbiographie* he relates "eine Zensur-Anekdote"[10] where he happened to come into contact with a former acquaintance, "einen Hofrat der Zensurshofstelle," who confessed to having been the one responsible for holding up for two years the approval of Grillparzer's most blatantly patriotic, pro-Habsburg play, *König Ottokars Glück und Ende*. When asked what he found so dangerous in the work, the Hofrat replied, "Gar nichts, ... aber ich dachte mir: man kann doch nicht wissen –!" Not surprisingly Grillparzer concluded from this incident, "[d]aß unter diesen Umständen in dem damaligen Österreich für einen Dichter kein Platz sei." Even a well-meant, loyal poem occasioned by a serious illness of the heir presumptive aroused the ire of the court, creating "ein[en] literarisch dynastisch[en] Aufruhr,"[11] as some read it as containing an irreverent allusion to the future Kaiser Ferdinand's dim-wittedness. As a consequence of this unintentional slight, Kaiser Franz I allegedly chose to bury Grillparzer's petition for a routine increase in salary. Hence, if he wanted to criticize the regime of his day, he would have to do it so clandestinely or so deviously that it would escape the scrutiny of the censor. Without securing official approval his plays could never reach the public.

A brief review of his works does disclose several instances where an intellectually gifted member of the lower class must contend with the whims, insults, arrogance or sheer stupidity of the ruling hierarchy. I have already discussed a brief but telling episode from *Des Meeres und der Liebe Wellen* involving a servant's claim to mental equality. Another clever servant, Leon, in his efforts to rescue the bishop's nephew, must overcome the latter's aristocratic biases. "Die Pferde hüt ich [Atalus] endlich weil ich muß, / Und weils ein edles, ritterliches Tier.[12] / Doch in der Küche? Eher hier am Platz / Laß ich mein Leben, gliederweis zerstückt" (828–31), i.e., he would rather die than condescend to do manual labor in a kitchen. As John Kautsky has pointed out, "Arbeit gilt als der bäuerlichen Welt zugehörig und ist folglich unter der Würde des Adligen, sie ist ehrlos und erniedrigend."[13] Of course, the comic mode and the fact that Grillparzer distanced *Weh dem, der lügt!* in both time and place by setting it in medieval France/Germany, not Austria, allowed the author to depict with impunity the noble knight either as an overindulged, useless member of human society or as a physically endowed but mentally deficient, inarticulate primitive: "EDRITA. Schmerzts noch etwa? / GALOMIR *nachuntenzeigend*: Uh!"(1384). The comedy notably concludes with Atalus's recognition of a kitchen boy's superiority, Leon's elevation to the nobility, and his successful conquest of the high-born girl whose love he won over two aristocratic suitors.

ATALUS   Ich denke, Herr, das Mädchen dem zu gönnen,
　　　　　Der mich gerettet, ach, und den sie liebt.
GREGOR   So recht, mein Sohn, und daß dir ja kein Zweifel
　　　　　Ob ihres Gatten Rang und Stand und Ansehn;
　　　　　Von heut an, merk! hab ich der Neffen zwei.
　　　　　Der König tut mir auch wohl was zu Liebe,
　　　　　Da frei er [Leon] immer denn das Häuptlingskind.　　　(1807–13)

And as a final illustration one should include the obvious ascendancy of a peasant farmer, Primislaus, celebrated for his "Klugheit" (1322) over the noble Wladiken, the "Toren" (1831) whom he leads by the nose in a manner reminiscent of Klesel's manipulation of the Austrian nobility. Although of humble birth, Primislaus, in his independence and pride of achievement, judges himself the equal of his aristocratic rivals for Libussa's hand: "Ich fühle mich als Herr in meinem Haus, / Und so brech' ich mein Brot. Ist doch der Pflüger, / Indem er Alle nährt, den Höchsten gleich" (1081–3). In fact, his opening speech at his second meeting with Libussa establishes the basis for a new peasant nobility, the productive "Sichel" replacing the destructive "Schwert," his "Schild" and "Wappen," a basket proudly displaying the fruits of his labor (an image at odds with the traditional aristocratic prejudice against manual work in the fields), his crown a "*Kranz von Ähren und Kornblumen*" (p.327) and his "Burg" his "Haus" (1261–70): "Und selbst der *Knecht* ist *Herr* in seinem Haus" (1033). On the basis of personal merit, a commoner acquires the coveted prize, Libussa's hand, and becomes Bohemia's ruler. "Er [Primislaus] ist mein Gemahl. / *Dient* ihm wie mir, wenn nicht noch mehr als mir, / Denn ich ich *dien'* ihm selbst als meinem *Herrn*. / Ich neige mich, folgt eurer Fürstin Beispiel" (1915–8). As in the other two plays, so here as well, Grillparzer could conceal out of fear of censorship his progressive liberal bourgeois tendencies behind the facade of a mythological past having ostensibly nothing to do with his contemporary Danube Monarchy, but in reality having much to do with it.

Klesel shares with his author peasant roots (the paternal/Grillparzer side of the family came from the country), a middle-class background (baker/lawyer) and a common professional career as a

"Federfuchser." However much Grillparzer may have resented the indignity of having to earn his daily bread as a civil servant, much to his regret, he could not survive solely on his art. But above all, the dramatist has equipped his cunning priest with his own insight and psychological acuity, mercilessly exposing the self-flattering delusions of the mind to bare the underlying egotistical motives. Hence, because of the writer's conflicting feelings toward the revolution – on the one hand, his desire for change and the recognition of its inevitability,[14] and on the other, his love of order, culture, and the fatherland – the resultant ambiguity may well have informed his portrayal of both the protagonist and his antagonist. While Rudolf attempts to make a *public* case for an autocratic state, a divinely ordained community which, according to Mason, really means "a subordination of society to imperial rule,"[15] in outlining the prerequisites for entry into his *secret* society of "Friedensritter," he rejects the very cornerstones of his class ideology, i.e., "Geburt,"[16] "Schwert," (1206)[17] and "Ehre" (1213),[18] and replaces them with highly ethical, altruistic standards of service to humanity (1209–10), no doubt indebted to the "Tugend-lehre" of the middle-class Enlightenment. Similarly, whereas Klesel's Machiavellian maneuvers frequently alienate the audience's sympathy and may even at times cast him in the role of the Mephistophelian villain, his character nonetheless provides a suitable vehicle to undermine the myth of aristocratic intellectual preeminence, and perhaps even an opportunity for subtle revenge on the class that more often than not put obstacles in the path of Grillparzer's bureaucratic and literary careers. Also, what would be more fitting or more ironic for an alleged "Kirchenfeind"[19] than to attack the Roman Catholic Church's worldly ambitions through the mouth of one of its own distinguished sons, the Archbishop of Vienna?

Rudolf's political strategy, if one may call it such, consists of isolating himself from all human contact, refusing to pay attention to reports from the outside world, and avoiding any decisive measures to deal with the growing unrest at home in the futile and seemingly naive hope that time will heal the wounds of religious dissent. His attempt to maintain imperial equilibrium by continuing to wage war against a foreign aggressor as a means to avoid civil war: "Fluch jedem Krieg! Doch besser mit den Türken, / Als Bürgerkrieg, als Glaubens-, Meinungs- Schlachten" (1193–4) is "Realpolitik, die einem heraldischen Träumer übel zu Gesicht steht … Außerdem ist dies eine Politik, die ihren Wirklichkeitscharakter bereits eingebüßt hat."[20] But even on a pragmatic level, would not such a policy, if continued indefinitely, only have decimated the ranks of the imperial army even further (almost one third we are told has already been lost) and simply postpone the day of reckoning? As for Rudolf's contradictory performance in the third act, Thompson summarizes aptly: "That he should eventually abandon his principles altogether and succumb to personal emotions provides the final ironic twist in the series of decisions which he takes in Act III. By his action he makes a mockery of his ideals and policies and of his noble efforts to adhere to these during the difficult circumstances which he has thus far encountered."[21] The conclusion seems obvious: as a practical politician, Rudolf is a disaster.

As we have observed, the tragedy has consistently and correctly associated the word "Politik" in the pejorative sense with Rudolf's antagonist, Klesel. In *Il Principe* Machiavelli maintains that moral principles may often be a hindrance or even fatal in the political arena and that the successful leader has to be willing to compromise his principles to obtain and maintain power. "There is a wide gulf between life as it is lived and life as it should be lived, and lessons drawn from the latter rather than the former will teach disaster rather than self-preservation. So it is that a ruler who intends to keep his office must learn the practice of wickedness for use, when necessary."[22] Consequently the effective leader should strive to unite in his person the cunning of the fox and the strength of the lion, "because the lion's strength alone will avail him little against gins, nor the wiles of the fox against the ferocity of wolves. The fox will avoid the snares and the lion will scare the wolves."[23] Klesel's major weakness lies in his precarious, dependent relationship to his master, i.e., he lacks the leonine qualifications to fulfil the Machiavellian model realized, for example, in Kleist's Hermann.[24] But no one can deny him the vulpine attributes; he has the cunning to rule through "die kluge Schrift" (2864). Even Rudolf himself concedes that success is all that really matters in politics, not one's intentions, however noble or superficially altruistic: "Erst der Erfolg des Wollens Wert bestimmt, / Der reinste Wille wertlos – wenn erfolglos" (1686–7), and from the point of view of success in the implementation of a preconceived plan, Klesel has a remarkably high rate of accomplishment beginning in Act I and continuing more or less unabated until his forced removal in Act V. Kleinstück even defends the priest's tactics as an insubordinate but nonetheless justifiable response to the chaotic conditions created by Rudolf's lack of decisive leadership.[25] Hence I would have to disagree with Thompson's position "that politically, Klesel's policy is no worse and no better than Rudolf's."[26]

If Klesel had been less politically vulnerable, could he have saved the day? Clearly he has no doubts himself as to the correctness or inevitable success of his policy: "ein fester Plan beherrscht das Ganze, / Und jeder Schritt führt näher an das Ziel" (2467–8),[27] and he enjoys at least Wassermann's support: "Er [Klesel] ist der einzige, der nach Rudolfs Tod das Reich und den Frieden erhalten könnte, als Macht hinter dem Thron, wenn er nicht dem Fanatismus und dem gekränkten Standesgefühl des Thronenwärters Ferdinand zum Opfer fiel."[28] In reaching a decision, one obviously has to weigh Klesel's behind-the-scene political maneuvers and achievements in the first four acts. The fifth act, generally ignored by the critics, discloses a cynical but pragmatic mind which, in marked contrast to Rudolf's, is extremely well-informed about both the domestic and foreign scene. He sees through the motivation of those attempting to thwart his conciliatory course of action but underestimates their influence on Ferdinand. With his practical grasp of political realities: "Erzwungen ist zuletzt ein jeder Friede; / Der Schwächere gibt nach" (2557–8), he confirms the unavoidable, terrifying alternative which renders peace so necessary: "Doch soll das Schwert / Nicht wüten bis zu völligen Vertilgung, / Muß Friede werden, der nur Friede ist / Wenn er gehalten wird, ob frei, ob nicht" (2558–61). In his desire to avert civil war by seeking accommodation and granting concessions, Klesel again approaches Rudolf's own position:

> Da stehts vor mir! Der Mord, der Bürgerkrieg.
> Was ich vermieden all mein Leben lang,
> Es tritt vor mich am Ende meiner Tage.
> Es soll, es darf nicht. Steckt die Schwerter ein,
> Vertragt euch mit dem Feind! (1673–7)

Circumstances compel the emperor to seek reconciliation while Klesel pursues by design a conciliatory objective from the beginning. One has the distinct impression that Rudolf is always obliged to react to an unforeseen, potentially dangerous situation and frequently personal emotions such as anger and revenge dictate the nature of his response, while Klesel always anticipates the turn of events and thus can manipulate it to serve his own ends with the one major exception. Even once he is deposed, his undiminished confidence, his valid prophetic pronouncements and his continued influence despite his absence convey a strong impression that if anyone could have preserved the empire and prevented the war, it would have to have been Klesel. This is all, of course, hypothetical, but the fact still remains that even if political intrigue has removed the secretary/servant from the effective seat of power, the social forces he personifies have nonetheless come out on top: "Zu oberst, weil zuletzt, der Sekretär" (2726). As Libussa foretells in her concluding vision capturing the mixed blessings of this eventuality, "Die lang *gedient* sie werden endlich herrschen, / Zwar breit und weit, allein nicht hoch noch tief" (2420–1).

CHAPTER SEVEN

Klesel's Antecedents

In one of the many melodramatic moments typical of *Miß Sara Sampson*, the faithful servant Waitwell finally convinces the titular heroine to read her father's letter: "Lieber alter Vater [i.e., Waitwell], ich glaube du hast mich überredet."[2] Having learned through Waitwell's intervention of Sir William's conciliatory response to her indiscretion, Sara expresses her gratitude to her father's mediator in the following terms: "Ich danke dir unterdessen für deine Mühe. Du bist ein rechtschaffner Mann. Es sind wenig Diener die Freunde ihrer Herren!" (L451) If one reviews the list of secondary characters from Lessing's dramas, including Waitwell, Norton, Betty, Just, Franziska or Al Hafi, the exceptions prove to be the rule. Whereas the cunning, pen-pushing servant of common origin, who is more a friend to himself than to his lord, will become the norm in several key works of the late eighteenth and the first half of the nineteenth century, Lessing's servants, drawn from the "Volk," exemplify the high ethical standards of the enlightenment's "Tugendlehre." However, as Waitwell points out in the same dialogue, the servants take their cue from their masters: "Wenn alle Herren Sir Williams wären, so müßten die Diener Unmenschen sein, wenn sie nicht ihr Leben für sie lassen wollten" (L451). In the master/servant relationship, the latter tends to embody an extension or reflection of the former.

The negative *Federfuchser* does not make an appearance in Lessing's *œuvre* and the only character to approximate this role is Marinelli from *Emilia Galotti*.[3] Significantly, this court intriguer, although exhibiting the diabolical features of the type, hails from a decadent, immoral aristocracy (he is a "Marchese" and "Kammerherr") and has no association with the main weapon of the bourgeoisie, the pen. I suspect that Lessing, as an adherent of German Enlightenment with its faith in the inevitable intellectual and ethical *Bildung* of his own class, would have found it difficult to ascribe self-serving, unscrupulous ambition to a representative of that same social class. Nevertheless, as we shall presently ascertain, *Miß Sara Sampson* already contains implications potentially destructive of the master/servant ideal it purports to expound.

Waitwell, as his descriptive name implies, represents the stereotypical faithful servant, an "alter ehrlicher Diener" (L411) whose honesty is beyond reproach. Unable to lie to his master: "Sagte ich das, so würde ich eine Lüge sagen; eine unverschämte böse Lüge. Sie könnte mir auf dem Todbette wieder einfallen, und ich alter Bösewicht müßte in Verzweiflung sterben" (L412), he only engages in falsehood as a last resort to bring about a reconciliation between the two people closest to his heart, Sara and Sir William: "Ja gewiß, ich glaube es ist in meinem Leben das erstemal, daß ich mit Vorsatz betrogen habe ... Das geht mir nahe, Miß. Ich weiß wohl, die gute Absicht entschuldigt nicht immer; aber was konnte ich denn tun? Einem so guten Vater seinen Brief ungelesen wieder zu bringen?" (L448) While the Machiavellian schemer frequently has recourse to the argument that the end justifies the means to conceal his self-interest, in this instance Waitwell's reluctant deception occurs in the best interest of someone else, "Einem so guten Vater," and thus really amounts to a form of self-denial since he must do violence to his moral integrity ("Das geht mir nahe, Miß."). Having cared for Sara as a child and having grown to love her as a daughter: "auf diesen meinen Armen habe ich dein Lächeln, dein Lallen bewundert" (L412), he has become a surrogate father or an extension of Sir William,[4] a relationship which she herself fully appreciates (L450). In this capacity he knows his young mistress well and does not hesitate to provide her with an unflattering but valid analysis of her motivation: "Es ist, Miß, als ob Sie nur immer an Ihren Fehler dächten und glaubten, es wäre genug, wenn Sie den in Ihrer Einbildung vergrößerten, und sich selbst mit solchen vergrößerten Vorstellungen marterten" (L448–9). Devoted to the welfare of his adopted family, he would never conceive of using this information for his own personal gain. The intimate knowledge that a servant acquires through consistent and close proximity to those he serves and the dependence such an association inevitably entails could place a less scrupulous person in a position of considerable influence.

In recognition of Waitwell's distinguished service Sir William, representing the well-to-do upper middle class, finally rejects the distinction between master and servant to proclaim equality in the here and now: "Betrachte dich von nun an, mein guter Waitwell, nicht mehr als meinen Diener. Du hast es schon längst um mich verdient, ein anständiger [sic] Alter zu genießen. Ich will dir es auch schaffen, und du sollst es nicht schlechter haben, als ich es noch in der Welt haben werde. Ich will allen Unterschied zwischen uns aufheben; in jener Welt, weißt du wohl, ist er ohnedies aufgehoben" (L457). The Bible and the writings of the early Christian Church do not repudiate the institution of slavery; for example, Paul wrote to the Ephesians, "Servants, be obedient to them that are your masters according to the flesh, with fear and trembling, in singleness of your heart, as unto Christ."[5] Therefore, the lord/servant relationship in its terrestrial context appears to bear the divine seal of approval. Equality only exists in heaven with the righting of accounts in the life after death. Sir William's pronouncement points, by concrete example, to the social feasibility and desirability of creating heaven on earth: two "good" people, for whom the barriers separating the served from the serving have become marginal, if not non-existent, complement each other. This same interdependence resulting from gratitude on the one hand and from selfless devotion on the other can be ascertained in Sara's expression of her indebtedness to her confidante: "Dein [Betty's] gutes Herz hat so oft mit mir geweint, nun soll es sich auch mit mir freuen. Ich werde wieder glücklich sein, und dich für deine guten Dienste belohnen können" (L455–6).[6]

Norton also comes across as a very positive, ethical figure who always appeals to his master's better self: "Ich [Norton] weiß besser, wo das Mitleiden hingehört" (L414). The fact that Mellefont has such a servant in his employ is an early sign to the audience that the master must have some redeeming qualities if he can still command the loyalty of such a man. Despite the temperament of his lord and the social limitations of his position: "in der Hitze Ihrer Leidenschaften, würde mir ein Wort den Hals gekostet haben" (L414), Norton has the courage to speak his mind when asked for advice on a moral issue and to take the side of his master's victim: "MELLEFONT. Rate mir doch, was soll ich tun? was soll ich sagen? / NORTON. Sie sollen tun, was sie [Sara] verlangen wird" (L416).[7] Far from taking advantage of Mellefont's dependency, he shows no interest in acquiring personal power or wealth at the expense of his moral integrity: "Ich wollte auch nicht dableiben, und wenn mir gleich jeder Augenblick mit Golde bezahlt würde" (L417).

Since the servant shares the fate of his master, including the consequences of the latter's crime, Norton voices his determination to speak out against Mellefont's inappropriate behavior, a decision which occasions the following exchange:

MELLEFONT. Nur vergiß nicht, wer du bist.

NORTON.   Ich will es nicht vergessen, daß ich ein Bedienter bin: ein Bedienter, der auch etwas Bessers sein könnte, wenn er, leider! darnach gelebt hätte. Ich bin Ihr Bedienter, ja; aber nicht auf dem Fuße, daß ich mich gern mit Ihnen möchte verdammen lassen.   (L462)

His determination not to share his employer's fate stands in direct opposition to Wurm's declaration in the concluding scene of *Kabale und Liebe*: "Arm in Arm mit *dir* [The Präsident; Schiller's emphasis] zur Hölle! Es soll mich kitzeln, Bube, mit *dir* [Schiller's emphasis] verdammt zu sein!"[8] As an aristocrat, Mellefont, in contrast to the upright *Bürger* Sir William, insists on maintaining the distance distinguishing the master from the servant. While Norton clearly knows his place, he still has a middle-class conscience and a sense of personal freedom attributable to his ethical nature. For instance, what Mellefont intended as a social "put-down": "Nur der Pöbel wird gleich außer sich gebracht, wenn ihn das Glück einmal anlächelt" (L462), Norton boldly turns back on its speaker: "Vielleicht, weil der Pöbel noch sein Gefühl hat, das bei Vornehmern durch tausend unnatürliche Vorstellungen verderbt und geschwächt wird" (L462).[9] And when Sara defends her lover by blaming herself, Norton asks, "Warum soll Mellefont niemals unrecht haben?" (L480).

This servant knows his master better than the latter knows himself. In fact Norton's familiarity with Mellefont's psychological make-up enables him to read his frame of mind with unnerving accuracy: "Und ich [Norton] will mich gern geirret haben, wenn Sie es nicht lieber gesehen hätten, der Vater wäre noch nicht versöhnt. Die Aussicht in einen Stand, der sich so wenig zu Ihrer Denkungsart schickt –" (L462). The audience is in a position to confirm this diagnosis after Mellefont's monologue in the preceding scene (IV/2). The *Diener* proves to be more perceptive, more clever than the *Herr* who persists in ignoring, to his own detriment, well-founded warnings: "Bedenken Sie [Mellefont] was Sie tun! Sie müssen sie [Marwood] nicht sprechen, oder das Unglück Ihrer armen Miß ist vollkommen" (L424). Whereas Norton directs his energies to an altruistic end, the welfare of his lord, the possibility of a Wurm or a Klesel is nevertheless present. It takes a mind trained by and accustomed to devious practices to recognize this potential for evil in the servant's superior insight: "Norton! Norton! du mußt ein erschrecklicher Bösewicht, entweder gewesen sein, oder noch sein, daß du mich [Mellefort] so erraten kannst. Weil du es getroffen hast, so will ich es nicht leugnen" (L462). The designation "ein erschrecklicher Bösewicht" already anticipates the satanic overtones which will characterize the Machiavellian schemer, for, to paraphrase the final line of *Emilia Galotti*, "[können] sich auch noch Teufel in [einen] Freund verstellen."[10]

This diabolical dimension remained a suggestion that Lessing chose not to develop in *Miß Sara Sampson* and his "bürgerliches Trauerspiel" concludes on a note reinforcing the stereotype of the loyal, lower-class servant devoted to his or her master/mistress. In Sara's death scene, the major characters lean heavily upon their servants in their supportive function: "Hilf mir auf, Waitwell, hilf mir auf" (L488) and the heroine's last two speeches reveal her concern for Waitwell and Betty: "Tröste deinen Herrn, Waitwell. Doch auch du stehst in einem trostlosen Kummer vergraben, der du in mir weder Geliebte noch Tochter verlierest?" (L491); "Noch denke ich an Betty, und verstehe nun ihr ängstliches Händeringen. Das arme Mädchen! Daß ihr ja niemand eine Unvorsichtigkeit vorwerfe, die durch ihr Herz ohne Falsch, und auch ohne Argwohn der Falschheit entschuldiget wird" (L491). The "Herz *mit* Falsch" of a servant, capable not only of discerning but also of exploiting "Falschheit" in others and anxious to rise above the social limitations imposed by a class society, would appear on stage twenty-eight years later in Schiller's *Kabale und Liebe*.

WURM IN SCHILLER'S *KABALE UND LIEBE*

The "erschrecklich[e] Bösewicht" disguised as a servant to whom Lessing alluded makes his first significant appearance in telling company. Most of the "Personen" from Schiller's *Kabale und Liebe* have descriptive names: all three parts of the designation Präsident von Walter (walten = to rule) point to the man of authority and power from the aristocracy. Since "Kalb" has the colloquial meaning of a ninny, Hofmarschall von Kalb already conveys the unsympathetic view the drama will present of the court and its values. In this context we read, "Wurm, *Haussekretär des Präsidenten*."[11] Schiller clearly intended to prejudice an audience against this type from the very outset by assigning him such an unattractive but fitting name. (Originally in mhd., ahd. and got., "Wurm" meant a snake, a meaning still retained in the vernacular). Indeed, "Wurm" suggests more a caricature than a characterization, a suspicion which the drama soon confirms. He is also immediately identified as the personal secretary to the Präsident, the man who rules. Just as we are encouraged, prior to his entrance, to see in Kalb a comic figure, similarly we are conditioned to regard this "Haussekretär" as a loathsome, subhuman being and, by extension, to associate these features with his profession.

Even before Wurm appears on stage, the first scene of *Kabale und Liebe* indicates the degree to which the written word can easily impress or intimidate some members from the lower class, especially ambitious mothers.[12] Whereas Frau Miller stands in obvious awe of the educated: "Solltest nur die wunderhübsche Billetter auch lesen, die der gnädige Herr an deine Tochter als schreiben tut" (s758), the pragmatic Miller classifies books as "Teufelsgezeug" (s758), a diabolical means to seduce his daughter away from her traditional moral standards, away from her modest home upbringing towards delusions of upward social mobility. In short, the written word already has a negative connotation.

When Wurm enters in the next scene, the underlying tension becomes immediately evident in the opening dialogue:

FRAU.   Ah guten Morgen, Herr Sekertare. Hat man auch einmal wieder das Vergnügen von Ihnen?

WURM.   Meinerseits, meinerseits, Frau Base. Wo eine Kavaliersgnade einspricht, kommt mein bürgerliches Vergnügen in gar keine Rechnung.

FRAU.   Was Sie nicht sagen, Herr Sekertare! Des Herrn Majors von Walter hohe Gnaden machen uns wohl je und je das Bläsier, doch verachten wir darum niemand.

MILLER.   (*verdrüßlich*).   Dem Herrn einen Sessel, Frau. Wollens ablegen, Herr Landsmann?   (s760)

Although the mother does show polite deference, she nevertheless endeavors to establish some distance between herself and her visitor by consistently addressing him by his calling (nine times in this scene), and by having recourse to the impersonal "man." In contrast, Wurm tries to ingratiate himself with her by seeming to put himself down, and by emphasizing a personal, family link when he addresses her as cousin to make her side with him out of a sense of family loyalty. His initial speech already implies the envy and resentment he harbors, as a member of the middle class, because of his inferior social status vis-à-vis an aristocrat: his allusion to Ferdinand signals the extent to which the new relationship irks him and does serious damage to his ego. He feels himself to have been unfairly (he cannot help his birth) upstaged by his noble rival. Frau Miller, choosing to ignore the familiar reference, insists upon his profession which she then proceeds to juxtapose with Ferdinand in all his aristocratic dignity – "hohe Gnaden." She no longer wishes to consider the suit of a mere "Herr Sekertare" since her daughter now has better prospects. Her insensitive and undiplomatic response demonstrates how easily titles impress the lower class: obviously proud of the new courtship, she does not hesitate to boast about it. Ironically, her improper pronunciation of a foreign "Modewort" ridicules her social aspirations and calls into question her concluding denial. For someone with Wurm's ambition and frustrated sense of self-worth, such an oblique but nonetheless painful humiliation would be difficult to ignore. Miller, annoyed by his wife's imprudent disclosure, attempts to divert the conversation away from such a sensitive issue by ostensibly welcoming Wurm into his home. Significantly, however, the form of address he employs, "Herr Landsmann," does create a common bond between them, but the most distant one possible, i.e., they are fellow countrymen.[13] As the conclusion of this scene will substantiate, Miller, while despising the Sekretär, still rightly fears his influence at court and realizes that he cannot afford to have him as an enemy.

Accepting Miller's invitation, Wurm "(*legt Hut und Stock weg, setzt sich*). Nun! Nun! und wie befindet sich denn meine Zukünftige – oder Gewesene? – Ich will doch nicht hoffen – kriegt man sie nicht zu sehen – Mamsell Luisen?" (s760). The "*Hut und Stock*" like the later reference to his "*Manschetten und Jabot*" (s760–1) are the visible signs of his claim to elegance and refinement, the outward marks of his superiority designed to impress his intended in this petty-bourgeois setting, where presumably he once could shine but where he has now been eclipsed by a brighter social light.[14] Part of his motivation for devising the later cabal stems from outraged love or denial of possession of what he considers to be his property.[15] With or without justification he has convinced himself that Luise will be his future bride but now he feels threatened by rumors which he hopes to invalidate. The magnitude of his emotional involvement becomes evident when the mother, in response to his continual prodding, finally divulges her view of the current situation: "Nu – Nu – ich dächte nur – ich meine (*hustet*) weil eben halt der liebe Gott meine Tochter barrdu zur gnädigen Madam will haben – Wurm (*fährt vom Stuhl*). Was sagen Sie da? Was?" (s761) Momentarily he forfeits his self-control in both gesture and speech.

Once Miller has managed to smooth some of Wurm's ruffled feathers, the latter, in an attempt to gain the father's support, retorts, "Auch hab ich es nicht um Sie verdient, Herr Musikmeister. Sie haben mich jederzeit den Mann von Wort sehen lassen, und meine Ansprüche auf Ihre Tochter waren so gut als *unterschrieben*" (s761). He begins with an implied threat – I have earned better treatment and greater respect – and then tries to flatter the father into compliance by obliging him to live up to his reputation for reliability. As neither father nor daughter has made such a commitment, Wurm is really putting words into Miller's mouth. Also, appropriately enough, the Sekretär voices his claim in terms of his profession: one cannot question a *signed* agreement; it assumes a tyrannical hold. Through this device, Wurm gives us the first hint of his main manipulative tool.[16] He then offers a résumé of his current and future prospects: "Ich habe ein Amt, das seinen guten Haushälter nähren kann, der Präsident ist mir gewogen, an Empfehlungen kanns nicht fehlen, wenn ich mich höher poussieren will" (s761). Proud of his office and his ability to provide for himself (and, by extension, for a family), he presents himself as a decidedly middle-class "Streber" with substantial political potential as a result of the influence he exerts upon those in power. The choice of "poussieren," suggestive of the precious, courtly world of eighteenth-century France,[17] effectively captures his drive to reach greater social heights. "Sie sehen, daß meine Absichten auf Mamsell Luisen ernsthaft sind, wenn sie vielleicht von einem adeligen Windbeutel herumgeholt –" (s761). Speaking the language of the "Spießbürger" he nonetheless cannot conceal his resentment at Ferdinand's interference, and he seeks to denigrate his rival in his absence, an all too obvious tactic. Since Wurm's emotions frequently win the upper hand over cunning calculation throughout this episode, the audience never senses that he has any real control of the situation.

Although Miller remains for the most part courteous to Wurm, the spectator easily detects the father's antipathy for this suitor which he inadvertently blurts out but quickly tries to cover up: "Ich zwinge meine Tochter nicht. Stehen Sie ihr an – wohl und gut, so mag sie zusehen, wie sie glücklich mit Ihnen wird. Schüttelt sie den Kopf – noch besser – in Gottes Namen wollt ich sagen – so stecken Sie den Korb ein, und trinken eine Bouteille mit dem Vater" (s761). Wurm's tactic here is too obvious: "Ein väterlicher Rat vermag bei der Tochter viel, und hoffentlich werden Sie mich kennen, Herr Miller?" (s762) He is sufficiently perceptive to realize the influence the father has over his daughter and therefore strives to ingratiate himself with Miller and to intimidate him as well – the latter part of his statement contains a veiled threat – in order that he will put pressure on Luise to accept his courtship. In other words, Wurm shows no moral qualms at using others to achieve his own personal goals. Miller, however, is not easily frightened when his daughter's welfare is at stake, and momentarily forgetting himself and resorting to the familiar form of address, he makes his aversion unmistakably clear: "Daß dich alle Hagel!'s Mädel muß Sie kennen. Was ich alter Knasterbart an Ihnen abkucke, ist just kein Fressen fürs junge naschhafte Mädel" (s762). Boldly, he also exposes Wurm's strategy and his low opinion of it: "Einem Liebhaber, der den Vater zu Hilfe ruft, trau ich – erlauben Sie, – keine hohle Haselnuß zu" (s762), but still appreciates the need to qualify his candidness – "erlauben Sie" – out of fear of the potential political power wielded by the Sekretär.

Ironically, when Miller outlines an ideal male suitor, one who pursues his courtship "hinter dem Rücken des Vaters" (s762), i.e., who directs it specifically at Luise, he accurately describes Ferdinand and his influence over his daughter. "Das nenn ich einen Kerl! Das heißt lieben! – und wers bei dem Weibsvolk nicht so weit bringt, der soll – – auf seinem Gänsekiel reiten" (s762). Schiller had a low opinion of the "Federnfuchser" (s762) or "Dintenkleckser" (s791) as also reflected in Karl von Moor's derogatory reference in *Die Räuber* to "diesem tintenklecksenden Säkulum."[18] In *Kabale und Liebe* he depicts a secretary not as an exemplary male ("Das nenn ich einen Kerl!") but as a scheming weakling who attempts to rule by the pen in contrast to Ferdinand, the real man of action associated with the sword.[19] The image of riding on a goose quill, since it originates with the popular superstition of the witch on her broom stick, also implies the feminine and the diabolical. Unable to face the unpleasant truth, Wurm "(*greift nach Hut und Stock, und zum Zimmer hinaus*). Obligation, Herr Miller" (s762) and escapes from the scene, thus confirming Miller's evaluation.

After Wurm has made his undignified exit, Miller is able to express his true sentiments: "Ist mirs doch wie Gift und Operment, wenn ich den Federnfuchser zu Gesichte krieg. Ein konfiszierter widriger Kerl, ab hätt ihn irgendein Schleichhändler in die Welt meines Herrgotts hineingeschachert" (s762–3). The Sekretär becomes the stereotype, if not the caricature, of his profession, a pejorative portrait pointing to death by deceitful means. Poison is the weapon of the underhanded villain, particulary of women – Lucretia Borgia, Marwood, Adelheid or Kunigunde come to mind.[20] This increases Wurm's resemblance to an effeminate, impotent weakling, one who, out of necessity, is more cerebral than physical. The satanic overtones contained in the assertion that Wurm does not rightly belong to a positive, divine world order become more explicit in Miller's description: "Die kleinen tückischen Mausaugen – die Haare brandrot – das Kinn herausgequollen, gerade als wenn die Natur für purem Gift über das verhunzte Stück Arbeit meinen Schlingel da angefaßt, und in irgend- eine Ecke geworfen hätte – Nein! Eh ich meine Tochter an so einen Schuft wegwerfe, lieber soll sie mir –" (s763). All of these details, the little malicious mouse eyes (mice or rats are the devil's minions), the red hair, the protruding chin, the general ugliness and the specific reference to "Schlingel" and "Schuft" proclaim Satan. In addition, there is the potentially comical situation of an older man – Miller calls Wurm "der Alte" (s763) – in love with a younger woman. The scene comes to a close with Miller's correctly judging that his wife's mouth has "got them into hot water": "und springt einem ein nasenweises Wort übers Maul. – Bumbs! habens Fürst und Matress und Präsident, und du hast das siedende Donnerwetter am Halse" (s763). One must handle with extreme circumspection people who can denounce others to those in authority, a realization that has figured prominently throughout this scene in Miller's at times seemingly contradictory treatment of the court informer.

As Miller predicted, Wurm informs against Ferdinand in order to force the Präsident to intervene and remove the opposition in the secretary's campaign to win for himself "[d]as schönste Exemplar einer Blondine" (s768). "Präsident (*lacht*). Er sagt mir, Wurm – Er habe ein Aug auf das Ding – das find ich" (s768). The laugh shows the callous nature of the master's attitude to a subaltern: he finds Wurm's predicament of having lost Luise to Ferdinand an amusing, and more importantly, a reassuring indication that his son will be able to conquer women with ease and will therefore excel at court. Far from being a naive, unintelligent master such as Mathias, the Präsident discerns his confidant's motive for the disclosure – the servant wants to use his superior to eliminate a dangerous rival: "Da Er meinen Sohn bei dem *Mädchen* [Schiller's emphasis] auszustechen Mühe haben möchte, soll Ihm der *Vater* [Schiller's emphasis] zur Fliegenklatsche dienen, das find ich wieder begreiflich – und daß Er einen so herrlichen Ansatz zum Schelmen hat, entzückt mich sogar – Nur, mein lieber Wurm, muß Er mich nicht mitprellen wollen" (s768). While rejoicing in his servant's machinations as long as the master is not on the receiving end, the Präsident, known for his cunning (Lady Milford calls him "der Hofschlaue Walter" [s780]), remains confident that he can keep Wurm on a short leash and exploit him to his own advantage. As the German proverb puts it, "Wie der Herr, so der Diener."

Throughout this scene Wurm consciously assumes the part of the sycophantic servant as signalled by his opening speech: "Ihro Exzellenz haben die Gnade, mir den Beweis zu befehlen" (s768) and by his gestures "Wurm (*verbeugt sich*). Ich mache hier gern den Bürgersmann, gnädiger Herr" (s769), i.e., he puts himself down by his actions, by the reference to his class and by his willingness to accept a deflowered Luise. However, the text does supply several hints that this man is not really intimidated. His conditional clause: "Wenn der Major Ihnen ebenso den *gehorsamen Sohn* [Schiller's emphasis] zeigt, als Sie ihm den *zärtlichen Vater* [Schiller's emphasis], so dörfte Ihre Anfoderung mit Protest zurückkommen" (s769) provides a glimpse into an independent, sarcastic mind. In a sense he is preparing for greater control of the intrigue: because he knows the state of affairs better than his master, he is certain that he will be vindicated. When the Präsident proposes testing Ferdinand by his reaction to the announcement of his imminent marriage to Lady Milford, Wurm, anxious not to provide the Major with an opportunity to conceal his true sentiments behind any sort of pretence, puts forward his own suggestion: "Ich ersuche Sie um eine schärfere Probe. Wählen Sie ihm die untadeligste Partie im Land, und sagt er ja, so lassen Sie den Sekretär Wurm drei Jahre Kugeln schleifen" (s770). Whereas he begins this speech with a further demonstration of obsequious deference: "Gnädiger Herr, ich bitte sehr um Vergebung" (s770), he concludes it by asserting his supreme confidence in his own analysis of the situation, one which contradicts his master's evaluation of the affair as a harmless flirtation.

The relationship between master and servant could be characterized as mutually beneficial in keeping with the German expression: "Eine Hand wäscht die andre." "WURM. Und daß der Dienst, Ihnen von einer unwillkommenen Schwiegertochter zu helfen – PRÄSI-DENT. Den Gegendienst wert ist, Ihm zu einer Frau zu helfen? – Auch das, Wurm" (s770). Having a specific goal in mind – to possess Luise – the secretary obtains the desired confirmation: "WURM (*bückt sich vergnügt*). Ewig der Ihrige, gnädiger Herr. (*Er will gehen*)" (s770). The stage direction *"vergnügt"* intimates his self-satisfied sense of accomplishment. He may appear to put himself down – he has no other choice given his background – but at the same time he remains convinced of his intellectual ascendancy and, most importantly, having persuaded his master to investigate the nature of Ferdinand's relationship with Luise, he has taken a decisive step towards disposing of a dangerous competitor.

An anticipation of the connection between Dorfrichter Adam and his Schreiber Licht can be heard in the following exchange: "PRÄSI-DENT. Was ich Ihm vorhin vertraut habe, Wurm (*Drohend*) Wenn Er plaudert – / WURM (*lacht*). So zeigen Ihr' Exzellenz meine falschen Handschriften auf (*Er geht ab*)" (s770).[21] The master draws assurance from the realization that he can blackmail his servant into compliance with his wishes, but by the same token, if the servant goes down, he could easily take his master with him. This creates a balance of powers. It is in each party's best interest to support the other as each could conceivably destroy the other. Wurm's laugh, another detail suggestive of the rogue, conveys his overweening confidence and an underlying sense of superiority even in the face of intimidation. Although his departing speech emphasizes the authority of the master over the servant, the laughter implies that he does not take the threat that seriously and thus belies his subequent words. Since at heart he feels quite secure and has achieved his objective, he can afford to be generous at his own expense.

The final comment of the scene made by the Präsident in Wurm's absence proves that the servant knows his master quite well. "Zwar du bist mir gewiß. Ich halte dich an deiner eigenen Schurkerei, wie den Schröter am Faden!" (s770). Wurm has successfully played to his exaggerated sense of authority, his desire to dominate and manipulate others and has put him in a confident frame of mind, but ironically the master has just become the unwitting victim of the cunning wiles of his servant and there is considerable doubt as to who really holds the reins of effective power.

Just before the first conversation between Ferdinand and his father is about to take place, the latter orders, "Laß Er uns allein, Wurm" (s772). Sending away his secretary may well signify the Präsident's growing insecurity. Since Wurm may be correct in his reading of the situation, the master wishes to spare himself the humiliation of losing face before a subordinate. The subsequent dialogue, although it demonstrates how the seasoned courtier takes it for granted that he can use people, even an only son, to achieve his political ends: "Mich laß an deinem Glück arbeiten, und denke auf nichts, als in meine Entwürfe zu spielen" (s772), also reveals Wurm's indirect influence in that the Sekretär's information enables the Präsident to test his son and to oblige him to follow the original plan of marrying the Prince's mistress.

The third act commences with a further consultation between the Präsident and Wurm in which the growing dominance of the servant over his master becomes increasingly evident. "PRÄSIDENT. Der Streich war verwünscht. / WURM. Wie ich befürchtete, gnädiger Herr. Zwang *erbittert* [Schiller's emphasis] die Schwärmer immer, aber *bekehrt* [Schiller's emphasis] sie nie" (s798). The secretary's response is the polite equivalent of "I told you so!" It definitely implies that he has a better understanding of the characters involved and could thus predict their reactions, much as will be the case with Klesel. Therefore, when the Präsident attempts to downplay Ferdinand's threat to expose his father's criminal past, Wurm responds emphatically, "Das denken Sie ja nicht. Der gereizten Leidenschaft ist keine Torheit zu bunt" (s799), i.e., "Don't be too sure of yourself!" He wants to frighten his lord in order to render him more receptive to his own counsel. The reference to aroused passion looks ahead to Wurm's correct diagnosis of his master's son: for Ferdinand to believe that Luise could betray him for the likes of Kalb is indeed a "Torheit" born out of "gereizte Leidenschaft." Clearly the Sekretär has made it a priority to know his opponent's strengths and weaknesses, including the grounds for his motivation and the source of his ideals: "Die Grundsätze, die er aus Akademien hieher brachte, wollten mir gleich nicht recht einleuchten. Was sollten auch die phantastischen Träumereien von Seelengröße und persönlichem Adel an einem Hof, wo die größte Weisheit diejenige ist, im rechten Tempo, auf eine geschickte Art, groß und klein zu sein. Er ist zu jung und zu feurig, um Geschmack am langsamen, krummen Gang der Kabale zu finden, und nichts wird seine Ambition in Bewegung setzen, als was groß ist und abenteuerlich" (s799). This provides a reasonably accurate psychological sketch notwithstanding the pragmatist's failure to appreciate the values attributable to youthful idealism. The glorification of individual greatness denigrated here by Wurm can all too easily lead to overt self-centeredness, as Ferdinand himself inadvertently confirms in an earlier statement of his own aspirations: "*Mein* Ideal von Glück zieht sich genügsamer in *mich selbst* zurück. In meinem *Herzen* [Schiller's emphasis] liegen alle *meine* Wünsche begraben" (s774). To the Präsident's query as to how such insight could possibly serve their purpose, Wurm responds, "Sie [Anmerkung] wird Euer Exzellenz auf die Wunde hinweisen und auch vielleicht auf den Verband. Einen solchen Charakter – erlauben Sie – hätte man entweder nie zum *Vertrauten* [Schiller's emphasis], oder niemals zum *Feind* [Schiller's emphasis] machen sollen" (s799). He must point out the obvious, specifically, one can get at an enemy by exploiting his weakness to one's own advantage. Since he is censoring his master's past behavior – the Präsident has already committed the two specified tactical errors by confiding in his son so that he can now destroy his father, and by transforming Ferdinand into an adversary through his treatment of Luise – the servant has to soften the blow "– erlauben Sie –" by making the usual deferential gesture.

Wurm continues to furnish evidence of an amazing grasp of the situation: "Er verabscheut das Mittel, wodurch Sie gestiegen sind" (s799), an observation which the final scene of the first act (I/7) fully corroborates. Particularly perceptive is his implied threat: "Machen Sie ihn durch wiederholte Stürme auf seine Leidenschaft glauben, daß Sie der zärtliche *Vater* [Schiller's emphasis] nicht sind, so dringen die Pflichten des Patrioten bei ihm vor. Ja, schon allein die seltsame Phantasie, der Gerechtigkeit ein so merkwürdiges Opfer zu bringen, könnte Reiz genug für ihn haben, selbst seinen Vater zu stürzen" (s799). Only three scenes later (III/4) Ferdinand gives substance to

Wurm's hypothetical scenario: "Er [Präsident] wird mich zwingen, den unmenschlichen Sohn zu machen. Ich stehe nicht mehr für meine kindliche Pflicht. Wut und Verzweiflung werden mir das schwarze Geheimnis seiner Mordtat erpressen. Der Sohn wird den Vater in die Hände des Henkers liefern. ... Höre, Luise – ein Gedanke, groß und vermessen wie meine Leidenschaft, drängt sich vor meine Seele –" (s807). The key word that Wurm harps upon is "Leidenschaft," because he already realizes Ferdinand's major weakness: his passion blinds him to such a degree that reason or common sense proves ineffective before its onslaught.

This scene also demonstrates the master's increasing dependency upon his servant. "WURM. Darf ich freimütig reden? / PRÄSIDENT (*indem er sich niedersetzt*). Wie ein Verdammter zum Mitverdammten" (s800). The inclusive self-condemnation strikes a responsive chord in the audience, for both speakers share diabolical characteristics such as a sadistic laugh. The Präsident's sitting down suggests not only his sense of defeat and despair but also his inferior position relative to Wurm. By putting himself into his servant's hands, the master makes himself more susceptible to his prompting. Since intrigue facilitated the Präsident's political rise, the secretary now proposes that his lord have recourse to the same underhanded tactics to conduct his domestic affairs for his own personal benefit. When Wurm relates some of the details of how Walter's predecessor was eliminated by lulling him into a false sense of security,[22] he stresses the importance of flexibility, the need to take advantage of or to anticipate any development, one of Klesel's main strengths. Master and servant are much closer in attitude and intellectual ability than in *Ein Brüderzwist* – both are immoral political and social opportunists, closer to the Adam/Licht constellation – but Wurm is more devious, more perceptive and hence more Machiavellian than the Präsident. The difference is one of degree only.

Just as Klesel avoids showing his hand and keeps largely to himself, Wurm recommends never revealing one's true colors: "Warum zeigten Sie Ihrem Sohne den Feind? Nimmermehr hätte dieser erfahren sollen, daß ich um seine Liebesangelegenheit wisse" (s800). If one openly declares one's hostility, one gives one's adversary too much warning and thus eliminates the option of surreptitiously undermining his position. "Sie hätten den Roman von Seiten des Mädchens unterhöhlt, und das Herz Ihres Sohnes behalten. Sie hätten den *klugen* General gespielt, der den Feind nicht am Kern seiner Truppen faßt, sondern Spaltungen unter den Gliedern stiftet" (s800). Cunning prescribes attacking the weaker, more vulnerable party, Luise, while one preserves the loyalty and affection of an important potential ally, Ferdinand. Also like Klesel, Wurm insists upon the main strength of the pen-pusher – his "Klugheit." Ironically, however, he uses a military comparison, one calculated to appeal to his aristocratic interlocutor, to make his point: intelligence will prevail over brute force.

As an answer to Walter's question: "Wie war das zu machen?" (s800), one which marks his putting himself in Wurm's power, the latter replies, "Auf die einfachste Art – und die Karten sind noch nicht ganz vergeben" (s800). Again, in anticipation of Klesel: "Eu'r [Mathias's] Spiel steht gut, ihr habt die Trümpfe, Herr! / Harrt aus!" (125–6), Wurm uses the image of a card game and in a similar vein he later asks his master, "wieviel [er] bei der fernern Weigerung des Majors auf dem Spiel [hat]" (s800). Gambling has frequently been linked to Satan, as for example in Faust's wager with Mephistopheles, and the Church has traditionally opposed games of chance as diabolical temptation.[23]

Although Wurm insists that the Präsident deny any paternal feelings for Ferdinand – such emotions would only jeopardize the attainment of their common objective – at the same time he advocates turning to account others' emotions. While recognizing how resistance to passion only increases its hold on its bearer, he also understands its vulnerability: "Überlassen Sie es *mir* [Schiller's emphasis], an ihrem eigenen Feuer den Wurm auszubrüten, der sie zerfrißt" (s800). He will exploit their own weakness, their passion, to destroy them. Appropriately, by "Wurm" he means his plan to appeal to Ferdinand's jealousy, a scheme hatched by his cunning mind: "Ich müßte mich schlecht auf den Barometer der Seele verstehen, oder der Herr Major ist in der Eifersucht schrecklich wie in der Liebe" (s800). The spectator already knows this appraisal to be valid from Ferdinand's question in I/4: "Wärest du ganz nur Liebe für mich, wann hättest du Zeit gehabt, eine Vergleichung [between herself and a woman from the upper class] zu machen?" (s766). The implication is clear: Luise's love for him should fully preoccupy and consume her.

Once Wurm learns the possible implications if the Präsident's plan to marry his son to the Prince's mistress were to fail – a loss of authority and perhaps even of Walter's life – the stage directions indicate a strange reaction under the circumstances: "*Munter*" (s801). Having heard what he wanted to hear, Wurm actually rejoices in the confessed weakness of his master since this only increases his own influence. But ever mindful of the need to play the dutiful servant, he begins with a polite introduction: "Jetzt haben Sie die Gnade und hören – Den Herrn Major umspinnen wir mit List. Gegen das Mädchen nehmen wir Ihre ganze Gewalt zu Hilfe. *Wir diktieren ihr ein*

Billetdoux an eine dritte Person in die Feder, und spielen das mit guter Art dem Major in die Hände [Schiller's emphasis]" (s801). The Machiavellian schemer, suitably casting himself in the role of the spider, has recourse to his main attribute – cunning – and his main instrument – the pen – to drive a wedge between the two lovers. Because, like Grillparzer's priest, he is well acquainted with the players, he knows what string to pull to gain the desired effect. Just as he reads Ferdinand quite accurately, he now boasts of his familiarity with Luise's personality: "Ich kenne das gute Herz auf und nieder" (s801) and specifies how to get to her: "Sie liebt ihren Vater – bis zur Leidenschaft möcht ich sagen" (s801). Indeed, he even foresees that she will relinquish Ferdinand – "Die Unmöglichkeit, den Major zu besitzen" (s801) – a renouncement that occurs before the Sekretär sets the cabal in motion.[24]

When Wurm outlines his intent to have the Miller family swear an oath to conceal the deception practiced against Ferdinand, the Präsident asks incredulously, "Einen Eid? Was wird ein Eid fruchten, Dummkopf?" to which the servant replies, "Nichts bei *uns* [Schiller's emphasis], gnädiger Herr. Bei *dieser* [Schiller's emphasis] Menschenart alles" (s802). The Präsident has little respect for his confidant and only resorts to him as a desperate last step, while Wurm, denying his own class, associates himself with his master and the court as a means to rise on the social ladder. "Und sehen Sie nun, wie schön wir beide auf diese Manier zum Ziel kommen werden" (s802). He sees their personal careers as inextricably bound to one another, for the servant is nothing without the protection and influence of the master, just as the latter cannot survive without the support and advice of his servant. In fact, after Wurm has fully explained his plan, the Präsident confirms the symbiotic nature of their relationship by stating that not only has the servant learned from his master but that he has even outdone him in the art of concocting diabolically clever courtly intrigues: "PRÄSIDENT (*lacht unter Kopfschütteln*). Ja! ich gebe mich dir überwunden, Schurke. Das Geweb ist satanisch fein. Der Schüler übertrifft seinen Meister" (s802).

In the first stage confrontation between Luise and Wurm, the latter "*tritt ... in das Zimmer und bleibt im Hintergrund stehen, ohne von ihr bemerkt zu werden*" (s810). Such a prelude reinforces his satanic image – the man in the background, observing what is transpiring and taking stock of his victim. Her reaction upon discovery of his presence both in action ("*tritt erschrocken zurück*") and word ("Schrecklich! Schrecklich!" [s810]) discloses her physical revulsion for the man. Aware that he is the one who exposed her liaison with Ferdinand, she also proves sufficiently prescient to discern his present intent:

"Ihre Braut von der Schandbühne abzuholen" (s811), an accusation which he denies but which the spectator knows to be true.[25]

In order to obtain Luise's compliance, Wurm pursues his preannounced tactic of securing "die Betäubung ihres Kopfes" (s801):

WURM.   Ich komme, geschickt von Ihrem Vater.
LUISE.   (*bestürzt*). Von meinem Vater? – Wo ist mein Vater?
WURM.   Wo er nicht gern ist.   (s811)

Cruelly he engages in a cat-and-mouse game, a sadistic approach calculated to make her more amenable to his stratagem. He realizes that her father comes first in her scale of values, a priority made clear to Ferdinand and the audience in an earlier scene (III/4): "So schweig und verlaß mich – Ich habe einen Vater, der kein Vermögen hat als diese einzige Tochter – der morgen sechzig alt wird – der der Rache des Präsidenten gewiß ist" (s808). Wurm is able to exploit the commitment contained in this statement almost as if he had been present when she made it. Similarly, when she raises the issue of Ferdinand, her other "tödliche Seit[e]" (s801), Wurm, continuing to depict her situation as hopeless, remarks, "Wählt Lady Milford oder Fluch und Enterbung" (s811). In the same earlier scene Luise divulged an almost pathological fear of the paternal curse: "Und der Fluch deines Vaters uns nach? – ein Fluch, Unbesonnener, den auch Mörder nie ohne Erhörung aussprechen, den die Rache des Himmels auch dem Dieb auf dem Rade hält, der uns Flüchtlinge, unbarmherzig wie ein Gespenst, von Meer zu Meer jagen würde?" (s808–9). Again, Wurm manages to strike his victim where she is most vulnerable. He seems to know instinctively how to manipulate Luise, partly because he is aware of her class's high ethical, religious standards. Only the threat of disinheritance in a material sense would have no effect on her. A loss of wealth would be a major consideration solely for the egoistic tormentor.

Refusing to let up on the pressure he is applying or to offer Luise any avenue of escape, Wurm successfully convinces his victim of the futility of her predicament. "Eine vollkommene Büberei," she notes, "ist auch eine Vollkommenheit" (s811). Wurm would seem to be the "perfect" villain, a purely negative character in appearance, deed, and word, without a single redeeming feature, in the tradition of the Shakespearian Machiavel, and as such he looks forward to Hebbel's Leonhard. Luise actually ends up feeling sorry for him: "Armer Mensch! Du treibst ein trauriges Handwerk, wobei du ohnmöglich selig werden kannst … ich möchte nicht *du* [Schiller's emphasis] sein" (s812). In keeping with the eighteenth century's near deification of "Tugend," the self-satisfying awareness of living with a good conscience readily triumphs over the unmitigated evil of a Sekretär whose values are material and self-serving.[26]

In this exchange Schiller touches upon another important aspect connected to the pen-pusher through Luise: "Was ist aber das? – Ich bin ein unwissendes unschuldiges Ding, verstehe mich wenig auf eure fürchterliche lateinische Wörter. Was heißt Kriminalprozeß?" (s812). The incident illustrates how knowledge, being synonymous with power, can be used to tyrannize the ignorant, since the simple people stand in awe of the learned, a scenario most memorably captured in Gretchen's reaction to Faust's attention:

> Du lieber Gott! was so ein Mann
> Nicht alles, alles denken kann!
> Beschämt nur steh' ich vor ihm da,
> Und sag' zu allen Sachen ja.
> Bin doch ein arm unwissend Kind,
> Begreife nicht, was er an mir find't.[27]

Goethe's dramatic poem also associates Faust's companion with academia and its diabolical potential: when Mephistopheles first appears to the learned doctor, he wears appropriately enough the costume of *"ein fahrender Scholastikus"*[28] and he later, in the second Studierzimmer scene, dons Faust's professorial robes in order to provide some satirical course counselling for the Schüler. Knowledge without an accompanying sense of responsibility to humanity can be profoundly corrupt and even evil.[29]

As a further proof of Wurm's manipulative skills, when Luise threatens to go and plead her case before the duke, he resorts to reverse psychology, another typical weapon in the psychological arsenal of the pen-pusher (cf. Klesel's feigned opposition to his master's candidacy to represent Habsburg interests). "WURM (*boshaft freundlich*). Gehen Sie, o gehen Sie ja. Sie können wahrlich nichts Klügeres tun. Ich rate es Ihnen." (s813). He is counting on her abandoning this course of action because he advises it, and, as usual, he correctly foresees Luise's reaction: "Etwas Abscheuliches muß es sein, weil dieser Mensch dazu ratet" (s813). Since he knows the inestimable value placed upon female chastity in the minds of people from the petty-bourgeoisie, he realizes beforehand that Luise will not be able to sacrifice her ethics, in other words, her virginity, even to save her father: "Deine Tochter kann für dich sterben, aber nicht sündigen" (s814). As in *Emilia Galotti*, virtue is more precious than life itself. Wurm then continues to appeal to her most vulnerable point, her love for her father, by making her believe that the situation is desperate, with no apparent escape, in the hope that she will turn to him for help to save herself and her family. The extent of her growing dependency upon the Sekretär becomes clear when, picking up on his fabrication calculated to arouse guilt and to appeal to her sense of filial responsibility: "'Meine Luise', sagte er mir, 'hat mich zu Boden geworfen. Meine Luise wird mich auch aufrichten'" (s814), she adopts the same image and line of argument: "*Ich* [Schiller's emphasis] hab ihn niedergeworfen. *Ich* [Schiller's emphasis] muß ihn aufrichten" (s814). Having surrendered to his will, she will obey his commands. Since he holds the key to the only solution: "Es ist nur *ein* [Schiller's emphasis] Mittel" (s814), she has no alternative but to accept it. This corresponds to Klesel's maneuver in the second act. The archdukes, after Klesel has brought them around to his perception of the problem, must adopt his plan as the only way to extricate themselves from their dilemma. The success of Klesel's strategy rests upon his considerable awareness of the personalities he is dealing with, enabling him to anticipate their reactions in the given circumstances which to a large extent he also created. Not only is Klesel a worthy successor to Wurm, but on a more sophisticated level, to quote the Präsident, "Der Schüler [Klesel] übertrifft seinen Meister [Wurm]." In *Ein Bruderzwist* there are more people involved and Klesel's character has greater depth and complexity than the caricature of evil, "diese[r] blutsaugend[e] Teufel" (s815), Wurm embodies.

Ferdinand must renounce Luise of his own accord, and to this end, the Sekretär turns to the visible signs of his influence: "Setzen Sie sich. Schreiben Sie! Hier ist Feder, Papier und Dinte" (s815). Blackmailing her by informing her that the letter is addressed "An den Henker [ihres] Vaters" (s815), he plays to her most vulnerable emotion and thus forces her to take his dictation. Interestingly enough, however, Luise does acknowledge the source of his power over her: "O du weißt allzu gut, daß unser Herz an natürlichen Trieben so fest als an Ketten liegt – Nunmehr ist alles gleich. Diktieren Sie weiter. Ich denke nichts mehr. Ich weiche der überlistenden Hölle" (s815). Submitting to the power of the pen, she surrenders to the *cunning* forces of hell. "Die wahrhaft diabolische Hinterhältigkeit in der Briefepisode aus *Kabale und Liebe*, observes Seidlin, "liegt in dem Umstand, daß das Opfer der Intrigue selbt zu ihrem Werkzeug gemacht wird, daß die Zerstörung auf des Schreibers eigenes Herz und Glück zielt."[30]

Wurm designs the incriminating letter with Ferdinand's temperament and background in mind. What could be more personally damaging to a man who has declared, "Ich fürchte nichts – nichts – als die Grenzen deiner Liebe" (s767) than to learn that he has been not only deceived but, even more humiliating, laughed at: "'Ich nahm meine Zuflucht zu einer Ohnmacht – zu einer Ohnmacht – daß ich nicht laut lachte'" (s816)? Wurm transfers his own diabolical reaction to ethical behavior – he *"lacht überlaut"* (s813) when Luise proposes to go to the duke to expose the intrigue – to his victim – she is supposed to have stifled a laugh at Ferdinand's attempt to defend her honor. Since he portrays her dealings with Ferdinand in terms of a "Maske" (s816), one of the devices which he himself employs in his deceptive games with his master and a traditional symbol of court life (cf. *Don Carlos* or *Maria Stuart*), he is counting on this contrived connection of Luise with the immoral practices of the aristocracy and Ferdinand's avowed aversion to them to poison his rival's affection for the "Bürgermädchen." Once Luise has completed the letter, she *"steht auf und betrachtet eine große Pause lang mit starrem Blick das Geschriebene, endlich reicht sie es dem Sekretär, mit erschöpfter, hinsterbender Stimme)* Nehmen Sie, mein Herr. Es ist mein ehrlicher Name – es ist Ferdinand – ist die ganze Wonne meines Lebens, was ich jetzt in Ihre Hände gebe – Ich bin eine Bettlerin!" (s816). Both her demeanor and her words underscore the overwhelming tyrannical potency of "das Geschriebene"; it dominates her reputation, her love, her happiness, everything she holds dear, including life itself.

The planted letter easily convinces Ferdinand of Luise's duplicity, for "wenn Himmel und Erde, wenn Schöpfung und Schöpfer zusammenträten, für ihre Unschuld bürgten – es ist ihre *Hand* [Schiller's emphasis]" (s817). One cannot deny the irrefutable evidence of "was man schwarz auf weiß besitzt." His emotional diatribe against Luise includes psychological/physiological signs that she did not in fact deceive him: "Da ich ihr die Gefahr unsrer Liebe entdeckte, mit welch überzeugender Täuschung erblaßte die Falsche da!" (s818). Turning pale constitutes an involuntary reaction over which one has no conscious control and which one can not summon on command. Nevertheless, in a highly irrational state of mind ruled by "Leidenschaft" rather than common sense, and despite Ferdinand's realization of what a wretched example of humanity the Hofmarschall von Kalb is, he still chooses to believe a written confirmation of his worst suspicions.[31]

Wurm is not the only one to exercise his authority through a letter. As soon as Lady Milford has made up her mind to break all the links between herself and the duke and to renounce Ferdinand, she *"setzt sich nieder und fängt an zu schreiben"* (s832) in order to steel her will, to force herself into compliance. She needs to put her decision on paper to make it irrevocable. But at the same time, she views her letter as one final manifestation of her power as she exalts at the prospect of the social upheaval it will undoubtedly unleash: "Das ganze Land wird in Gärung kommen" (s832). Seeing a way out of her predicament, Luise also plans to make use of a "Billett" (s836) which she asks her father to deliver to Ferdinand. When Miller threatens to read it, she retorts, "Wie Er will, Vater – aber Er wird nicht klug daraus werden. Die Buchstaben liegen wie kalte Leichname da und leben nur Augen der Liebe" (836). The pen-pushers – "O! sie sind pfiffig, solang sie es nur mit dem Kopf zu tun haben, aber sobald sie mit dem Herzen anbinden, werden die Bösewichter dumm" (s836) – with all their cleverness cannot hope to resurrect dead letters upon the page; only love can make them meaningful and give them life, essentially the same message Rudolf proclaims when he reluctantly signs the "Majestätsbrief": "Hier meine Unterschrift. Da ihr / Den toten Zügen einer toten Hand / Mehr traut als dem lebendig warmen Wort, / Das von dem Mund der Liebe fortgepflanzt, / Empfangen wird vom liebedurst'gem Ohr, / Hier schwarz auf weiß" (1652–7).

Whereas Rudolf wants people to trust his word rather than an impersonal written paper, Ferdinand, as a sign of his delusion, reverses the priorities: "Ihr mißtraut meinen Worten? So glaubt diesem schriftlichen Zeugnis. (*Er wirft Luisen den Brief an den Marschall zu*)" (s841). From the audience's point of view, his comments concerning the letter are often replete with irony, for example: "Daß er [der Brief] in die unrechte Hände fiel? Gepriesen sei mir der Zufall, er hat größere Taten getan als die klügelnde Vernunft, und wird besser bestehn an jenem Tag als der Witz aller Weisen" (s842). The letter fell into the very hands for which "klügelnde Vernunft" intended it, and it was not chance but cunning design that sought to discredit Luise and thus alienate the two lovers. The signed document of the pen-pushing servant has become the instrument to rule over the lives of others: "Ihr [Mathias] habt die Schrift, / Die euch zum Herren macht in diesem Land" (1071–2). Therefore, when Luise is compelled to confess, "Ich schrieb ihn [den Brief]" (s843), i.e., the truth but not the whole truth, she would appear to condemn herself and to sign her own death warrant in Ferdinand's eyes. The written word has a formidable influence in *Kabale und Liebe* – the final scene begins "PRÄSIDENT (*den Brief in der Hand*)" (s856) – and without exception it is an agent of destruction. Through a letter Lady Milford shatters the false harmony of the court and Ferdinand wreaks havoc on his father's ambitious plans, but above all, Wurm ruins the happiness of the two young protagonists by undermining the trust that once existed between them: "Ein entsetzliches Schicksal," one engineered by a pen-pushing Sekretär, "hat die Sprache [ihrer] Herzen verwirrt" (s854).

When, in the concluding scene, the Präsident attempts to put the blame on his servant, Wurm, refusing to be the scapegoat, responds in kind: "Über mich [die Verantwortung]? (*Er fängt gräßlich an zu lachen*) Lustig! Lustig! So weiß ich doch nun auch, auf was Art sich die Teufel danken. – Über mich, *dummer* Bösewicht?" (s857–8). "The gloves are off." The diabolical laugh, as if the audience needed reminding at this late stage, again puts him in the devil's company, but he rightly tars his master with the same brush and even goes one significant step further. Whereas Wurm, constrained earlier by his dependent social status, did not respond to his master's pejorative address "Dummkopf" (s802) and simply swallowed the insult, he now calls his superior a stupid villain. By implication the secretary is the smart one and, in this sense, he parallels Klesel: Wurm insists upon his intellectual pre-eminence based on his own sense of self-worth. "War es *mein* [Schiller's emphasis] Sohn? War *ich* [Schiller's emphasis] sein Gebieter?" (s858) He implies that the only issue at stake was to ensure Ferdinand's compliance with his father's political ambitions, as if the whole affair did not involve or stand to benefit Wurm in any way. The audience realizes, however, that he had hoped to win Luise for himself by compromising her, and then offering himself as an expedient to rehabilitate her reputation. Moreover, his rhetorical questions raise another important consideration. The master elected to follow his servant's lead and thus must bear the consequences, but the query: "War *ich* sein Gebieter," while attempting "to pass the buck," does raise the issue of effective command.[32] Although only a servant, Wurm nonetheless devised and orchestrated the whole scheme and did successfully manipulate his master into circumstances where the social inferior could indirectly control his social superior by using him to pursue his own objective – the possession of Luise.

In the final moments of the tragedy, Wurm declares his independence. "Jetzt *will* [Schiller's emphasis] ich verloren sein, aber *du* [Schiller's emphasis] sollst es mit mir sein" (s858). At the moment of his downfall, he refuses to be intimidated and assumes responsibility for his own life. He still feels that he can *will* his fate, and as a manifestation of his power, he will take his master down with him, i.e., he still retains sufficient influence to destroy him. Because of the increased interdependence between master and servant, a relationship emerges in which the roles can be reversed. Once Wurm threatens to divulge his secrets: "Ich will Geheimnisse aufdecken, daß denen, die sie hören, die Haut schauern soll" (s858), the play points again to the mutual dependence founded on a balance of fears as noted earlier. Since each party is privy to information compromising to the other, if one falls, the other will inevitably follow: "Arm in Arm mit *dir* [Schiller's emphasis] zum Blutgerüst! Arm in Arm mit *dir* [Schiller's emphasis] zur Hölle!" (s858) They once formed this unholy alliance only because it served their respective interests, and it quickly dissolves when one party tries to eliminate the other. The master made the mistake of rendering himself subject to his servant just as the latter forfeits his influence as soon as he is deprived of the master's support. Since the servant now has nothing to lose, he has no reason to keep up the pretense of subservient obedience and he can indulge in the sadistic pleasure of exacting his revenge by imposing the same harsh sentence upon his social superior. "PRÄSIDENT (*hält ihn*). Du wirst doch nicht, Rasender? / WURM (*klopft ihn auf die Schultern*). Ich werde, Kamerad! Ich werde – … Es soll mich kitzeln, Bube, mit *dir* [Schiller's emphasis] verdammt zu sein! (*Er wird abgeführt*)" (s858) The patting of his master on the shoulder, the familiar ("Kamerad"), the derogatory ("Bube") forms of address and the common use of the intimate "du" throughout this exchange further underline the relative social equality that now exists between master and servant. Since, however, the Präsident tries to hold Wurm back and thus demonstrates his dependence, the Sekretär's parting gesture is an act of condescension and a public proclamation of superiority in defeat along the lines of Klesel's final words: "Mir bleibt der Vorrang, wär's in Ketten" (2700). Both Wurm and Klesel are put under arrest, but whereas the former is led off as a common criminal without any vestige of sympathy on the part of the dramatist, the latter *"geht mitten durch die Trabanten ab. Seyfried [the arresting officer] folgt"* (p.474). This contrast again points to Grillparzer's ambivalent attitude to his pen-pusher.

In writing *Kabale und Liebe*, Schiller is said to have been inspired by Freiherr Otto von Gemmingen's *Der deutsche Hausvater* (1780)[33] and Heinrich Leopold Wagner's *Die Reue nach der Tat* (1775).[34] The former, a melodrama designed as an apology for the aristocracy and conservative politics,[35] and having as its central character a "Hausvater, [e]in biederer thätiger, deutscher Mann, bekannt mit der Welt; antiker Grundsätze über seine Familie, aber doch mehr ehrlicher Mann als Edelmann,"[36] stands in marked contrast to Schiller's tragedy with its explicit social criticism of the upper class and its implicit revolutionary message. The only character to come close to Wurm is the Amtmann who spends most of his time in the city showing off his family's finery ("sie blitzen wie 'n Pfau vor schöne Kleider"[37]). Proud of his legal expertise ("Euer Hochgräflichen Excellenz wissen, daß ich mich auf mein *jus* verstehe"[38]) he specializes in exploiting the decent, hard-working, loyal peasants and makes his one and only brief appearance in the play before his master with a document in his hand: "Was haben Sie [Amtmann] da für ein Papier?"[39] Significantly, this short dialogue concludes with the Hausvater's repudiation of his steward: "Herr, ich wollte, Sie wären bloß ein Narr und nicht auch ein Schurke."[40] This pen-pusher, although exhibiting some of the key features of his type, is clearly no match for his honest master and his sole function would seem to be to accentuate, by negative example, the admirable social conscience of the titular hero. In Wagner's *Die Reue nach der Tat*, a drama glorifying the Habsburg regime – "WALZ [Miller's equivalent]: Heisa! es leb' die Kaiserin, Königin! es leb' unser Kaiser!"[41]" – there is simply no male equivalent to Wurm. The diabolical schemer proves to be the main protagonist's socially ambitious mother, the Justizrätin: "Sie müßte ein Teufel sein, wenn sie sich so hätte verstellen können; unmöglich!"[42] While the play contains two people associated with the pen, they are the positive central character, Assessor Langen: "*Ein Schreibtisch mit Schriften, Akten und Büchern beladen; … Lange, vor einem Tisch sitzend,*"[43] and his confidant: "*Werner sitzt am Schreibtisch und ist beschäftigt, Papiere in Ordnung zu bringen*"[44] who demonstrates his genuine friendship and loyalty in his efforts to bring the lovers, Langen and Fridericke, together. If anything, Wurm looks back to Lessing's Marinelli or one of Schiller's own creations, Franz von Moor, the calculating, rationalistic materialist, but the latter's domestic intrigue, conducted in part by letter, has a different social background based on sibling rivalry and, as previously noted, the "Marchese" belongs to the morally corrupt nobility. Therefore, Wurm's characterization establishes an influential model for all subsequent pen-pushers, one which would undergo several variations such as that represented by Klesel. This line of descent has an ironic twist if one bears in mind how Grillparzer, after having witnessed a performance of *Kabale und Liebe* at the Burgtheater, repudiated the tragedy as "das elendeste Machwerk, das je ein Mann der doch, und zwar nicht ohne Grund, Anspruch macht unter die Matadors seiner Nation gezählt zu werden, aus bunten, glitzenden Lumpen zusammen[ge]flickt hat, und an dessen breiten Worten und hohen Stelzen man unmöglich die Absicht des Verfassers ein Meisterwerk liefern zu wollen erkennen kann."[45]

THE SEKRETÄR IN GOETHE'S
DIE NATÜRLICHE TOCHTER

According to Gerhard Fricke, Schiller had no need of literary models or sources when he wrote *Kabale und Liebe* (first version completed in 1783): "hier gab ihm einmal die eigene Erfahrung alles, wessen er bedurfte. Für die Atmosphäre dieser absolutischen Residenz, ihre Günstlings – und Mätressenwirtschaft, ihre Intrigen und Skrupellosigkeiten, ihre Üppigkeit und Verschwendungssucht, ihre brutale Ausbeutung und Vergewaltigung der Untertanen boten Karl Eugen und seine Stuttgarter Hofhaltung dem Dichter im ganzen wie in zahlreichen nachweislichen und nachgewiesenen Einzelheiten alle Farben, die er für sein grelles, aber wahres Gemälde verwendete."[46] In other words Schiller drew his inspiration for "dieses realistisch-revolutionäre, anklägerische Gegenwartsstück"[47] from his experiences before the outbreak of the French Revolution but in anticipation of many issues highlighted by this, the most far-reaching development of the eighteenth century. Goethe's *Die natürliche Tochter*, completed in 1803 as the first part of a trilogy which he never saw to completion, owes its creation to the *Mémoires historiques de Stéphanie de Bourbon-Conti, écrits par elle-même* which he first became acquainted with while visiting Schiller in 1799. Josef Kunz has outlined in detail Goethe's quite considerable debt to his source, including even the title.[48] Commenting upon his conception of the tragedy, Goethe noted in the "Tag– und Jahresheften" for the year 1799, "In dem Plane bereitete ich mir ein Gefäß, worin ich alles, was ich so manches Jahr über die französische Revolution und deren Folgen geschrieben und gedacht, mit geziemendem Ernste niederzulegen hoffte."[49] Hence, while Schiller's "bürgerliches Trauerspiel" foresees the Revolution, Goethe's "Trauerspiel" seeks to reevaluate it with the wisdom of hindsight. Not surprisingly then, *Ein Bruderzwist*, allegedly dealing with the most catastrophic European upheaval of the seventeenth century, but more likely reflecting its author's concern with the contemporary social and political unrest that culminated in the Revolution of 1848, contains numerous points of contact with its two dramatic precursors, not least of which is the emergence and increasing influence of the pen-pushing secretary as a natural consequence of these social changes. Since Grillparzer first began working on the drama as early as 1824,[50] completed H^1 and H^2 in 1848, but still revised the manuscript in 1849–50, *Ein Bruderzwist* looks both forward to a revolution (*Kabale und Liebe*) and back at it (*Die natürliche Tochter*).

While reading Kunz's commentary on *Die natürliche Tochter*, I was struck by several observations which sound as if he were describing *Ein Bruderzwist*. For example, "An sich geht es, wenigstens dem vordergründigen Geschehen nach, um eine Familientragödie. Aber sie war durch viele Fäden mit den geschichtlichen Ereignissen des Zusammenbruchs der Monarchie und des Beginns der Revolution verbunden."[51] One would be hard pressed to find a more succinct description of the thematic considerations in both the fore – and background of Grillparzer's tragedy. Common as well to the two works is their authors' obvious attraction to the central figure – Eugenie/Rudolf – who mirrors in her/his individual fate a historical progression on a more general, universal scale. Whereas Grillparzer portrays these developments from the conservative, socio-political perspective of a divinely ordained "Ordnung" set opposite anarchy or "Aufruhr," Goethe, equally conservative in his preference for evolution over revolution, but strongly influenced by his scientific studies, has recourse to an organic model to depict these changes as a conflict between "Gestalt" and "Element," or "Form" and Chaos." Yet, strangely enough, despite their divergent points of departure, they arrive at essentially the same conclusion: "Damit eine solche [Struktur] ihr eigentümliches Leben entfalten kann, dazu ist vor allem eins nötig: daß das Telos des Ganzen … also jene Instanz, in der sich der Sinnbezug dieses Lebensgefüges darstellt, auch die Energie besitzt, um den Zusammenhang des Ganzen gewährleisten zu können. Versagt diese – und das geschieht in diesem Drama [*Die natürliche Tochter*] in beklemmender Weise –, dann zerfällt das Gefüge, indem die Glieder den Bezug zum Ganzen verlieren und den Lebenssinn nur mehr in der Behauptung ihrer besonderen, vom Ganzen abgelösten Existenz zu erblicken vermögen."[52] Although Rudolf asks his confidant, "Nun Herzog Julius, fühlt ihr noch die Kraft / Das Schwert zu schwingen in der alten Rechte?" (1482–3) and goes on to claim, "Mich selbst befällt ein Hauch der Jugendzeit / Und an der Spitze, denk' ich, meiner Treuen / Hinauszuziehn, um Stirne gegen Stirn / Den *Aufruhr* zu befragen was sein Ziel" (1484–7), the same speech signals symbolically the passive nature of his regime in the current location of his sword: "Er [Degen] lehnt am Tisch zunächst am meinem Bette" (1496). The weak, senile old man of his first stage appearance clearly lacks the prerequisite will and energy to win his subjects' support for his cohesive vision of his rule, which "einig mit dem Geist des All, / … / Den Gang nachahmt der ewigen Natur" (1280–2), or to prevent the impending dissolution: "Der Reichsfürst will sich lösen von dem Reich" (1236), the nobles from the princes and the burghers from the nobles, while everyone seeks only his/her own advantage: "Auch mir mein Teil, vielmehr das Ganze!" (1252).

Kunz distinguishes two major themes in *Die natürliche Tochter*: "die Bedeutung des geschichtlichen Geschehens im allgemeinen d.h. der Anspruch und der Verfall einer hierarchisch – organischen Ordnung" (as we have observed, a concern shared by *Ein Bruderzwist*), and, secondly, the fate of the main protagonist, "dieses zu verstehen im Sinne des Märchenmotivs vom edlen Blut in Exil."[53] Eugenie, as her name implies, personifies a guarantee for a rebirth of her class. There is hope that the aristocracy will be rejuvenated through her, the one who is "well-born," but, in the meantime, she must remain hidden, collecting her forces and preserving the positive values of her heritage, just as an organism in a state of "Verfall" regains its vitality during a dormant period. Rudolf also recognizes "Verborgenheit als das Gesetz dieser Stunde"[54] and therefore feels the need to hide himself from a world in decline: "Damit ich lebe muß ich mich begraben, / Ich wäre tot, lebt' ich mit dieser Welt" (1160–1). However, in contrast to Goethe's optimistic, organic view, the emperor sees his own epoch as apostasy, a falling away from God, the unifying principle of which he is the earthly representative. Confident that the Deity will eventually show the way: "Da hält man sich denn ruhig und erwartet / Bis frei der Weg, den Gott dem Rechten ebnet" (1177–8), he endeavors to safeguard the best of the old traditions. Whereas Goethe's tragedy leaves the audience with the promise of a better future, but one still based on an aristocratic hierarchical system, the final act of *Ein Bruderzwist* presents Rudolf as the *pharmakos* demanded by an inexorable historical process, and suggests the end of an era and the inevitable ascendancy of the pen-pushing servant. As we shall subsequently see, Goethe appreciated the danger embodied by the secretary but elected not to ascribe to his role the central importance discernible in Klesel's characterization.

The first act of *Die natürliche Tochter* frequently anticipates the socio-political climate depicted in the various dialogues of *Ein Bruderzwist*. In his opening speech the König concedes, "Der edle Hirsch, hat über Berg und Tal / So weit uns irr'geführt, daß ich mich selbt, / Obgleich so landeskundig, hier nicht finde,"[55] thus implying symbolically his general disorientation. Unable to find himself, he is not in control. Terms such as "Ahnherrn königlicher Gnade" (G10) or "Lehnsmann deines Reiches" (G11), appearing in the Herzog's first words, indicate a feudal system similar to the one depicted by Rudolf. Like the emperor, the König speaks on behalf of the divine right of kings and the need for solidarity amongst the ruling elite – an aristocratic order designed to serve the best interest of the whole community, including the masses:

Sie [die Menge] ist bedeutend, mehr noch aber sind's
Die wenigen, geschaffen, dieser Menge
Durch Wirken, Bilden, Herrschen vorzustehn.
Berief hiezu den König die Geburt,

So sind ihm seine nächsten Anverwandten
Geborne Räte, die, mit ihm vereint,
Das Reich beschützen und beglücken sollten.   (G303–9)

But the ruling head of state also formulates very early in Goethe's drama the central issue of *Ein Bruderzwist in Habsburg* contained within its very title: "O träte doch in diese Regionen / Zum Rate dieser hohen Wächter, nie / Vermummte Zwietracht, leise wirkend, ein!" (G310–12). In view of this internal threat, the König invites a socially rehabilitated Eugenie to join the "Chor der Treuen, die an [s]einer Seite / Das Rechte, das *Beständige* beschützen" (G359–60). He stands for the constant or the permanent, that which is because it is and therefore is the just and correct way. Rudolf resorts to a similar argument when he pleads with the Standesherren not to meddle with "das Beständige," for to do so would be to risk unleashing the forces of anarchy.

Und aus dem Wechselspiel von hoch und niedrig,
Von Frucht und Schutz erzeugt sich dieses Ganze,
Des Grund und Recht in dem liegt, daß es ist.
Zieht nicht vor das Gericht die heil'gen Bande,
Die unbewußt, zugleich mit der Geburt,
Erweislos weil sie selber der Erweis,
Verknüpfen was das Klügeln feindlich trennt.   (1612–18)

Rudolf's fear of the encroaching democratization process which "alles Große, / Die Kunst, die Wissenschaft, den Staat, die Kirche / Herabstürzt von der Höhe, die sie schützt, / Zur Oberfläche eigener Gemeinheit, / Bis alles gleich, ei ja, weil alles niedrig" (1270–4) finds an exact parallel in the König's warning:

O diese Zeit hat fürchterliche Zeichen:
Das Niedre schwillt, das Hohe senkt sich nieder,
Als könnte jeder nur am Platz des andern
Befriedigung verworrner Wünsche finden,
Nur dann sich glücklich fühlen, wenn nichts mehr
Zu unterscheiden wäre, wenn wir alle,
Von einem Strom vermischt dahingerissen,
Im Ozean uns unbemerkt verlören.   (G361–8)

A plea for the recognition of the quality of life exemplified in the class system (the word aristocracy derived from the Greek signifies the rule of the best) and threatened by the self-debasement of the reigning minority unites the two sovereigns, as well as the painful realization that the ship of state is rotten from within. "Aus eignem Schoß," proclaims the emperor, "ringt los sich der Barbar" (1269) while the King exhorts two of his family members, "Laßt endlich uns den alten *Zwist* vergessen, / Der Große gegen Große reizt, von innen / Das Schiff durchbohrt, das gegen äußre Wellen / Geschlossen kämpfend nur sich halten kann" (G372–5). The two rulers may identify the problem facing the nation and possess the selfless desire to act in its best interest, but both ultimately lack the strength to put their ideal aspirations into effect as the König admits already in the first act: "O wäre mir zu meinen reinen Wünschen / Auch volle Kraft auf kurze Zeit gegeben" (G417–8). The Herzog, a fervent adherent of the old order, points out in a subsequent scene the crisis facing the country: the König is too moderate, too weak, to be an effective leader (G435–8), for he has made himself dependent on advisors and administrators whose motives are anything but "rein," and who strive primarily to enhance their own influence: "Des Königs Milde zeugt Verwegenheit" (G434). The audience has thus been adequately prepared for "die Gegenwelt in [dem] Raum des dramatischen Geschehens,"[56] the Sekretär.

His initial speech at the beginning of the second act already demonstrates the tactics of the Machiavellian schemer: "Verdien' ich, das du [Hofmeisterin] mich, im Augenblick, / Da ich erwünschte Nachricht bringe, fliehst?" (G649–50). His first two words: "Verdien' ich" infer that on the basis of past favors granted, he has earned better treatment. Having nurtured a sense of obligation in the Hofmeisterin, he plays on her sense of love, loyalty, and gratitude at the appropriate moment in order to induce her to do what he wishes. His intended victim, however, is sufficiently perceptive to recognize the manipulative technique: "Entfliehen laß mich der *Gewalt*, die, sonst / Durch Lieb' und Freundschaft wirksam, fürchterlich / Wie ein Gespenst mir nun zur Seite steht" (G655–7). It is surely no accident that the word "Gewalt" is mentioned so early in their exchange. The Sekretär has gained the Hofmeisterin's support: he has promised her marriage but in return she must do violence to her emotions, i.e., betray her beloved mistress. He has exploited sex to capture a pawn for use in a morally questionable intrigue. When she proves impervious to this approach, he attempts to bribe her into submission by painting a picture of domestic bliss: "Verlangst du Wohnung, mitten in der Stadt, / Geräumig, heiter, trefflich ausgestattet, / Wie man's für sich so wie für Gäste wünscht" (G670–2), an image of "sichres Glück" (G683) founded on the material values ("Sparsamkeit" [G683]) of the middle class. This dialogue, located immediately after the conversation between the König, Herzog and Eugenie, must be seen as a consciously designed contrast to the more noble, abstract concerns such as honesty and loyalty displayed in the previous act: "Leb' wohl, mein Vater, folge deinem König / Und sei nun auch um deiner Tochter willen / Sein redlicher Vasall, sein treuer Freund" (G607–9).

The Hofmeisterin, in her integrity and affection for her charge, does not allow the prospect of future material happiness to cloud the issue; her conscience intervenes: "Und was ein solch Verbrechen mir erwarb, / Ich sollt' es je mit freier Brust genießen?" (G690–1). This prompts the Sekretär to adopt a different tack:

Doch wenn das Mächtige, das uns regiert,
Ein großes Opfer heischt, wir bringen's doch,
Mut blutendem Gefühl, der Not zuletzt.
Zwei Welten sind es, meine Liebe, die,
Gewaltsam sich bekämpfend, uns bedrängen.   (G706–10)

He rationalizes an unconscionable act as something demanded by the one in power, and therefore hides behind the master/servant relationship, i.e., the servant must be prepared to make a great moral sacrifice for his lord. As loyal followers, they have no alternative. However, the choice of the abstract, general term "das Mächtige" lends itself to various interpretations, the most obvious of which is the König; the text has already supplied several hints that this particular ruler is ineffective – "Die Kraft," notes the Herzog, "entgeht vielleicht dem späten Zweige" (G440) – and does not really have command of the situation. It could also mean the demands of the moment, "Not," which the Sekretär will doubtlessly know how to turn to his advantage. Moreover, the implied "Not kennt kein Gebot" contains a Machiavellian aspect: the Hofmeisterin is expected to sacrifice moral principle to political expediency. The Sekretär then proceeds to portray himself and his interlocutor as unwitting victims caught in the middle of two feuding factions: the Herzog, representing the older generation and its respect for traditional ideals, including strong leadership from above, and his dissolute son who stands for the egocentric values of the new times (cf. Don Cäsar). It is an era of dissolution, of suspension of historical loyalties, a period like the one deplored by Rudolf: "Der Reichsfürst will sich lösen von dem Reich, / Dann kommt der Adel und bekämpft die Fürsten" (1236–7). The König, in his weakness, would seem to side with the son's party through the implied intervention of the Sekretär. The latter has switched his allegiance to the profligate son and the feeble king since the servant can easily manipulate them but not the duke, his current master. By his independent views and behavior, the Herzog has shown that he has a mind of his own. Since he is not the least sympathetic to recent trends, he must be prevented from gaining greater control over the König through his daughter at the expense of his son. A young man known for "rohes, wildes Wesen, / Verworrenheit, Verschwendung, starren Trutz" (G56–7) would be easier to manage than an "edlen Herzog," a man of principles as the preceding act has amply indicated. The Hofmeisterin gives indirect credence to this analysis when she later warns Eugenie, "Doch die Partei die seinen [the son's] Groll bestärkt, / Auf ewig steht sie deinem Wunsch entgegen" (G1109–10). The Sekretär's faction views her as a threat to their puppet, the brother, with whom they seek to gain influence by catering to his worst attributes. Finally, by using the first-person plural "uns," the Sekretär tries to ingratiate himself further with the Hofmeisterin: she shares his fate both in victory and defeat, and hence she has much to gain by casting her lot in with him.

One feature does distinguish Goethe's secretary from Schiller's: "Warum, o! schuf dich die Natur von außen / Gefällig, liebenswert, unwiderstehlich, / Wenn sie ein kaltes Herz in deinen Busen, / Ein glückzerstörendes, zu pflanzen dachte?" (G723–6). Whereas Wurm's outer appearance reinforces or reflects his inner diabolical disposition, the secretary's physical attractiveness, an effective weapon to solicit the collaboration of women, only serves to conceal his calculating, sadistic heart. Despite the appealing outer shell, he exhibits his share of satanic characteristics, not least of which is his exploitation of sex (cf. Leonhard): "und bin ich [Hofmeisterin] nicht / Mir auch ein Rätsel, daß ich noch an dir / Mit solcher Neigung hänge, da du mich / Zum jähen Abgrund hinzureißen strebst?" (G719–22). One detects the Mephistophelian seducer responsible for the victim's fall into the bottomless pit. Clearly the Sekretär has attempted several times to pressure his lover into joining his conspiracy, but with limited success because of her loyalty to and love for the Herzog and his daughter.

In response to the Hofmeisterin's, as it turns out, naive contention that Eugenie should be granted "das Glück des Rechts" (G755), the intriguer retorts,

> Geliebte, Teure! Sprichst du doch so leicht,
> Durch diese Mauern von der Welt geschieden,
> In klösterlichem Sinne von dem Wert

Der Erdengüter. Blicke nur hinaus;
Dort wägt man besser solchen edlen Schatz.   (G756–60)

This anticipates Klesel's conversation with the religious bigot Ferdinand whose dogmatically naive Christian point of view blinds him to the self-interest of others and to his own underlying dynastic ambitions: "Auch ist der Seeleneifer und der Eigennutz / Nicht gar so unvereinbar als man glaubt. / … / Und wie der Adler, der der Sonne nächst, / Holt er sich Kräftigung durch ird'sche Beute" (2531–5). The sheltered existence led by the Hofmeisterin has ill-equipped her to measure real life by material standards; the world of the self-serving, middle-class pen-pusher places more store in the "Wert / Der Erdengüter," "ird'sche Beute" than in intangible, ideal concepts such as truth and loyalty. As Klesel observes in this respect, "Man sieht sich vor; die Zeiten schlagen um" (2504). The old aristocratic principles such as justice, self-sacrifice or fidelity to one's word now constitute a source of ridicule, since pragmatic self-interest has come to dictate one's attitude and actions: "Der [Bürger] dehnt sich breit," Rudolf comments sarcastically, "und hört mit Spottes-Lächeln [cf. the Sekretär's response to "das Glück des Rechts"] / Von Toren reden, die man Helden nennt, / Von Weisen, die nicht klug für eignen Säckel, / Von allem was nicht nützt und Zinsen trägt" (1241–4).

The Seckretär goes on to point out how *Geldsackgesinnung* has pervaded all levels of society, including the aristocracy, where greed has created selfish individuals with no appreciation for the cohesive nature of the family, and even the clergy, "Selbt der Geistliche," he remarks, "vergißt, / Wohin er streben soll, und strebt nach Gold" (G765), a preparation for the later appearance of the Weltgeistlicher and a valid summary of at least part of Klesel's motivation:

So lang der Kirche Gold und Rang und Ansehn
Euch [Klesel] noch ein Lohn schien, der des *Strebens* wert,
Und habt, so sagt die Welt, nicht nur von Glaubens-*Schätzen*,
Auch von den Schätzen dieser ird'schen Welt
Ein Artiges gehäuft in euern Speichern.   (2499–53)

The Church's involvement in power politics touched on by Ferdinand becomes an issue later in the dialogue between the Hofmeisterin and the Seckretär when the latter, to contravene the former's suggested expedient that Eugenie be put in a convent, replies, "Im Kloster nicht; wir mögen solch ein Pfand / Der Geistlichkeit nicht anvertrauen, die / Es leicht als Werkzeug gegen uns gebrauchte" (G805–7).[57] Since the Sekretär and people of his ilk judge others by their own priorities, they regard envy, jealousy and greed as normal responses to a threat to their own advantage:

> Verdächte man's dem Prinzen, der sich stets
> Als einz'gen Sohn gefühlt, wenn er sich nun
> Die Schwester nicht gefallen lassen will,
> Die, eingedrungen, ihm das Erbteil schmälert?
> Man stelle sich an seinen Platz und richte. (G766–70)

I am reminded of Mephistopheles's reaction to Faust's reluctance to initiate the seduction of Gretchen by leaving behind a chest of jewels a hidden treasure being one of the customary sources of the devil's power: "Fragt Ihr viel? / Meint Ihr vielleicht den *Schatz* zu wahren? / Dann rat' ich Eurer Lüsternkeit, / Die liebe schöne Tageszeit / Und mir die weitre Müh' zu sparen."[58] Unable to comprehend Faust's dawning awareness of Gretchen as a human being, not just as a sex object, Satan, judging by his own standards, assumes that Faust's hesitancy is due to his desire to keep the bait for himself.

When the Hofmeisterin asks why the prince cannot spare a small portion of his extensive inheritance to win the love and support of his sister, the Sekretär's retort discloses the immoral depths to which the worship of Mammon can lead: "Willkürlich handeln ist des Reichen Glück! / Er widerspricht der Forderung der Natur, / Der Stimme des Gesetzes, der Vernunft, / Und spendet an den Zufall seine Gaben" (G776–9). As we would say today, money talks. It grants one the means to indulge one's merest whim, to fly in the face of nature, law and reason. It removes the obligation to act in a morally responsible fashion, as one becomes a law unto oneself. At the heart of the matter, however, lies power, i.e., what the secretary and his class aspire to. Significantly, he refers to "des Reichen Glück," because the rich man need not be a nobleman.[59] Already in the eighteenth century wealth had begun to shift away from land holding, the traditional source of aristocratic income, towards industry and commerce, the strengths of the bourgeoisie. In addition, the aristocracy had become a casualty of its customary extravagance and the squandering of its inheritance: "Genug besitzen hieße darben. Alles / Bedürfte man! Unendlicher *Verschwendung* / Sind ungemeßne Güter wünschenswert" (G780–2), but, as Rudolf cautions, "Den [Adel] gibt die Not, die Tochter der *Verschwendung* / Drauf in des Bürgers Hand, des Krämers, Mäklers, / Der allen Wert abwägt nach Goldgewicht" (1238–40). The duke's son, in his spendthrift ways, is actually being true to his heritage: "In der adligen Ideologie wird Sparen … als

geizig und knauserig, als unehrenhaft und unadlig angesehen. An-
dererseits ist prunkhafte Zurschaustellung von Reichtum und Groß-
zügigkeit bis zur *Verschwendung* lobenswert."[60] In order to sustain
such expensive habits, however, the nobleman inevitably contracted
"debts of honor" rendering him increasingly dependent upon the
moneyed middle class, and, in this respect as well, the servant, the
one offering a financial service, could easily become the master.
Rudolf paints a grim picture of this social transformation as a warning of what could happen since he disapproves of the consequences,
describing them as a "Scheusal ... gräßlich anzusehn / Mit breiten
Schultern, weitgespaltnem Mund, / Nach allem lüstern und durch
nichts zu füllen" (1246–8). In contrast, the Sekretär welcomes this
same development as a reality which one cannot ignore and from
which he clearly hopes to profit. Such a process, since it will ultimately weaken the ruling class, will give the Sekretär and the bourgeoisie greater authority in the new age.

The Sekretär continues in his efforts to oblige his lover to side with
his party by putting her on the spot and presenting her with only
two options: "Hier denke nicht zu raten, nicht zu mildern; / Kannst
du mit uns nicht wirken, gib uns auf" (G783–4). She must declare
herself either for or against them and, endeavoring to put her mind
at rest while enticing her with sensual pleasure: "Dein Liebling kann
auch drüben [in exile] glücklich sein, / Und dich erwarten hier Genuß
und Wonne" (G812–13), he again seeks to minimize what later turns
out to be certain death, and to lure her into compliance with an
implied bribe: "Was wir gesonnen, führe du es aus: / Klein wird das
Übel werden, groß das Glück" (G834–5).

Another typical trait shared by all scheming secretaries is their
intimate knowledge of all that is going on at court (or in town).
Nothing of major importance remains concealed for long from the
Sekretär:

> Der Herzog scheint gewiß, daß ihm der König
> Am nächsten Fest die hohe Gunst gewähren
> Und seine Tocher anerkennen wolle;
> Denn Kleider und Juwelen stehn bereit,
> Im prächt'gen Kasten sämtlich eingeschlossen,
> *Wozu er selbt die Schlüssel wohl verwahrt*
> Und ein Geheimnis zu verwahren glaubt;
> Wir aber wissen's wohl und sind gerüstet.   (G838–45)

However, there would appear to be one crucial exception: the where-
abouts of the key.

Who broke the royal imposition of silence: "Am Throne glänze dein [Eugenie's] Geschick. / Doch bis dahin verlang' ich von euch [Herzog and Eugenie] beiden / Verschwiegenheit. Was unter uns geschehn, / Erfahre niemand" (G404–6)? If it were Eugenie, she would certainly have announced her good news to her confidante and surrogate mother, the Hofmeisterin: "HOFMEISTERIN. O möchtest du mir alles gleich vertrauen! / EUGENIE. Von allen Menschen dir zuerst" (G920–1),[61] but the exchange of II/1 proves that the Hofmeisterin learns of her charge's future social elevation first of all through her lover. Aware of the atmosphere of envy and distrust at court (G468f) the Herzog cautioned his daughter to trust no one: "Hier ist der Schlüssel! den verwahre wohl; / Bezähme deine Neugier! öffne nicht, / Eh' ich dich wiedersehe, jenen Schatz. / Vertraue niemand, sei es, wer es sei" (G541–4). It is thus extremely unlikely, given the vehemence of this warning, that he would divulge details capable of destroying his daughter's happiness. In other words, the guilty party had to be the king himself. As a further substantiation, the one detail which the Sekretär has wrong is the location of the key: he assumes incorrectly that the Herzog still has it in his possession, while we know from the subsequent dialogue between father and daughter, (I/6) at which the König was absent, that the Herzog has surrendered the key to her – the only piece of information to which the König was not privy and which the Sekretär appears to ignore. Since only three people shared the secret, Goethe has skillfully included the necessary circumstantial evidence to point to the culprit.

One senses the Hofmeisterin's growing alienation from the man who has used her in her description of his diabolical scheme: "Auf düstern Wegen wirkt ihr tückisch fort" (G848), and in her suggestion that a superior avenging force could easily thwart his plans. While the Sekretär acknowledges the possible existence of "ein Herrschendes" (G853), he asks rhetorically, "Doch wer hat sich zu seinem hohen Rat / Gesellen dürfen? Wer Gesetz und Regel, / Wonach es ordnend spricht, erkennen mögen?" (G856–8). Since no one can know the will of the higher being, any interpretation is equally valid and, by implication, the authorities of the past and their view of a morally governed world order have been called into doubt and perhaps even superseded. "*Verstand* empfingen wir, uns mündig selbst / Im ird'schen Element zurechtzufinden, / Und was uns nützt, ist unser höchstes *Recht*" (G859–61). Above all, as the pen-pusher before him and those to follow him, the Sekretär claims the right to assert his god-given intelligence, the one aspect enabling him to distinguish himself and to gain dominance over his social masters. As Klesel succinctly puts it, "Niemand soll zittern! / Vor allem der im *Recht* ist und der *klug*" (2573–4). Glorying in the mental maturity enabling the human race to control and exploit the earth, the Sekretär advocates a selfish ultilitarianism with the arrogance born of the intellect. The emperor's worst fears have been realized: the materially motivated burghers ridicule those "die nicht *klug* für eignen Säckel, / Von allem was nicht *nützt* und Zinsen trägt" (1243–4) and demand as the majority their "Recht!" (1254). Whereas Rudolf similarly acknowledges his limitations: "Fragst aber du [Ferdinand]: ob sie mir selber kund, / Die hohe Wahrheit aus der Wesen Munde? / So sag' ich: nein" (418–20), in direct contrast, he has what Goethe's Sekretär lacks – "Ehrfurcht / Für das daß Andre mächtig und ich nicht" (423–4). Rudolf's ideal, as captured in his proposed order of "Friedensritter" (1207), emphasizes altruism – "Aus Männern, die nicht dienstbar ihrem Selbt" (1209) – and a belief in the innate goodness of human feelings, the compassion of the human heart, as the source of the ethical voice in each of us – "Nicht außen auf der Brust trägt man das Zeichen, / Nein innen wo der Herzschlag es erwärmt, / Es sich belebt am Puls des tiefsten Lebens" (1217–19). This parallels the Hofmeisterin's concept of the Divine: "Und so verleugnet ihr das Göttlichste, / Wenn euch des Herzens Winke nichts bedeuten" (G862–3). Since the pen-pusher, denying his better self, remains deaf to the promptings of his heart, he responds only to the cold dictates of self-serving cunning. As an instance of retrospective irony, the Herzog earlier warned Eugenie, "Vertraue niemand, sei es, wer es sei. / Die *Klugheit* rät's, der König selbt gebeut's" (G544–5). "Klugheit" has taught the difficult lesson that at court, trust can be a liability. Intelligence, not feeling, holds sway and, as a specific illustration, the very man who established a trust based on silence is the one to betray it.

When the Hofmeisterin's sense of human decency, her love and loyalty win the upper hand, she stands up to the Sekretär and expresses her resolve to arm herself "gegen Macht und List" (G866), the intriguer's objective and the means to achieve that objective.[62] Faced with her resistance, he resorts to his knowledge of the affection she feels for Eugenie to ensure her participation in the complot. He claims that she alone can avert a greater disaster from befalling her beloved surrogate daughter: "dies ihr Heil vermagst / Du ganz allein zu schaffen, die Gefahr / Von ihr zu wenden, magst du ganz allein" (G870–2). By forcing her to choose the lesser evil, as if there were no other choice, he engages in a form of emotional blackmail comparable to that employed by Wurm. Then, as an intensification of his psychological warfare, he again attacks where she is most vulnerable: "Du schauderst, / Du fühlst, was ich zu sagen habe. Sei's, / Weil du mich drängest, endlich auch gesagt: / Sie zu entfernen, ist das Mildeste" (G876–9), i.e., I would prefer to spare you the gruesome details but your reluctance to comply forces me to disclose them. It's really your fault. This is all part of a mental strategy devised to take advantage of her love for the victim, to make her feel guilty as if she were somehow responsible, and thus to put her in a more subservient, receptive frame of mind for his machinations. To paraphrase Luise's observation regarding Wurm's cruel exploitation of human feeling, "[er] versteh[t] [sich] darauf, Seelen auf die Folter zu schrauben" (s815).

When, in the last speech of the scene, the Sekretär raises the spectre of Eugenie's ineluctable death if the Hofmeisterin does not participate actively in "diesen Plan" (G880), he touches on another common attribute of the pen-pushing secretary. His calculating mind always looks to the future, has figured the odds and does everything to accomplish the desired goal: Wurm's cabal to alienate the affection between Ferdinand and Luise, Leonhard's strategy to get ahead in the town community by impregnating women who stand to further his career, or Klesel's declaration: "ein fester Plan beherrscht das Ganze / Und jeder Schritt führt näher an das Ziel" (2467–8) come to mind. With great tenacity and determination they all adhere to the plan regardless of the illegality or loss of human life it may entail.

The third act also commences with a dialogue between the Sekretär and one of his instruments, in this case, the Weltgeistlicher. Early in their conversation, the latter asks, "Und wem vertraut ihr solch ein schwer Geschäft [i.e., Eugenie's abduction]?" to which the Sekretär replies, "Dem klugen Weib, das uns angehört" (G1168–9). He confidently designates his lover as their willing tool and extends to her his own main characteristic, but in so doing, he judges by his own norm of cleverness – she must see that it is in her own best interest to subscribe to our scheme – and therefore underestimates her. On the basis of his personal philosophy: "Und was uns nützt, ist unser höchstes Recht" (G861), he is unable to conceive of a loyal servant who would put her mistress's well-being before her own. This tendency to project one's own motives or attitudes onto others and thus to misrepresent those one seeks to manipulate – other examples would include Wurm's failure to appreciate the intensity of feeling between Luise and Ferdinand, the Sekretär's or Leonhard's inability to comprehend Klara or Klesel's faulty assessment of Ferdinand – is another common characteristic to be added to the figure of the *Federfuchser*.

The Secretary must persuade the secular priest to do his part in the plot, specifically to convince people of Eugenie's tragic death. But beforehand, worried that his fellow conspirator may be weakened by remorse, the masterplanner sounds him out:

SEKRETÄR.	Ein innres Unbehagen fügt sich oft,
	Auch wider unsern Willen, an die Tat.
WELTGEISTLICHER.	Was hör' ich? du bedenklich? oder willst
	Du mich nur prüfen, ob es euch gelang,
	Mich, euern Schüler, völlig auszubilden?
SEKRETÄR.	Das Wichtige bedenkt man nie genug. (G1191–6)

Although the Weltgeistlicher at first appears incredulous at his master's reservations, he soon hits upon the real intent: has he truly sold his soul to the conspiring faction? The Sekretär, taking nothing for granted, wants to consider every angle of his plan to ensure its successful realization. He can afford no weak links.

In describing how he was enlisted, the Weltgeistlicher uses the same image of the *hortus conclusus* (G1202) to describe his earlier innocence as does the Hofmeisterin (G757), the other agent. This sheltered existence proved to be an inadequate preparation for the priorities of the real world beyond the confines of the garden, by implication, the realm of the Sekretär. Even though both recruits speak of ethical goodness and the power of the human heart to combat evil, (G1208), they nevertheless were eventually won over "mit schmeichlerischem Wesen, / Mit süßem Wort" (G1214–5), the technique the audience already witnessed in operation at the beginning of the second act.

SEKRETÄR.	Wir brachten dir so manche Freude zu.
WELTGEISTLICHER.	Und dranget mir so manch Bedürfnis auf.
	Nun war ich arm, als ich die Reichen kannte;
	Nun war ich sorgenvoll, denn mir gebrach's;
	Nun hatt' ich *Not*, ich brauchte fremde Hilfe.
	Ihr wart mir hilfreich, teuer büß' ich das. (G1218–23)

In order to gain supporters, the Sekretär, like his mentor, the devil, appeals to the worst features of human nature – envy, ambition and greed in the case of the priest, extravagance and "Groll" (G1109) in the case of the duke's son. As we noted earlier, "Not, die Tochter der Verschwendung" puts the aristocracy "in des Bürgers Hand" (1239), while, in this particular instance, it is a representative of the masses (G1660) whom the middle-class Sekretär has managed to corrupt. Having thus built up an enormous sense of psychological obligation and/or financial dependence in the Hofmeisterin and the priest, the Sekretär transforms them into instruments of his will, into slaves – "Zum Sklaven, sollt' ich sagen, dingtet ihr / Den sonst so freien, jetzt bedrängten Mann" (G1225–6) – a well-known phenomenon outlined by Hobbes in *Leviathan*: "benefits oblige; and obligation is thraldome; and unrequitable obligation, perpetuall thraldome."[63] Indicative of the priest's moral degeneracy is his refusal to be "ein gefühllos Werkzeug" (G1234) any longer. He demands to play a more active part in the conspiracy, vying for ascendancy in the power vacuum created by ineffectual leadership: "Von nun an fordr' ich, mit im Rat zu sitzen" (G1239). At least in terms of his designs and his insight into the larger picture, he has the potential to become a Klesel: "Wenn ich bedenke, wie, verborgen, ihr / Zu mächtiger Parteigewalt euch hebt / Und an die Stelle der Gebietenden / Mit frecher List euch einzudrängen hofft" (G1255–8). Eugenie's individual fate, when juxtaposed with this grandiose political perspective of assuming power through cunning, pales in significance: the end justifies the means. But interestingly enough, this Klesel in embryo has the same prophetic function Grillparzer assigns to his cardinal – he becomes the dramatist's spokesman in the last important speech of the dialogue, to emphasize the negative side of the process to which he has willingly subscribed: "Nicht ihr allein; denn andre streben auch, / Euch widerstrebend, nach demselben Zweck. / So untergrabt ihr Vaterland und Thron; / Wer soll sich retten, wenn das Ganze stürzt?" (G1259–62). The consequences could entail the collapse of the monarchy and its supportive hierarchical structure with chaotic consequences for society in general. The Weltgeistlicher is still concerned about his own fate when the traditional structure begins to crumble, but, somewhat inconsistently, he does not regard the threat of anarchy, the dissolution of the existing order from which the middle class hopes to profit, as a positive development. The Sekretär has no opportunity to respond to this doomsday scenario, since the duke's imminent arrival leaves it dangling ominously in the air.

This same ambiguity, also associated with Klesel, continues to surround the personality of the Weltgeistlicher in his subsequent conversation with the Herzog. The priest has the task of comforting the bereaved father and, to that end, he observes,

Wie heftig wilde Gärung unten kocht,
Wie Schwäche kaum sich oben schwankend hält;
Nicht jedem wird es klar, dir aber ist's
Mehr als der Menge, der ich angehöre.
O zaudre nicht, im nahen Sturmgewitter
Das falsch gelenkte Steuer zu ergreifen!
Zum Wohle deines Vaterlands verbanne
Den eignen Schmerz.   (G1657–64)

It is almost as if he were speaking out of turn or being carried away by his own enthusiasm. He presents the lower class, to which he belongs himself, and its agitators in an unfavorable light, acknowledges how weak the king's hold on power is, and portrays the current royal policy as ill-advised. The Herzog must consequently assume command of the ship of state to save the nation. Is this speech simply out of character, i.e., contrary to the self-indulgent image evident in his dialogue with the Sekretär, or perhaps more in character, i.e., in keeping with the moral integrity of the time spent in the *hortus conclusus*? Or is he scheming to create additional instability by inciting his interlocutor to challenge the king's authority? Since the duke has traditionally opposed his sovereign's policies, is this high-sounding rhetoric: "O bringe deinen Jammer, deinen Kummer / Auf dem Altar des allgemeinen Wohls" (G1669–70) merely a guise to conceal an appeal to foment open revolt within the ruling hierarchy and thus the ultimate temptation?

The Sekretär or his creature, the Weltgeistlicher, do not appear in the last two acts of the tragedy, although the spectator can nonetheless sense the former's presence or influence. The object around which the final scenes revolve is the *lettre de cachet*. It renders Eugenie *persona non grata* in the realm and offers the alternative of either exile or death, unless she chooses a mésalliance, making her politically harmless. This document comes to symbolize arbitrary power exercised by the king to remove what has been presented to him as a threat to his authority: "Nicht ist von Recht, noch von Gericht die Rede: / Hier ist Gewalt! entsetzliche Gewalt, / Selbt wenn sie *klug*, selbt wenn sie weise handelt" (G1747–9). The fact that all hinges upon a piece of paper, together with the reference to "klug," tends to point to the cabals of the secretary. Klesel also has no qualms to interpret or bend the law, or even to hide behind it if it suits his purpose: "Niemand soll zittern! / Vor allem der im Recht ist und der *klug*" (2573–4).

The Hofmeisterin sees in the Gerichtsrat a way out of the dilemma. On the spur of the moment, that is to say on the basis of feeling and not of deliberation, he must agree to marry Eugenie: "Der Rettende faßt an und klügelt nicht" (G1831). Since "Klügeln," Klesel's domain, leads in Rudolf's estimation to dissension, distrust and civil war, the emperor stands for "Verknüpfen was das Klügeln feindlich trennt" (1618). It follows that the irrational side of the Gerichtsrat's personality leads him to agree to a union with the heroine whereas the mind, "Klugheit," would have counselled caution and delay to consider the matter at greater length: "Ich weiß, ich fühle deinen Zustand, kann /

Und mag nicht mit mir selbst bedächtig erst, / Wie Klugheit forderte, zu Rate gehn!" (G1857–9). Feeling again comes across as the better part of the person: "die Neigung spricht für dich" (G1902), not the calculating intellect which always pursues its selfish advantage.

Nevertheless, the drama definitely associates the Gerichtsrat, as his descriptive professional title implies, with the rule of law and order based on a judicial model endorsed by the middle class to protect its own interests: "In abgeschloßnen Kreisen lenken wir, / *Gesetzlich streng*, das in der Mittelhöhe / Des Lebens wiederkehrend Schwebende" (2009–11). In direct contrast he considers the rule of the aristocracy to be founded on arbitrary decision, without consultation or even judgment: "Was droben sich in eingemeßnen Räumen / *Gewaltig* seltsam hin und her bewegt, / Belebt und tötet ohne Rat und Urteil, / Das wird nach anderm Maß, nach andrer Zahl / Vielleicht berechnet, bleibt uns rätselhaft" (G2012–16). Might is right. To the man of law, the noble legal system flies in the face of that which is intellectually explicable, verifiable, or defensible. As in Klesel, so too in the Gerichtsrat one senses the frustration of the gifted man from the middle class who feels powerless: "Der obern Macht ist schwer zu widerstehen" (G2066) before an arbitrary, absolute power: "entsetzliche Gewalt" (G1748) which runs counter to "Rat und Urteil" (G2014), but which he must nevertheless acknowledge and submit to. He cannot but feel impotent before this unfair, secret imposition of "Willkür" (G2087).

When Eugenie reaches her decision to remain "In Verborgnen … als reinen Talisman" (G2852–3) of a better future, one can still detect the Sekretär, or at least what he embodies:

> Diesem Reiche droht
> Ein jäher Umsturz. Die zum großen Leben
> Gefugten Elemente wollen sich
> Nicht wechselseitig mehr mit Liebeskraft
> Zu stets erneuter Einigkeit umfangen.
> Sie fliehen sich, und einzeln tritt nun jedes
> Kalt in sich selbst zurück. Wo blieb der Ahnherrn
> Gewalt'ger Geist, der sie zu einem Zweck
> Vereinigte, die feindlich kämpfenden?   (G2825–33)

Whereas this speech owes a considerable debt to Goethe's organic studies, it also anticipates the conflict between Rudolf and Klesel: the protagonist who tries in vain to unite the internally warring factions against a common external enemy, and who views his rule as that of a loving, self-sacrificing patriarch ("Ich will allein das Weh für Alle tragen" [2411]) and his antagonist, the pen-pusher, who, together with Goethe's Sekretär, "tritt … [k]alt in sich selbst zurück" in his pursuit of power. Both the king and the emperor, despite their good intentions, make arbitrary, bad decisions and are ultimately brought down by a combination of their own weakness and the influence of the times, the dominant feature of which Rudolf sees as self-interest: "Nein, Eigendünkel war es, Eigensucht, / Die nichts erkennt, was nicht ihr eignes Werk" (336–7).

Because *Die natürliche Tochter* depicts on a universal scale socio-political developments prior to a cataclysmic revolution, its players tend to assume a more symbolic role as indicated by the functional, non-personalized names. *Ein Bruderzwist* also depicts monumental historic events leading up to the outbreak of the Thirty Years' War, and, if one reads between the lines, the Revolution of 1848. However, Grillparzer's characters come across as much more individualized or more complex than Goethe's, partly , one suspects, out of the latter's consuming interest in the overall process of which the characters, including the heroine, exist primarily as manifestations. Notwithstanding this major contrast, the Sekretär shares with Wurm or Klesel many common tactics, attitudes and ambitions. In the final work examined, the social background is quite different – the aristocracy disappears as a significant factor in the life of a small town[64] – but the same figure, indeed two manifestations of it, still has a central role in *Maria Magdalene.*

THE TWO SECRETARIES IN HEBBEL'S
MARIA MAGDALENE

Whereas Goethe drew extensively from the mémoires of Stéphanie de Bourbon-Conti to write *Die natürliche Tochter,* Hebbel was able to construct *Maria Magdalene* on the basis of his first-hand knowledge of the petty-bourgeois milieu,[65] just as Schiller derived much of the material for *Kabale und Liebe* from his acquaintance with the Stuttgart court. Hebbel went one step further: he depicted specific situations and experiences from his own early career, including a period in which he served as a secretary. His father's death – Hebbel was only fourteen at the time – plunged the family into dire economic straits, obliging the surviving son to seek employment. J.J. Mohr, a local official, offered to provide room and board, while, in return, Hebbel was expected to perform minor duties for his benefactor. As soon as Mohr became aware of Hebbel's ability, he exploited the young man, deputizing him to act on his behalf in minor cases, and employing him as his confidential clerk in frequently deplorable working conditions. On one occasion, as Hebbel himself later reported, he was expected to sleep with the coachman despite the fact that the latter was afflicted with an infectious disease. Hebbel's pride suffered substantially during this seven-year stage of his life, for it was the time that he discovered his true calling, began to write poems and gained confidence in his talent.[66] When, years later, Mohr had the temerity to claim credit for having once patronized the now celebrated dramatist residing in Vienna, Hebbel wrote a devastatingly cutting letter to his former employer, a copy of which appears in his diary. He felt so bitter and humiliated that even with the passage of twenty years, the indignation he suffered under his master still rankled him:

Ich bin *nicht* [Hebbel's emphasis] in Ihrem Hause aufgewachsen, ich kam in meinem vierzehnten Jahr, mit vortrefflichen Schulkenntnissen ausgerüstet, zu Ihnen, und leistete Ihnen vom ersten Tage an Dienst, die anfangs zwar gering waren, die Sie aber sehr bald in den Stand setzten, Ihren Schreiber zu entlassen und mich an seiner Statt zu verwenden. Dadurch ersparten Sie den nicht beträchtlichen Gehalt, den Sie ihm zahlen mußten und ich erhielt als Äquivalent Ihre abgelegten Kleider und die Beköstigung am Gesindetisch; für meine Bildung aber thaten Sie gar nichts, wenn Sie es sich nicht etwa als Verdienst anrechnen, daß Sie mir Ihre paar Bücher nicht geradezu aus der Hand rissen und auch später trugen Sie zu meinen Studien nicht das mindeste bei.[67]

One easily detects the resentment of the secretary forced by circumstances to submit to an intellectually inferior master, as well as the unmistakable signs of the *Streber*. This incident brought out the worst in Hebbel as he sought to blackmail Mohr into a retraction by threatening to make public how he seduced his servant girl and then tried to bribe his "Schreiber" into assuming paternity. The writer comes across as arrogant, trumpeting his independence, fame and association with the upper class (Fürst Schwarzenberg).

The second episode from his biography which left its mark on *Maria Magdalene* occurred during his stay at the home of a carpenter, Anton Schwarz, where Hebbel witnessed the dark cloud of shame that descended upon a typically lower middle-class family after the local constabulary entered the premises to arrest the son. Hebbel had contracted an intimate relationship with Schwarz's daughter, Beppi. When she confessed to him a former affair, he refused to forgive her and mercilessly upbraided her. "An jenem Sonntag-Abend, wo Du [Beppi] mir die Geständnisse machtest, war es wohl menschlicher Kraft unmöglich, jedes bittre Gefühl auf einmal zu unterdrücken (cf. "Darüber kann kein Mann weg!"[68]) und Deine aus dem tiefsten Herzen kommende Bitte: 'Ach Gott, verzeih's mir' zu gewähren."[69] In this case, the incident did not result in the tragic consequences of the drama which it no doubt inspired, but, once again, the socially ambitious Hebbel found himself cast in a role which he later assigned to a secretary.

Within the petty-bourgeois setting outlined in such detail in *Maria Magdalene*, the *Herr/Diener* dynamic still has a major function, but not in the format of a contrast between *Adel* and *Bürgertum*. Although the king guarantees his subjects "Gerechtigkeit" in return for "Treue und … Gehorsam" (H357), he only acts as a remote final court of appeal with no direct influence upon everyday community affairs. The social hierarchy depicted in this tragedy originates more with century- old traditions going back to the medieval guilds and Christian teachings. For instance, in the face of death, one pleads to God "wie ein Diener den Herrn anfleht, die schlecht gemachte Arbeit noch einmal verrichten zu dürfen, um am Lohntag nicht zu kurz zu kommen" (H332). As this comparison implies, economics and religion largely determine the speaker's point of view.[70] The older generation regards the master/servant relationship of dominance/submission as the norm confirmed by daily experience. Because the mother unquestioningly supports this arrangement, she strongly urges her daughter to accept Leonhard, for "er ist so gesetzt! Wenn er nur erst etwas wäre! Zu meiner Zeit hätt er nicht lange warten dürfen, da rissen die Herren sich um einen geschickten Schreiber, wie die Lahmen um die Krücke, denn sie waren selten" (H334). Even before the audience has the opportunity to see the first secretary of the play, we learn of the respect he enjoys for his writing ability. Once the masters were anxious to obtain a "Schreiber" and were dependent upon him to the extent that they were unable to function adequately, were lamed, without his assistance. The mother goes on to point out how the cunning secretary was in a position to profit from the illiteracy of several members within the same family: the son employed him to write a greeting to his father and the recipient secretly engaged his services to read it: "Das gab doppelte Bezahlung" (H334). "Da waren die Schreiber *obenauf* und machten das Bier teuer" (H334). In other words, the prophecy contained in *Ein Bruderzwist*: "Zu *oberst*, weil zuletzt, der Sekretär" (2726), has not only been fulfilled but has gone several steps further: "Jetzt ists anders, jetzt müssen wir Alten, die wir uns nicht aufs Lesen und Schreiben verstehen, uns von neunjährigen Buben ausspotten lassen! Die Welt wird immer klüger" (H334). The ascendancy of the clever, those who wield power through the pen, has taken place and is, moreover, commonplace in town society. Education has become an effective weapon capitalized on by the lower class to prosper, even at the expense of one's own kind, and has led to the pride and arrogance evident in Grillparzer's priest. The fact that Meister Anton harps upon his illiteracy: "wenn ich schreiben könnte" or "unwissend, wie ich bin" (H347) intimates the resentment and self-consciousness he feels at his lack of formal schooling and thus at his inferior position in relation to Leonhard, and particularly his son: "Ja, wir Alten sind dem Tod vielen Dank schuldig, daß er uns noch so lange unter euch Jungen herumlaufen läßt, und uns Gelegenheit gibt, uns zu bilden" (H341). A major part of his personal problem lies in his inability to deal with a changing, unstable world, one that is becoming "klüger." Forfeiting some of the authority and respect he once enjoyed, he feels left out or left behind, and thus sees in *Bildung* a threat to the old ways. *Schreiben*, synonymous with *Klugheit*, has developed into a highly esteemed talent in this petty-bourgeois society and, as we shall presently ascertain, two secretaries, a negative and a more positive example, exert substantial influence upon this narrow community.

Leonhard, of course, embodies the negative case along the line of Schiller's Wurm,[71] "von Haus aus eine gemeine Natur ... ein Lump,"[72] as his own creator conceded. Like his predecessor he derives sadistic pleasure from manipulating others, particularly the heroine of this "bürgerliche Trauerspiel." "So frei fühlst du dich von mir? Mir kanns recht sein! Dann *Mit Beziehung* hat dein Zahnweh von neulich nichts zu bedeuten gehabt!" (H336). He knows that he has complete power over Klara and revels in that awareness. He sees her as a possession he wants to secure: "Nicht recht, daß ich mein höchstes Gut, denn das bist du, auch durch das letzte Band an mich fest zu knüpfen suchte?" (H336). As with Goethe's Sekretär, he shows no hesitation to use sex to secure his material advantage, for Klara, his "höchstes Gut," only has appeal as long as marriage to her will advance his own prospects. Yet another feature of the type surfaces in his pejorative description of his rival, the Sekretär (cf. Wurm's designation of Ferdinand as an "adligen Windbeutel" [S761]). Having sought to better himself by attending the "Akademie," the Sekretär has surpassed a mere village "Schreiber," who therefore envies his intellectual and social superior and fears a threat to his property: "Mir kam das kleine, lächerlich-runde Gesicht des Gecken, ich bin erbittert auf ihn, ich verhehle es nicht, er hat mir lange genug bei dir im Wege gestanden" (H337). His seduction of Klara did not occur out of love or even passion but as a coldly calculated manipulative tactic to force her to make a decision, to demonstrate his authority over her, and to render her fully dependent upon him: "Noch diesen Abend stell ich sie auf die Probe! Will sie mein Weib werden, so weiß sie, daß sie nichts wagt. Sagt sie nein, so –" (H337).

In order to achieve their self-serving objectives, all three secretaries of the other plays discussed so far have carefully devised a plan to that end. Leonhard is no exception: "Um so leichter glückte mein Plan" (H340). In this instance he is referring to his strategy to obtain the post of "Kassierer" (H338), every detail of which was carefully worked out in advance, leaving nothing to chance. He fabricated a quarrel with his fiancée to justify a fourteen-day absence, pretended to court the ugly niece of the mayor – "Das dauerte so lange bis ich dies [the niece] in Händen hatte" (H339) – and arranged for a few friends to get the other candidate drunk, i.e., he eliminated the opposition through cunning. A significant difference between Klesel and Leonhard is the scale of their preconceived projects. The former functions on the world political stage, "die große Welt," and relies upon his master only to furnish the social front while the latter operates in the petty-bourgeois domain, "die kleine Welt," but still must show some deference to the town leaders, those with either wealth or influence such as the mayor (whose hand he obsequiously kissed, "obgleich sie nach Tabak roch" [H339]). He shows respect to Meister Anton only as long as he stands to gain a dowry, the main reason for his courtship of Klara, from his prospective father-in-law. As soon as he learns of its non-existence, his attitude changes accordingly: "Also doch weg! Nun, so brauch ich mir vor dem alten Werwolf auch nichts gefallen zu lassen, wenn er mein Schwiegervater ist" (H345). Theoretically, at least, Leonhard has the possibility of becoming a leading community figure provided he plays his cards wisely.

Other shared attributes include his pride in his cleverness: "Sei du [Klara] ohne Falsche wie die Taube, ich will *klug*, wie die Schlange sein" (H339); diabolical allusions: like Wurm or Licht he *"lacht"* (H339) with sadistic glee at the misfortune of others for which he was responsible; inordinate emphasis on material wealth: money represents for him "einen so wichtigen Punkt" (H340) and it is surely a conscious design of the dramatist that this secretary intends to earn his living as a treasurer; a sarcastic exploitation of religion: he is quite adept at quoting scripture to suit his own purpose, even to the extent of momentarily deluding Meister Anton by using the Bible to justify his greed[73] (H345); and a tremendous faith in and reliance upon the signed document as a source of security and power: "hier ist sie [die Bestellung] selbst, unterschrieben und besiegelt!" (H339)

The authority of the written word remains an underlying theme throughout the first act. The stage directions encourage one to asso-

ciate reading with Leonhard *"der bisher im Wochenblatt gelesen hat"*
(H348). *"Zu dem lesenden Leonhard,"* Meister Anton enquires, "Was
Neues?" (H349), i.e., his inability to read renders him dependent
upon his daughter's fiancé, a situation which clearly annoys him.
When Adam enters to search the house, he receives his authorization
from a papier: "ADAM *zeigt ein Papier.* Kann er geschriebene Schrift
lesen? / MEISTER ANTON. Soll ich können, was nicht einmal mein
Schul*meister* [i.e., *Meister* Gebhardt] konnte?" (H351) A "Gerichts-
diener," a servant of the court holding an office customarily viewed
as disreputable, can lord it over a master carpenter because of the
authority granted by the pen. Leonhard, of course, sees the disgrace
after Karl's arrest as a convenient opportunity to break his word:
"Schrecklich! Aber gut für mich!" (H351) Since marriage to Klara
would now bring no financial advantage, and since he lacks the
courage to face her directly, he resorts to the written word to do his
"dirty work":

EINE MAGD   *tritt ein mit einem Brief, zu Klara.* Von Herrn
                                                Kassierer Leonhard!
MEISTER ANTON. Du brauchst ihn nicht zu lesen! Er sagt
                                          sich von dir los!
          Schlägt in die Hände.   Bravo Lump!
KLARA   *hat gelesen.*   Ja! Ja! O mein Gott!   (H352)

Friedrich, whom the text always designates by his calling, "Sekretär," and whose arrival acted as a catalyst setting the tragic train of
events in motion: "O, wenn der nicht zurückgekommen wäre –"
(H361), also has a strong link with book learning. In his presence
Klara feels inadequate: "Ich dächte, man vergäße solche Dinge, wenn
man hundert und tausend Bücher durchstudieren müßte" (H361).
Presenting schooling as a form of mental seduction and an escape
from life, he portrays the pen-pusher as a physical weakling, "mager
und blaß" (H362) and, in contrast, praises the world and the joy of
existence: "Wodurch willst du denn für das Leben danken, als
dadurch, daß du lebst? Jauchze, Vogel, sonst verdienst du die Kehle
nicht" (H363). While acting as an antithesis to Klara's attitude which
sees hope only in death (II/2), this positive, life-affirming outlook
also runs counter to the usual image of the dark, spider-like intriguer
spinning his web of deception in the background. However, there are
indications that this secretary also has serious limitations or weaknesses. Like his pen-pushing predecessors, he believes that he can
read accurately the motivation of those around him: "daß du [Klara]
seit acht Tagen schwerer atmest, wie sonst, begreif ich wohl, ich

kenne deinen Alten" (H363), but he overestimates his abilities and does not fully appreciate either the duress under which Klara is suffering or the emotional tyranny of which Meister Anton's damaged pride is capable. In wishing to be the bearer of good news (Karl's release), he expects a reward, a show of gratitude from Klara, and from this point of view his dialogue with her is mildly manipulative from the outset.

On more than one occasion Friedrich shows himself to be almost as self-centered as Leonhard. "O Mädchen, warum hast du mir das getan! Und doch – habe ich ein Recht, mich zu beklagen? Sie ist, wie alles Liebe und Gute, alles Liebe und Gute hätte mich an sie erinnern sollen, dennoch war sie jahrelang für mich, wie nicht mehr in der Welt" (H363). All the men of the drama think in the first instance only of themselves, of their reputation or advantage, in their relationship to the heroine. Klara's engagement was a personal affront to the Sekretär. Then, after his spontaneous outburst, indicative of his true feelings, he pauses (signaled by the dash), regains conscious control and admits his own responsibility – his failure to appreciate her worth and his neglect during his university days. This will become his pattern: he initially reacts on the basis of ingrained social values upholding male domination, but then, because of basic decency and honesty, he places the blame where it rightly belongs and acknowledges his own guilt. Soon, however, he reverts to his social model: "Dafür hat sie – Wärs nur wenigstens ein Kerl, vor dem man die Augen niederschlagen müßte! Aber dieser Leonhard –" (H363–4), i.e., I who loved and love you, I, who am worthy of you and can value your true merit, how could you insult me by agreeing to marry such a man?! Friedrich's own ego takes precedence over any genuine concern for Klara's well-being and expresses itself in an arrogance at least in part attributable to his recently acquired status.

In her review of the pressures that led to her agreeing to Leonhard's suit, Klara inadvertently exposes the class prejudices within the petty-bourgeoisie itself. "Spott und Hohn von allen Seiten, als du auf die Akademie gezogen warst und nichts von dir hören ließest" (H365). Schooling offers the means to improve one's prospects for advancement: "Es ist wenig, aber es kann mehr werden" (H364), but at the same time, as noted earlier, the newly emerging ambitious academics, see themselves and are seen to be superior to the rest of their own class, a development causing a growing schism between the educated and the non-educated members of the same social group. "Und dann die Mutter! Halte dich zu deinesgleichen. Hochmut tut nimmer gut! Der Leonhard ist doch recht brav, alle wundern sich, daß du ihn über die Achsel ansiehst" (H365). Education, according to the mother, has placed the Sekretär beyond Klara's reach; therefore, Leonhard would be a more modest but nonetheless excellent catch within the context of the community since he does have a promising career. What with family pressure, village ridicule and Friedrich's silence, Klara had little choice in the matter. Again in anticipation of the conclusion, her interlocutor confesses his guilt: "Ich bin schuld" (H365; cf. H391) but compounds it even further with his infamous response when Klara discloses her pregnancy: "Darüber kann kein Mann weg!" (H366). Here he demonstrates his lack of compassion and his social limitations. Ultimately he is more concerned with his public image, his reputation as a man: "Vor dem Kerl, dem man ins Gesicht spucken mögte, die Augen niederschlagen müssen?" (H366) His solution, to eliminate "den Hund, ders weiß" (H366) in order to avoid the potential for social embarrassment Leonhard could cause him, ignores the desperate plight of the real victim.

Caught between two secretaries, Klara, in her soliloquy, perceives her fate as hinging upon a letter: "Ich bettle ja nicht um ein Glück, ich bettle um mein Elend, um mein tiefstes Elend – mein Elend wirst du mir geben! Fort – wo ist der Brief?" (H367). If Leonhard takes the letter back, she will experience the personal hell of being married to a man she rightly despises while loving another, and if he refuses, she must destroy herself in order to prevent her father from making good his suicide threat.

The third act opens in a *"Zimmer bei Leonhard"* with the latter *"an einem Tisch mit Akten, schreibend"* (H367). The tragedy thus associates him visually with the trappings and the gestures of the pen-pusher as seen in *Kabale und Liebe* or *Ein Bruderzwist*. "Das wäre nun der sechste Bogen nach Tisch! Wie fühlt sich der Mensch, wenn er seine Pflicht tut!" (H367). Industriously working at home, a sign of his keenness to get ahead, Leonhard boasts of his clerical accomplishments and displays an exaggerated sense of self-importance and a fair measure of hypocrisy. While he maintains, like Klesel, that he is performing his duty, a claim provoking only an ironic response in the spectator who knows him to be a scoundrel, one can be reasonably confident that whatever he does will promote his own career as well. "Jetzt könnte mir in die Tür treten, wer wollte, und wenns der König wäre – ich würde aufstehen, aber ich würde nicht in Verlegenheit geraten!" (H367). In his overt pride in himself and his position, Leonhard becomes the fulfilment of another of Klesel's prophecies: "Ich werde nicht vor Menschen feig erzittern, / Und wärens Könige – im Land der Zukunft" (2570–1), but its worst possible manifestation.

The lengths to which he is prepared to go to satisfy his ambition become particularly evident in his calculated exploitation of the mayor's niece: "Vor allen Dingen die Sache mit dem kleinen Buckel nur recht fest gemacht, damit die mir nicht entgeht, wenn das Gewitter ausbricht! Dann habe ich den Bürgermeister auf meiner Seite, und brauche vor nichts bange zu sein!" (H367) A real Machiavellian schemer, he shows no reluctance to seduce a woman in order to gain the support of the local ruler, the mayor. With His Worship and the authority he wields on side, Leonhard needs fear no one. One senses the frustrated ambition of the man of lowly circumstances who will stop at nothing to make a name for himself in the town hierarchy. He was smart enough to become "Schreiber" to the mayor, i.e., he elected to serve the most influential person in the community in order to have direct access to the local power base. His eagerness to facilitate his rapid rise in influence closely parallels Klesel's relationship to the archdukes.

In the final dialogue between Leonhard and Klara, a document again provides an important focal point. The former almost immediately enquires, "Hast du meinen Brief nicht erhalten?" (H367). His instinctive reaction to her unexpected entry is to hide behind his letter, the means by which he seeks to exercise his authority.

KLARA.   Ich komme, um dir deinen Brief zurückzugeben! Hier ist er. Lies ihn noch einmal!

LEONHARD *liest mit großem Ernst.*   Es ist ein ganz vernünftiger Brief! Wie kann ein Mann, dem die öffentlichen Gelder anvertraut sind, in eine Familie heiraten, zu der *Er verschluckt ein Wort* zu der dein Bruder gehört? (H368)

Symptomatic of the pen-pusher is his insistence upon the intelligence associated with the written word and the dignity and trust of his confidential office. As a sign of the times he has chosen to be close to the real source of power in the new commercial-industrial age: money. Once more the audience is in a position to reject this argument as hypocritical – Leonhard has obtained his post through immoral and specious means; he invokes civic responsibility only to camouflage self-serving ambition. Since it suits his purpose, he continues to defend his stance on the basis of irrefutable evidence: "Eben weil ich ein Mann von Wort bin, muß ich dir antworten, wie ich geantwortet habe. Dir schrieb ich vor acht Tagen ab, du kannst es nicht leugnen, der Brief liegt da. *Er reicht ihr den Brief, sie nimmt ihn mechanisch*" (H370). Like Klesel, he is able to conceal his highly suspect motives behind the "Schrift," to exploit it to his benefit and to rationalize his stance on ethical grounds. Whereas Klesel argues that it is in the best interest of the nation to sign a treaty despite the illegality of making peace without the emperor's consent, Leonhard maintains that an office of trust does not permit him to marry the sister of a thief. In both cases the documents are a mere pretence to increase one's power: the peace treaty constitutes one of several carefully planned steps to secure the absolute authority of the master and, by extension, of the servant, while the letter provides the pretext to rid Leonhard of an obligation in order to pursue a more financially and politically desirable mate. Rudolf offers to give his word as a guarantee, but the Standesherren demand a signed commitment. Appealing to his legal right before the law, Leonhard does not recognize any obligation to honor a verbal contract; he is only as good as his written word: "In diesen acht Tagen knüpfte ich ein neues Verhältnis an; ich hatte das *Recht* dazu, denn du hast nicht zur rechten Zeit gegen meinen Brief protestiert, ich war frei in meinem Gefühl, wie vor dem *Gesetz*" (H371). He thus embodies the most despicable features of "die krummen Wege ... / Auf denen Selbstsucht geht und die Gemeinheit" (1473–4): insistence upon one's individual rights, vindication through the written word and strict adherence to the letter of the law[74] in order to gratify the self at the expense of the community.

The all-important letter, a visual leitmotif and a link between the scenes, reappears in Klara's hand upon her return home. Karl "*entreißt ihr Leonhards Brief. Her damit!*" (H375); "KARL *der den Brief gelesen hat*. Donner und – Kerl, den Arm, der das schrieb, schlag ich dir lahm!" (H376). Clearly a focal point in this scene as well, the letter confirms Leonhard's base nature since even the normally egoistic Karl reacts violently to its content as it relates to his sister.

While the spectator preserves a grudging respect for Klesel, especially in defeat, Leonhard has no saving grace whatsoever. Typical of his tendency to view all of life in economic terms, and indicative of the immoral depths to which he can plunge, he blames Meister Anton for Klara's predicament: "Wer die Aussteuer seiner Tochter wegschenkt, der muß sich nicht wundern, daß sie sitzenbleibt ... Was auch daraus entsteht, er hats zu verantworten, das ist klar!" (H371). The text compares him to a worm (cf. *Kabale und Liebe*), a mad dog (H373), and finally a snake: "Ich [Klara] danke dir, wie ich einer Schlange danken würde, die mich umknotet hätte und mich von selbst wieder ließe und fort spränge, weil eine andere Beute sie lockte" (H371). This association with Mephistopheles' "Muhme, die berühmte Schlange"[75] is one of numerous diabolical allusions contained in this dialogue. In the same speech, Klara remarks, "mir ist, als hätt ich durch deine Brust bis in den Abgrund der Hölle hinuntergesehen" (H371), but Leonhard himself establishes the most direct link to his satanic prototype: the dramatist has him paraphrase the devil's cruelest comment from Goethe's *Faust*: "Du sprichst, als ob du die erste und letzte wärst!" (H369).[76] This *Federfuchser* in particular, both in terms of his general attitude and his use of force over others, has much in common with Mephistopheles' cynicism, cruelty, and ego-centricity: [D]er Teufel ist ein Egoist / Und tut nicht leicht um Gottes willen, / Was einem andern nützlich ist."[77]

Maria Magdalene does not conclude on a note totally unsympathetic to the pen-pusher, for I suspect that Hebbel portrayed aspects of his own ambitious but difficult rise from poverty into prominence through Friedrich, the Sekretär.[78] The tragedy thus has recourse to the positive representative of the type to pronounce, as *raisonneur*, the final judgments: "Er [Meister Anton] hat sie [Klara] auf den Weg des Todes hinausgewiesen, ich, ich bin schuld, daß sie nicht wieder umgekehrt ist" (H391). He condemns Meister Anton for his moral rigidity, his obsession with his social image, and he condemns himself for having made himself dependent upon the same public opinion. Although Friedrich must pay for his moral prejudice with his life, the very recognition of his guilt shows promise and hope and offers a lesson to be learned by the audience. Despite Meister Anton's self-centered repartees, the spectator's sympathy tends to lie with the Sekretär and his condemnation of a father's insensitivity towards his daughter.

CHAPTER EIGHT

Conclusion

On the basis of this examination of the *Federfuchser* as he appears in four dramas covering the period from 1783 till 1850 (Schreiber Licht from Kleist's *Der zerbrochne Krug* should also be borne in mind), there emerges a comprehensive portrait of the outstanding features common to what has clearly become a literary type. At the end of the eighteenth and the beginning of the nineteenth century the pen-pusher owed his growing prominence to a period of political and social instability, a gradual dissolution of an aristocratic, hierarchical system. Since the middle-class Enlightenment placed greater emphasis upon education, a new intellectual elite began to gain recognition, and knowledge became increasingly synonymous with power. The old order was declining, but even those writers who stood to gain most from a reformed social order greeted the approach of the new with mixed feelings.

A bright, capable member of the bourgeoisie, jealous and resentful of those in authority, seeks employment as secretary to a political head of state or a local official in order to exert influence upon his less gifted master. Having acquired considerable insight into the power structure, be it of an empire, a country, a principality, or a town, the secretary rules indirectly through his lord by dint of superior intelligence. Above all he insists upon and is proud of his cleverness (*Klugheit*) made manifest either through the pen or through intrigues where the written word figures prominently. Closely aligned to the devil by his association with the snake, the rogue, and the gambler, or by his propensity to indulge in sadistic laughter, the secretary has adopted a cold, rational, pragmatic approach to life in his pursuit of power and material advantage (*Schatz/Lohn*) resulting in the deification of and dependence upon the letter of the law and his commitment to act according to a carefully devised plan. Because he has an intimate knowledge of his master and those near him, i.e., he knows the players well, he is able to predict or anticipate their reactions and views and turn them to account, while, at the same time, he also possesses the mental flexibility and agility to profit from unexpected turns of events.

Since the pen-pushing secretary follows an end-justifies-the-means approach to life, he has no qualms of conscience in exploiting people to achieve his goals. From his psychological arsenal, he has recourse to flattery, reverse psychology, emotional blackmail, and builds up a sense of obligation or appeals to the worst possible motives in his victim. He must at all times perform the difficult balancing act of allowing his master the illusion of being in control while, at the same time, maneuvering his superior into a position or a frame of mind where, in reality, the master only does what the servant desires. In this regard the *Federfuchser* is an expert at presenting his solution as the only way out of a dilemma or as the lesser evil. The pen or the bourgeois intellect that moves it proves to be mightier than the sword or the aristocratic prowess that once wielded it: "Nicht mehr mit blut'gen Waffen wird man kämpfen, / Der Trug, die Hinterlist ersetzt das Schwert" (*Libussa*, 2382–3). If the pen-pusher has one major flaw, it is his tendency to make assumptions and to judge others by his own scale of values, and thus to underestimate the moral strength or bias of his opponent. The dramas in question all leave the audience with the underlying message that, if not the specific individual, then the type will ultimately prevail, even though he may go down to temporary defeat.

In the second half of the nineteenth century, Theodor Fontane, who had a first-hand acquaintance with the Prussian *Junkertum*, has Botho von Rienäcker's conservative uncle, Baron Kurt Anton von Osten, ein "Märkischer von Adel,"[1] take to task Fürst Bismarck for his Machiavellian political tactics in a sarcastic allusion to the Ems telegram. "[Bismarck] ist ein Federfuchser. Aber nicht die Federfuchser haben Preußen groß gemacht. War der bei Fehrbellin ein Federfuchser? War der bei Leuthen ein Federfuchser? War Blücher ein Federfuchser oder Yorck?"[2] In other words, Bismarck is sufficiently prescient to recognize the new emerging social order – in *Effie Briest* we learn that he has recently purchased a paper factory. The "Feder" belongs more appropriately to the secretary and the clever, ambitious and wealthy, but frustrated and disenfranchised, middle class he comes to champion. Ferdinand's phrase "die kluge Schrift" (2864) captures both the essence of the secretary's function in *Ein Bruderzwist* and that of his literary predecessors. While Klesel the person may have fallen from power, the development he represents has nevertheless gained the upper hand. As one of the play's most far-reaching ironies, the archduke, the man responsible for the cardinal's elimination, proclaims the ineluctable decline of his own class and its values: "Die Feder schlägt oft sicherer als die Waffe" (2865), an unwitting but nonetheless fitting testimony to the career of a *Federfuchser*.

Notes

1 Quoted in Kleinstück, "Don Cäsar," 207.

2 Thompson, "An Off-Stage Decision," 137.

3 Nadler, *Franz Grillparzer*, 425.

4 Naumann, *Das dichterische Werk*, 42. The French critic Claude David also lavishes high praise on *Ein Bruderzwist*: "Die österreichische Literatur besitzt kein schöneres Drama als dieses von seinem Autor verworfene Stück" (*Ordnung des Kunstwerks*, 77).

5 Fricke, *Studien*, 281.

6 Ibid., 284. According to Grillparzer's own scale of values, he would not have held *Ein Bruderzwist* in very high esteem as a play's success or failure depended in his view entirely upon its performability. In 1872 Heinrich Laube reported, "Er [Grillparzer] hat nie ein Drama geschrieben, ohne es in der Theatererscheinung vor sich zu sehen, und er wies mit Geringschätzung alle sogenannten Buchdramen ab" (*Werke*, 3:821).

7 Hering, "Zum Thema," 41.

8 Griesmayer, *Das Bild*, 300. Even the detractor Volkelt admired the portrayal of the emperor, calling him "vielleicht der am tiefsten gedachte und durchgefühlte Charakter Grillparzers." Quoted in Kleinstück, "Don Cäsar," 207.

9 Sternberger, "Politische Figuren," 1150.

10 Wells, *The Plays*, 125.

11 Naumann, *Das dichterische Werk*, 54.

12 Kleinstück, "Don Cäsar," 226.

13 Mason, "A New Look," 102–15.

14 David, *Ordnung des Kunstwerks*, 94.

15 Langvik-Johannessen has argued that all the characters are reflections of the main protagonist ("Versuch einer Offenlegung," 34).

16 Sengle, *Das historische Drama*, 141. Cf. "Gegenspieler dieser anonymen schicksalhaften Macht, die noch das Widerstreitendste zusammenfaßt und die Grillparzer 'Zeit' nennt, ist allein der Kaiser" (von Wiese, "Geschichte und Gottesordnung," 443).

17 Wells proposes yet another candidate, Mathes Thurm: "It is not Rudolf but Thurm, the clever calculating egoist, the Protestant counterpart to Klesel, who thinks that he can control his actions so that they lead only to such consequences as are desirable for him" ("The Problem," 163).

18 Kleinstück, "Don Cäsar," 211.

19 Baumann, "Ein Bruderzwist," 430. Wassermann also refers to Klesel as Rudolf's "zeitweise erfolgreicher Gegenspieler" ("Kaiser Rudolf," 276).

20 Politzer has provided the most extensive analysis of Don Cäsar's importance in "Grillparzers Bruderzwist," 173–94.

21 Naumann, *Das dichterische Werk*, 55–6.

22 Fülleborn, "Geschichtsdrama," 196.

23 Wells, *The Plays*, 112.

24 David, *Ordnung des Kunstwerks*, 90.

25 Baumann, "*Ein Bruderzwist*," 432.

26 Langvik-Johannessen, "Versuch einer Offenlegung," 37.

27 Fülleborn, "Geschischtsdrama," 196.

28 Müller, "Grillparzer," 135.

29 Politzer, "Götterdämmerung," 360.

30 Sternberger, "Politische Figuren," 1146.

31 Yates, *Grillparzer*, 246.

32 Thompson, "Grillparzer's Political Villains," 101. Thompson further notes, "Grillparzer had read his Machiavelli, both *The Prince* and the *Discourses* by 1820" (110).

33 I have dealt with this model as it relates to Kleist's dramas in *Pursuit of Power*. Zawisch closely parallels Hohenzollern in *Prinz Friedrich von Homburg* while Klesel has his most obvious Kleistian predecessor in Schreiber Licht from *Der zerbrochne Krug*.

34 Grillparzer, *Werke*, 3:813–14.

35 Ibid., 3:812.

36 van Stockum, "Grillparzers *Ein Bruderzwist*," 29.

37 David, *Ordnung des Kunstwerks*, 90.

38 Grillparzer, *Sämtliche Werke*, "Selbstbiographie," 4:109.

39 For a list of sources, see Grillparzer, *Werke*, 3:824–7. In his "Selbstbiographie," the dramatist saw the following relationship between history and creative invention: "Der Dichter wählt historische Stoffe, weil er darin den Keim zu seinen eigenen Entwicklungen findet, vor allem aber um seinen Ereignissen und Personen eine Konsistenz, einen Schwerpunkt der Realität zu geben, damit auch der Anteil aus dem

Reich des Traumes in das der Wirklichkeit übergehe" (*Sämtliche Werke*, 4:118).

40 Grillparzer, *Werke*, 3:754–823.

41 Ibid., 760.

42 Ibid., 815.

43 Grillparzer, *Werke*, 3:2568–9. All subsequent references to *Ein Bruderzwist* and Grillparzer's other plays will be drawn from this edition and verse numbers will be included directly in the text. Italics will be used to indicate stage directions and my own emphases unless otherwise indicated. In the case of dramas other than *Ein Bruderzwist*, the volume numbers will also appear.

44 Grillparzer, *Werke*, 3:812–13.

45 Ibid., 3:814. Cf. also: Jedermann wünschte, daß ihn [Klesel] der Teufel hohlen und in den Abgrund der Hölle führen sollte" (3:801).

46 Ibid., 3:805.

47 Ibid., 3:772.

48 Ibid., 3:773.

49 Cf. "Eine beabsichtigte Zusammenkunft beider Brüder vor Mathias Abreise von Prag, verhindert Klesel." Ibid., 3:794.

50 Ibid., 3:779.

51 Ibid., 3:829–33.

52 Ibid., 3:833.

53 Thompson outlines the obvious points of comparison between Shakespeare's Wolsey and Klesel ("Grillparzer's Political Villains," 108).

54 Wassermann, "Kaiser Rudolf," 276.

55 Grillparzer, *Sämtlichte Werke*, 4:108. A paragraph from Grillparzer's "Erinnerungen aus dem Revolutionsjahre 1848" in which he describes Metternich as "von Hause aus ein liebenswürdiger, geistreicher, aber, in seiner ersten Epoche leichtsinniger, und sein ganzes Leben lang durch seine Gelüste (im bessern Sinn des Wortes) bestimmter Mann" provides a summary of his ambivalent attitude towards the Prince (*Sämtliche Werke*, 4:2060).

56 Thompson, "Grillparzer's Political Villains," 108.

57 Ibid., 109.

58 Duckworth, *Roman Comedy*, 250.

59 Gomme, *Greek History*, 286–7. Duckworth also supports the view that "the Plautine slave, with his gaity, cleverness, and unscrupulousness, is the creation of Roman comedy" (250).

60 Duckworth, *Roman Comedy*, 251.

61 Scott-Prelorentzos, *The Servant*, 1.

62 Ibid., xii.

63 Kommerell, "Betrachtungen über die Commedia dell'arte," 164. Features of the cunning slave can be found in the "Zanni" of the *commedia*

dell'arte. "Und nun setzt sich in der unersättlichen Umkehr des Diener-Herrnverhältnisses die Dümmlings- und Halunkengöttlichkeit der Zanni, die böse sind, aber doch nur das Aufgeblasene straucheln machen, die dumm sind, aber doch der Wahrheit ins Gesicht sehen, die Verwirrung stiften, wo die Ordnung keinen Pfennig wert ist" (169–70).

64 Scott-Prelorentzos, *The Servant,* xii.

65 Cf. Scott-Prelorentzos, *The Servant,* xiv-xv.

66 Schiller, *Die Räuber, Sämtliche Werke,* 1:502.

67 Bancbanus belongs to the country gentry, but Grillparzer still portrays him in word and gesture as a pedantic, although thoroughly ethical, "Federfuchser." He appears at the outset of the second act *"Schriften in der Hand"* (2:p.530) and later in the same episode, surrounded by "Schriften," he asks, "Die Feder ist wohl stumpf? / *Halt sie vors Auge.* Nu, nu, sie geht! / Nur Ordnung, sag ich euch!" (2:534–5).

68 Baumann, *"Ein Bruderzwist,"* 424.

69 Shklar, *Freedom and Independence,* 60–1.

70 Horowitz and Horowitz, *"Everywhere They Are in Chains,"* 18.

71 Ibid., 21.

72 This message can be drawn from either the *Discours sur les origines* or the *Contrat Social.*

73 Rousseau, *Du Contrat Social,* 3:351.

74 Rousseau, "Lettres écrites de la Montagne," Huitième Lettre, 3:841–2.

75 Shklar, *Freedom and Independence,* 66.

76 Norman, *Hegel's Phenonenology,* 49–50. To use Hegel's own words, "Es [das Bewußtseyn] ist darin [i.e., the fear of death] innerlich aufgelöst worden, hat durchaus in sich selbst erzittert, und alles Fixe hat in ihm gebebt. Diese reine allgemeine Bewegung, das absolute Flüssigwerden alles Bestehens, ist aber das einfache Wesen des Selbtbewußtseyns, die absolute Negativität, das reine Fürsichseyn, das hiermit an diesem Bewußtseyn ist" (*Phänomenologie,* 156).

77 Hegel, *Phänomenologie,* 156.

78 Shklar, *Freedom and Independence,* 66.

79 Hegel, *Phänomenologie,* 156.

80 Norman, *Hegel's Phenomenology,* 50.

81 Hegel, *Phänomenologie,* 155.

82 For Hegel, "both principles [slave/master] are equally vital in the progress of the spirit towards its destiny: if Marx developed one side of this dichotomy, Nietzsche seized upon the other" (Kelly, "Notes in Hegel's 'Lordship and Bondage,'" 799).

83 "Indem ich von diesen Eindrücken voll [his readings on Napoleon] meine sonstigen historischen Erinnerungen durchmusterte, fiel mir eine obgleich entfernte Ähnlichkeit mit dem Böhmenkönige Ottokar II

in die Augen. Beide wenn auch in ungeheuerm Abstande, tatkräftige Männer, Eroberer, ohne eigentliche Bösartigkeit durch die Umstände zur Härte, wohl gar Tyrannei fortgetrieben, nach vieljährigem Glück dasselbe traurige Ende" (*Sämtliche Werke*, 4:117).

84 I do not propose to examine Licht in the context of this monograph as I have already dealt with him as a Machiavellian schemer in a chapter entitled "Ein dunkles Licht" in *Pursuit of Power*, 9–22, but he clearly belongs to this tradition.

85 Cf. "Das Selbstbild des Schwächlings, der leben, alles erringen möchte und es doch im Grunde nicht vermag, ist von Grillparzer objektiviert in *Der Traum ein Leben*. Rustan, der maßlose Träumer und Schwächling im Handeln, wird vorangetrieben von einem dunklen Prinzip, dem Sklaven Zanga, der seinen Wünschen Gestalt verleiht. Dieses Paar wird hier [in *Ein Bruderzwist*] wiederholt. Mathias, begleitet von seinem Ratgeber Klesel, verkörpert den Lebenswunsch nach Selbtbehauptung und Macht, der nur der Eitelkeit des Ich und keinem allgemeinen Ziel dient" (Naumann, *Das dichterische Werk*, 44). Although the parallel is valid, the usual critical bias against Klesel as a character worthy of independent consideration underlies this comparison. The dream Zanga is after all a dark manifestation of Rustan's own unconscious mind, while the same may not be said of Klesel in his relationship to Mathias.

86 Goethe, *Faust I*, 1646–8.

87 Ibid., 1716.

88 Ibid., 1651–5.

89 Nietzsche, "Zur Genealogie der Moral," 2:190.

CHAPTER TWO

1 Langvik-Johannessen, "Versuch einer Offenlegung," 34.

2 Cf. "Sowie sich der Vorhang gehoben hat, wird mit aller Deutlichkeit, deren das Theater fähig ist, der Zusammenhang zwischen Rudolf und Don Cäsar hergestellt – und sogleich durchbrochen" (Politzer, "Götterdämmerung," 361). Langvik-Johannessen also deals with this dialogue ("Versuch einer Offenlegung," 54).

3 "At several points in the play the epithet 'wildverworren,' so often applied to the times, is applied to Cäsar himself, bringing out the fact that his untutored passion is symbolical of the turbulent age in which he lives" (Wells, "The Problem," p.169).

4 Cf. "And it is just the prevalence of preoccupation with self to which he [Rudolf] attributes the upheavals of the age ... His speeches in the third act of the play amount to a tirade against selfish passion." (Wells, "The Problem," 164). In the same vein, Naumann writes, "Der Wahl-

spruch des Ordens lautet: 'Nicht ich, nur Gott' (1221). In diesen Worten ist der Sinn der konservativen Haltung des Dichters zusammengefaßt. Das Ich des Einzelnen, Eigendünkel, Eigensucht ist die Quelle aller Verkehrtheit der Zeit" (*Das dichterische Werk*, 56).

5 The description of this order of knights (1205–15) evokes the high ideals of Camelot and the Knights of the Roundtable, also chosen "aus den Besten aller Länder," and, not surprisingly, self-serving passions also destroyed this ideal community.

6 Several critics, notably Langvik-Johannessen, Politzer, and Mason, have seen Don Cäsar as reflecting the irrational, antisocial aspect in the emperor himself. Mason, for example, puts forward the following thesis: "My contention is that Don Cäsar represents the Emperor himself so truly as to frighten Rudolf at what this mirror reveals to him" ("A New Look," 113).

7 Cf. "[Klesel] ist der Diener, der die Schwäche seines Herrn nutzt, selber die Macht zu üben, der Minister, der den König am Zügel führt, vor allem der Emporkömmling, der auf solchem subalternen Umweg seine eigene Machtgier stillt" (Sternberger, "Politische Figuren," 1147).

8 Of course, other critics have used this image to characterize the relationship between Mathias and Klesel. "Mathias ist nur eine Marionette in seinen [Klesel's] Händen" (Fülleborn, "Geschichtsdrama," 196).

9 Grillparzer, *Werke*, 3:794.

10 David, *Ordnung des Kunstwerks*, 90.

11 Baumann, "*Ein Bruderzwist*," 430. Baumann substantiates this designation, with which I fully concur, only in the most general terms: "sorgfältig berechnet er seine Schritte und hartnäckig verfolgt er das Ziel; der Waffenstillstand mit den Türken im zweiten Aufzug liefert ihm nur den erwünschten Vorwand, die Herrschaft dem ihm hörigen Mathias zuzuspielen" (430–1).

12 Thompson, "Grillparzer's Political Villains," 108.

13 Naumann, *Das dichterische Werk*, 44.

14 Cf. "Es ist völlig durchsichtig, wie der ehrgeizige Klesel Mathias nur als Werkzeug gebraucht, sich selbt durchzusetzen, die Gebärde erweist unwiderleglich, wie er ihm seine Rolle souffliert, den halb Widerstrebenden mitreißt" (Baumann, "*Ein Bruderzwist*," 423).

15 Schäble, *Franz Grillparzer*, 125. Thompson adds another interesting slant to Rudolf's dilemma, seeing it as a choice between surrender to pressure from his relatives and his better judgment, i.e., "Klugheit" (412) ("An Off-Stage Decision," 141). But ironically the drama consistently associates intelligence, here synonymous with political astuteness, with his real antagonist, Klesel.

16 Kleinstück, "Don Cäsar," 223–4.

17 Hence circumstantial evidence would seem to point to Ferdinand's being
a target of Klesel's machinations as well. Thus van Stockum's analysis
contains only half of the truth: "Rudolfs Vetter Ferdinand von Steiermark
jedoch weiß bei [Rudolf] ein Unterkommando für Mathias bei der
Armee in Ungarn zu erwirken" ("Grillparzers *Ein Bruderzwist*," 26).
18 Thompson, "An Off-Stage Decision," 137–8.
19 This successful appeal to a base emotion gives further credence to the
view that the earlier invocation of ideal values, "Habsburgs Heil, das
Heil der Kirche, / ... unser Aller Heil" (132–3), really amounts to an
appeal to Mathias's vanity.
20 In interpreting this line, Langvik-Johannessen comments, "Daß Mathias
hier als Symbol dient, ist auffallend, aber richtig; auffallend, weil wir *nie
mehr von ihm als dem ruhesuchenden Fürsten* hören; richtig, weil Mathias
von Klesel zur geistigen Hybris verleitet wird" ("Versuch einer Offenlegung," 51–2). However, the last scene of the tragedy clearly refutes
the "striking" uniqueness of this frame of mind: "Ich [Mathias] aber
brauchte Stille / Tönts doch in meinem Innern laut genug; / ... / O
Bruder, lebtest du und wär' ich tot!" (2898–9; 2904). As for intellectual
hubris, Mathias's description of his Dutch adventure and his aspiration
"Sich einen Thron erbaun" strongly suggest that the arrogance and
pride were already present before Klesel arrived on the scene. The latter
had only to exploit or encourage an inherent tendency in his master.

CHAPTER THREE

1 Thompson, "Grillparzer's Political Villains," 106.
2 Cf. "Then in a moment of inspiration he realizes that if he lets Mathias
put *his* [Thompson's emphasis] case for continuing the war (presumably badly) the others will recognize the futility of such a course"
(Ibid., 106). Yates makes essentially the same point: "The Emperor
regards him [Klesel] as cunning (1403); and indeed he is a born politician, and an opportunist, as we see from the way he turns his disagree-
ment with Mathias to advantage" (*Grillparzer*, 240).
3 David, *Ordnung des Kunstwerks*, 78. And yet, at the end of the meeting,
the archdukes are not fully aware of the extent to which they have
been duped.
4 Cf. Wells, *The Plays*, 114; Schäble, *Franz Grillparzer*, 126; Baumann, "*Ein
Bruderzwist*," 431; or Politzer, "Götterdämmerung," 371. Only Naumann, in my view incorrectly, tries to make a case for the alleged master: "Mathias ist im ganzen Akt [II] gegenwärtig [and yet we see Klesel
before Mathias], er ist der Feldherr des Lagers [but not in the view of
the soldiers] und der Mittelpunkt der Verhandlungsszenen [only osten-

sibly]. Er wächst an als Gegenspieler des Kaisers [really Klesel's role] in einer gegenläufigen Bewegung, die ihn heraushebt, aber nicht persönlich vergrößert und die ihn im letzten Akt in die Mitte stellt" (*Das dichterische Werk*, 52).

5 Thompson, "Grillparzer's Political Villains," 106.

6 Ibid., 106.

7 Although several recent critical appraisals of Rudolf have been extremely harsh (Cf. Mason), many of his utterances as distinguished from his actions owe much to the ideal of 18th-century enlightened despotism. For example, Rudolf's recognition of the dependence of his will upon God's echoes Nathan's reaffirmation of faith: "Ich stand! und rief zu Gott: Ich will! / Willst du nur, daß ich will!" (Lessing, *Nathan der Weise*, 3:680–1).

8 Baumann refers to "die vorbereitete Resolution, die Klesel aus seiner Busentasche hervorzieht, ein Gebärdenspiel aus Behäbigkeit und Schläue, Eifer und Entrüstung, vor allem jedoch die Doppelung aus Vorgespieltem und Echtem" ("*Ein Bruderzwist*," 432).

9 In this context, Wells contends, "As the archdukes see it, if Mathias were anxious to oust Rudolf, he would argue for peace and for power to enforce it. As he in fact argues for war, they feel confident that he is without ulterior motive" (*The Plays*, 117). This line of reasoning omits, in my opinion, two more important considerations. The archdukes see Mathias as being very "kindisch" (881) and totally unreasonable in wanting to maintain hostilities with only half the surviving army. Their confidence, moreover, is based upon the deceptive appearance that he has the independence to go against Klesel's advice.

10 Schäble, *Franz Grillparzer*, 127.

11 Thompson, "Grillparzer's Political Villains," 107.

12 Ibid., 106–7.

13 Naumann, *Das dichterische Werk*, 55. Essentially Naumann offers a summary or paraphrase of Rudolf's argument before the "böhmischen Stände" (1587–1650).

14 "Freilich bleibt diese aus Selbstmitleid geborene Erkenntnis an der Oberfläche haften und macht Mathias zur Puppe des Politikers Klesel" (Politzer, "Götterdämmerung," 360).

15 Cf. "Max, Ferdinand and Leopold naturally suspect the truth, namely that he [Klesel] is trying to ensure that these powers be accorded to his master, Mathias, who will then be able not only to oppose Rudolf, but to do so with the backing of the most powerful members of his family" (Wells, *The Plays*, 116).

16 Thompson, "Grillparzer's Political Villains," 107. The "unacceptable" would have to refer to Leopold although his candidacy is never raised in this exchange. Others have broadly recognized Klesel's successful

tactic here. For example, "Natürlich trägt er [Klesel] zuerst ihnen [arch-dukes] dieses Amt an ... Doch weder Max noch Ferdinand wollen in den Verdacht kommen, nach der Kaiserkrone zu streben" (Schäble, *Franz Grillparzer*, 127).

17 Cf. "Rudolf trägt durch seine Inaktivität Schuld an der Rebellion, die sich gegen ihn vorbereitet. Und er selbst hat ihr in Mathias ein Haupt gegeben" (Kleinstück, "Don Cäsar," 225). Not disagreeing with the first sentence, I would, however, nominate Klesel as the character who creates in Mathias a figure head for the revolt against the emperor.

18 Cf. "[D]eklariert doch der 'Bruderzwist in Habsburg' die bürgerlich-liberale Opposition zum zerstörenden Faktor einer idealisierten Feudalordnung, in der statt der 'toten Hand' (V.1653) das 'lebendig warme Wort' (V.1654) gelte" (Gregolin, "Habsburg ohne Zwist," 274). If one classifies a letter as a document, then Seidlin reaches a similar conclusion in his analysis of letters in Schiller's early plays: "[Der Brief] hat, wie alle echte menschliche Sprache, die Aufgabe, ein wahres aus-zusagen, aber da er nicht menschliche Sprache ist, kann er seine Wahr-heit nur indirekt an den Tag treten lassen. Diese Indirektheit nun, der mittelbare Charakter des Briefes, öffnet der Korruption Tor und Tür" ("Schillers 'Trügerische Zeichen,'" 248).

19 Goethe, *Faust I*, 1966–7.

20 Ibid., 1716–9; 1726–30.

21 Ibid., 1736–40.

22 Cf. "Hätt' ich [Mephistopheles] mir nicht die Flamme vorbehalten, / Ich hätte nichts Aparts für mich" (Ibid., 1377–8).

23 Another good example is Mathias's entrance in the second act. "He declares he will not lay it [Hungarian peasant coat] aside until he has restored his reputation, but he dons another coat when it is brought – a little detail that shows how readily his resolution is undermined" (Wells, *The Plays*, 106).

24 Thompson, "Grillparzer's Political Villains," 106.

CHAPTER FOUR

1 Cf. "His [Rudolf's] insight is repeatedly revealed by his ability to discern character. He sees through Klesel, 'jener listige Priester', and he sees through the heretic to the 'Ehrenmann' beneath in Julius" (Wells, "The Problem," 169). Rudolf may correctly assess Klesel's character, but because he does not keep himself informed of the political situation, his discernment comes too late to have any influence on the chain of events unleashed by the bishop.

2 Wells has argued that Rudolf's views reflect the theological ethic of his age whereby God supplies the absolute standard. Klesel represents the

new ethic of utility or reciprocity ("The Problem," 164). Mason ("A New Look") has cast some doubt upon this assessment, calling Rudolf's first long speech inspired by the stars "homemade astrological poetry, not traditional belief" (106) and concluding "that Rudolf really means by 'göttliche Ordnung' a subordination of society to imperial rule" (108).

3 Thompson, "An Off-Stage Decision," 138.

4 Politzer, "Götterdämmerung," 357. Although Politzer implies a diabolical seduction, he and the rest of the critics have overlooked the possible indebtedness to Goethe's *Faust*.

5 Thompson, "An Off-Stage Decision," 138.

6 Fülleborn, "Geschichtsdrama," 65.

7 Cf. "But Grillparzer's Rudolf retains our sympathy since we see the strongest provocation is necessary before anger can obscure his judgement here" (Wells, *The Plays*, 120).

8 Baumann, *"Ein Bruderzwist,"* 440–1. Thompson has written an informative article to justify relegating in part this decision to the off-stage location: "To place such a critical decision off-stage was clearly a bold and original step, possibly without parallel in European, least of all German drama" (An Off-Stage Decision," 140). However, I should point out that in *Prinz Friedrich von Homburg* the audience never knows exactly when the Elector decides to spare Homburg and that the latter's decision to accept his execution takes place essentially off-stage. Also, interestingly enough, just as Homburg and the Elector never really engage in face-to-face dialogue, the same could be said of Klesel and Rudolf.

9 Schiller, *Maria Stuart*, 9:3220–3248.

10 Goethe, *Faust I*, 1728–9.

11 Politzer, "Götterdämmerung," 360.

CHAPTER FIVE

1 Baumann, *"Ein Bruderzwist"* 446–7. Cf. Also: "Der fünfte Akt des *Bruderzwist* lebt unter dem Schalten eines nicht mehr Anwesenden" (Hering, "Zum Thema," 42).

2 Cf. "Its [the fifth act's] function is to vindicate Rudolf by showing how catastrophe ensues when his policy is abandoned" (Wells, *The Plays*, 124) or "Er selbst, der Dichter, gibt dieses urteil ab, es ist das Ziel seines Weges. Hier im *Bruderzwist* zeigt er es als die weitertreibende Zeit, die Auflösung die kommt, Wallenstein, den Dreißigjährigen Krieg, die Rudolf rechtfertigen und das Tun seiner Feinde verurteilen" (Naumann, *Das dichterische Werk*, 61).

3 Yates, *Grillparzer*, 238.

4 Naumann, *Das dichterische Werk*, 60.

5 Baumann, *"Ein Bruderzwist,"* 447.

6 Thompson, "Grillparzer's Political Villains," 108.

7 Ibid., 108.

8 David, *Ordnung des Kunstwerks*, 82. When David alleges that Mathias "will niemanden, nicht einmal seine Vertrauten, sehen," this is not completely true. He commands, "Schickt nach dem Kardinal!" (2776) but Ferdinand and the Catholic party have removed the one "Vertrauten" upon whom Mathias is accustomed to depend totally, and this in part explains his isolation: he is like a child without his father: "Wär Klesel hier er wüßte des wohl Rat" (2795).

9 Cf. "Wenn irgendwo 'Absicht' vorhanden ist und an ihr Ziel kommt, dann hier [in Klesel]. Erst in der letzten Szene tritt Klesel ein überlegener Wille in Ferdinand entgegen und macht seine weiteren 'Absichten' zunichte" (Fülleborn, "Geschichtsdrama," 196). Moreover, "jene kluge Politik des konfessionellen Ausgleichs," according to Sternberger, was historic ("Politische Figuren," 1147).

10 The historic Melchior Klesel became "Rektor" of the University of Vienna in 1616.

11 I largely disagree with Eibl's contention: "im Kontext ergibt das banale Argument kaum einen Sinn, es wird in Klesels Mund zur Karikatur der Herrscherwürde, oder auch zur Schutzwehr des zynischen 'Realpolitikers.'" The latter observation strikes closer to the mark in my view. ("Ordnung und Ideologie," 78).

12 Goethe, *Faust I*, 285–8.

13 Ibid., 300.

14 Ibid., 324–6.

15 Ibid., 315–17.

16 Thompson, "Grillparzer's Political Villains," 108. Cf. "Klesel too [i.e., together with Mathias] is motivated by self-interest, at a different level: it emerges in the last act that as well as gaining high ecclesiastical office he has consistently safe-guarded his material interests (2500–8)" (Yates, *Grillparzer*, 240). The hypocrisy evident in standing for spiritual, other-worldly values but at the same time attending to one's material comfort appears to have particularly annoyed Grillparzer. During his return visit to Rome (1819), he talks of the beautiful view from his window, "die nur dadurch gestört wird, daß gerade unter ihm der Garten der Jesuiten liegt und [er] die Herren, die [er] nicht recht wohl leiden mag, vor [seinen] Augen herumgehen sehen muß. Eine eigene Equipage samt einem Bedienten zur Disposition, kurz prosaisches Wohlergehen ohne Ende!" (*Sämtliche Werke*, 4:331).

17 Cf. "L'intérêt parle toutes sortes de langages, et joue toutes sortes de personnages, même celui de désintéressé" (La Rochefoucauld, *Maximes*, no. 39, 15).

18 I have documented Kleist's more pragmatic view of human nature in my monograph *In Pursuit of Power*. Büchner presented all human activity as originating with the pleasure principle, really a variation of the self-interest thesis: "Jeder handelt seiner Natur gemäß d.h. er thut, was ihm wohl thut" (*Dantons Tod*, 1:27).

19 Kleist, *Sämtliche Werke und Briefe*, 2:806.

20 Ferdinand has an obvious predecessor in Lessing's Patriarch of Jerusalem who also "strebt, zu herrschen, damit jener herrsche" and for whom "Seeleneifer" and "Eigennutz" are intimate friends indeed. One could also point to Voltaire's *Mahomet* (1741) which exposes religious fanaticism as a sublimation or variant of the will to power.

21 Cf. "Das reicht bis zur parodistischen Verzerrung. Um sein (und des Baiernfürsten) Talent zu rechtfertigen, frommes Tun mit Mehrung des eigenen Nutzens zu verbinden, bedient er sich des alten Bildes von der Sonnennähe des Adlers – und ergänzt es um dessen Gefräßigkeit" (Eibl, "Ordnung und Ideologie," 78). I would simply add that Klesel obviously includes Ferdinand in the equation.

22 Goethe, *Faust I*, 2836–8.

23 The one exception, of course, is his decisive treatment of his natural son, Don Cäsar, which according to Wells occurs in the "private" as opposed to the "political" sphere. "[F]rom the beginning Rudolf has punished the immorality and selfishness of the individual, but failed to deal effectively with that of the group, the sect, the class" (*The Plays*, 122). However, he expresses a strong sense of will at the end of his life but this volition only relates to and reinforces his religious views and values: "Ich *will* allein das Weh für Alle tragen" (2411). In fact his final words of the play are, "Ich *will*," willing his entry into the "himmlisch Vaterland" (2426).

24 Grillparzer, *Werke*, 3:815.

25 Cf. "Erst in der letzten Szene tritt Klesel ein überlegener Wille in Ferdinand entgegen und macht seine weiteren 'Absichten' zunichte" (Fülleborn, "Geschichtsdrama," 196).

26 Even at the beginning of our current century (1915), Anthony Ludovici made a similar claim in his *Defence of Aristocracy*: "[If] bodily beauty is the creation of order lasting over generations, then since the spirit is but the emanation of the body, a beautiful spirit must likewise depend upon the same laws that govern the production of a beautiful body, and the two are inseparable" (13).

27 In his *Selbstbiographie* Grillparzer writes of the "Grausamkeit, einen jungen Menschen am Eingange des Lebens, einen Hausgenossen, in einer solchen Lage hilflos zu verlassen" (*Sämtliche Werke*, 4:65).

28 Cf. "Hier [having just concluded the first act of *Medea*] wurde ich über 4 Wochen unterbrochen, durch den Verdruß über die Übergehung in

der Beförderung, die mir zukam und die mir die Hofkammer aus altem Groll verweigerte. Ich wollte die Staatsdienste verlassen, aber der wackere Graf Stadion widerriet mirs" (*Sämtliche Werke*, 4:350).

29 Grillparzer's particular *bête noire* was Josef Graf von Sedlnitzky, responsible for censorship. "Der Umstand, daß [Metternich] allein es war, der den elenden Polizeipräsidenten Grafen Sedlnitzky stützte und hielt, reicht für sich schon hin um allen Lobrednern Metternichs Stillschweigen aufzuerlegen" ("Meine Erinnerungen aus dem Revolutionsjahre 1848," *Sämtliche Werke*, 4:206).

30 Ibid., 220.

31 Sternberger, "Politische Figuren," 1147.

32 Ibid., 1147.

33 The prohibition against mésalliances was based on the belief that aristocratic excellence depended upon keeping the blood line pure and not defiling it by marriage beneath one's station. Cf. "Die Sorge der Adligen um die Reinheit ihres Blutes drückt sich auch in den Verboten gegen Mißheiraten mit Nicht-Adligen aus, eine leicht zu durchschauende Maßnahme, um den bestehenden Abstand zu diesen zu unterstreichen" (Kautsky, "Funktionen," 12).

34 Grillparzer, *Werke*, 4:545. The clear note of defiance based on confidence in one's own superior worth comes through in this diary entry (Paris, 1836) and may be seen to anticipate a comparable attitude in Klesel's parting words: "Mir bleibt der Vorrang, wär's in Ketten" (2700), i.e., "they're not going to get me down!"

35 Goethe, *Faust I*, 1224; 1237.

36 Nietzsche, *Zur Genealogie der Moral*, 2:185.

37 Ibid., 2:190.

38 Nietzsche, *Jenseits von Gut und Böse*, 2:41.

39 Griesmayer, *Das Bild*, 305.

40 Grillparzer, *Werke*, 3:804–5.

41 Cf. "In der Korrespondenz mit den apokalyptischen Visionen des Protagonisten ... läßt auch die pathetische Schlußrede des Intriganten einzig erkennen, wie sehr dessen Position als eine Hypothek auf dem heimgesuchten Feudalismus lastet" (Gregolin, "Habsburg ohne Zwist," 276). While the two speeches I have compared outline the major distinction between the active Klesel and the passive Rudolf, the similarities are also quite striking both in content and tone, and the priest's "Schlußrede" thus gains in standing from the comparison.

42 Sternberger refers to Wallenstein "als das militarische Pendant des geistlichen Klesels, überhebliche Fürstendiener beide, die ihren Platz und ihr Amt nicht kennen und Unmögliches begehren" ("Politische Figuren," 1148). Cf. also "As he [Mathias] depended on Klesel, so will Ferdinand become the creature of Wallenstein" (Wells, *The Plays*, 125).

43 Thompson, "Grillparzer's Political Villains," 109.

44 Cf. "Wie er unversehens weggeführt wird, gibt er sich zunächst einschmeichelnd, listig, zuletzt aber bauernstolz und nicht ohne Würde;
   er ist die einzige Figur, die etwas wie eine Entwicklung erfährt, bei
   den übrigen enthüllt sich nur, was sie wahrhaft sind" (Baumann, "*Ein
   Bruderzwist,*" 447). Baumann's assessment runs counter to that
   expressed by David: "Diese wenig nuancierte Gestalt gehört nicht zu
   den besten des Trauerspiels" (*Ordnung des Kunstwerks*, 90). However,
   I would contend that it is not Klesel who shows development but
   rather our attitude towards him as the drama progresses. His character
   remains essentially the same; we simply learn more about it.

45 Grillparzer, "Meine Erinnerungen aus dem Revolutionsjahre 1848,"
   Sämtliche Werke, 4:220.

46 Cf. "Als aber am dritten Tage die Ungarn kamen und sich von der
   Gesamt-Monarchie losrissen und die Menge, die das wußte, ihren Vivats
   und Eljens zurief, da merkte ich, daß die Dummheit, oder vielmehr
   Unbesonnenheit mit Unwissenheit gepaart, gefährlicher ist als die
   Schlechtigkeit und war überzeugt, daß wir verloren seien" (Ibid., 219).

47 Cf. "The Obligation of Subjects to the Sovereign, is understood to last
   as long, and no longer, than the power lasteth, by which he is able to
   protect them (*Leviathan*, 114).

48 Cf. "Arbeit gilt als ... unter der Würde des Adligen, sie ist ehrlos und
   erniedrigend" (Kautsky, "Funktionen," 9).

49 Shakespeare uses the famous image of the stomach in his *Coriolanus* to
   express the same idea of the central but nonetheless unproductive role
   of the aristocracy.

50 *Bible*, St. Mark, 10:31.

51 He does show some reluctance in connection with signing the "Vollmacht" and arresting Klesel.

CHAPTER SIX

1 Politzer, "Götterdämmerung," 360.

2 Fülleborn, "Geschichtsdrama," 195.

3 Wassermann, "Kaiser Rudolf," 276.

4 Sengle, *Das historische Drama*, 122.

5 Sternberger, "Politische Figuren," 1151.

6 Gregolin, "Habsburg ohne Zwist," 278.

7 Naumann, *Das dichterische Werk*, 61. Cf. also "Its [the fifth act's] function is to vindicate Rudolf by showing how catastrophe ensues when
   his policy is abandoned" (Wells, *The Plays*, 124). I shall subsequently
   argue that the same case can be made for Klesel's policy and, if anything, with greater political justification.

8 Mason, "A New Look," 115. Mason's assessment contains considerable insight but represents, in my view, an oversimplification. There are other important psychological and intellectual factors involved in Rudolf's indecision.

9 Kleinstück, "Don Cäsar," 225. Mathias may be the figure-head but Klesel is clearly the brains.

10 Grillparzer, *Sämtliche Werke*, 4:130. All the quotations referring to this incident appear on the same page.

11 Ibid., 160.

12 Cf. "Der Jagdfalke und der Jagdhund und besonders das Pferd des Adligen sind 'edel.'" (Kautsky, "Funktionen," 11).

13 Ibid., 9.

14 Grillparzer, *Sämtliche Werke*, 4:204.

15 Mason, "A New Look," 108.

16 Cf. "Hinweise auf 'Zucht,' 'edles Blut' und 'hohe Geburt' und über-haupt die Vorstellung der Aristokratie als einer erblichen Klasse – alle diese Dinge sind Ausdruck des aristokratischen Anspruchs auf ihre biologische Besonderheit" (Kautsky, "Funktionen," 12).

17 Cf. "Was das Kriegswesen betrifft, so können Adel und Militär praktisch identisch sein" (Ibid., 5).

18 Cf. "Die Begriffe Dienst und Pflichterfüllung sind eng verbunden mit dem Begriff der Ehre, einem zentralen Bestandteil adliger Ideologie, der aber für Nicht-Aristokraten schwer zu verstehen ist" (Ibid., 8).

19 One of the most dramatic events in Grillparzer's life occurred in 1868 when, as a member of the upper house, he resolved to attend parliament in order to cast his vote against the Roman Catholic attempt to block the repeal of the Concordat. He thus helped to pave the way for new, more liberal marriage legislation and became an instant public hero cheered by crowds gathered in the Spiegelgasse.

20 Politzer, "Götterdämmerung," 356.

21 Thompson, "An Off-Stage Decision," 144–5.

22 Machiavelli, *The Ruler*, 83.

23 Ibid., 91.

24 Cf. Reeve, *In Pursuit*, 97–111.

25 Cf. "Zwar geht Klesel nicht den Weg des geltenden Rechts, aber wie sollte er ihn auch gehen in einer Situation, wo es 'nicht Ordnung, Kundschaft und Befehl' gibt? Oder sollte er wie Rudolf nichts tun?" (Kleinstück, "Don Cäsar," 224–5).

26 Thompson, "Grillparzer's Political Villains," 108.

27 Cf. "But Klesel clearly believes that his policy would have prevented war had not Ferdinand intervened. As far as he is concerned he has nothing to be penitent about, and his anger [at his arrest] expresses his frustration at having been deprived of the prize within his grasp" (Ibid., 109).

28 Wassermann, "Kaiser Rudolf," 277.

CHAPTER SEVEN

1 A German translation of the Latin: "Plane qualis dominus, talis et servus" from Petronius. *Satiricon* (58).

2 Lessing, *Miß Sara Sampson*, *Werke*, 1:450. All subsequent references to *Miß Sara Sampson* will be drawn from this edition and page numbers preceded by L will be included in the body of my text.

3 Cf. "Lessings Marinelli können wir als eines der Vorbilder des Sekretärs Wurm ansprechen" (Schafarschik, *Erläuterungen*, 70).

4 Both master and servant live with the consciousness of their advanced age and imminent death: "Wie herzlich vergnügt es mich, Sir, Sie vor meinem Ende wieder zufrieden zu wissen!" (L457) Throughout the drama the one complements the other.

5 *Bible*, Ephesians, 6:5.

6 A very open, seemingly democratic relationship exists between Minna and Franziska.

7 In contrast Hannah, more or less an echo of Marwood, flatters her mistress in an attempt to restore her self-confidence: "Ach, Madame, was sind Sie für eine Frau! Den möchte ich doch sehn, der Ihnen widerstehen könnte" (L435). Hannah would appear to have been adversely influenced by the corrupt practices of the upper class while Norton has managed to preserve his moral principles and a sense of independence even though, as he confesses, he has not always lived by those principles (L462).

8 Schiller, *Kabale und Liebe*, 858.

9 This theme will continue well into the nineteenth century. For example, Fontane's *Irrungen, Wirrungen* (1887) sets up a contrast between a healthy, industrious and vital "Volk" (Lene) versus a decadent, unproductive and passive aristocracy (Botho).

10 Lessing, *Emilia Galotti*, *Werke*, 1:710.

11 Schiller, *Kabale und Liebe*, *Sämtliche Werke*, 1:756. All subsequent references to *Kabale und Liebe* will be drawn from this edition and page numbers preceded by s will be included in the body of my text.

12 Hebbel's *Maria Magdalene* will develop this thesis even further and pursue it to its tragic conclusion.

13 Cf. "Miller verwendet den sehr allgem. Ausdruck, der jeden bezeichnen kann, um keine Vertraulichkeit zu zeigen" (Schafarschik, *Erläuterungen*, 12).

14 With respect to his costume, Rolf Martin-Kruckenberg, in an attempt to explain "das Unmenschliche in [Wurm] als das Produkt der Gesellschaft, in der er sich befindet," argues, "Auch Wurm wird sich mit

dem Lohn seiner Tätigkeit Attribute der Hofgesellschaft aneignen wollen: eine modische Kleidung und kostbaren Schmuck beispielsweise. Das Kostüm ist etwas, was deutlich sichtbar über die Figur erzählend in Erscheinung tritt. Also scheuen wir nicht, einen modisch gekleideten Wurm zu zeigen. Die Motive seines Handelns werden um so verständlicher" ("Über die Darstellung des 'Bösen,'" 13f).

15 Almost all the characters lay claim to Luise. In this dialogue the mother continually (four times) emphasizes "meine Tochter" – "Sie ist eben in die Mess, meine Tochter" (s760). Ferdinand and Miller also see her as their possession.

16 The importance of getting something in writing, of having it signed and sealed, also becomes evident in the Präsident's announcement of the proposed union between Ferdinand and Lady Milford: "HOFMARSCHALL. Denken Sie! – Und das ist schon richtig gemacht? PRÄSIDENT. *Unterschrieben* (Schiller's emphasis], Marschall" (s772). The latter can thus confidently spread the news throughout "die ganze Stadt." The signed document acquires the aura of an incontestable authority which will brook no opposition. Cf. "Allein ein Pergament, beschrieben und beprägt, / Ist ein Gespenst, vor dem sich alle scheuen" (*Faust I*, 1726–7).

17 Cf. "*poussieren*: frz. pousser 'stoßen, fördern' dt. im 18. Jh. 'aufrücken, aufsteigen'" (Schafarschik, *Erläuterungen*, 13).

18 Schiller, *Die Räuber*, 1:502. Cf. "[Karls] allerersten Worte schon, die Verwünschung des 'tintenklecksenden Säkulum', sein Zornesausbruch gegen eine Lebensform, die an Stelle der Unmittelbarkeit und vitalen Direktheit heroisch offenen und spontanen Fühlens und Handelns ängstliche Kritik und kleinliche Besserwisserei setzt, klingt wie eine ahnungsvolle Zurückweisung des verklatschten und pharisäischen Tintengekleckses, mit dem in der Hand Franz zu Beginn des ersten Aktes die Bühne betrat" (Seidling, "Schillers 'Trügerische Zeichen,'" 252).

19 The drama contains several instances linking Ferdinand to his sword, the symbol of his aristocratic heritage. One of the highpoints of the tragedy occurs when he draws his sword and defends Luise against his father and the "Gerichtsdiener." "FERDINAND. Wenn es denn sein muß (*indem er den Degen zieht und einige von denselben [Gerischtsdienern] verwundet*), so verzeih mir, Gerechtigkeit! PRÄSIDENT (*voll Zorn*). Ich will doch sehen, ob auch ich diesen Degen fühle" (s797–8). Later in the play, when convinced of Luise's infidelity he has poisoned her and himself, he performs a telling gesture: "FERDINAND (*fängt an stärker zu gehen, und beunruhigter zu werden, indem er Schärpe und Degen von sich wirft*" (s852). He forsakes the signs of his noble birth in favor of a "Liebestod" union with the "Bürgermädchen."

20 Ferdinand's use of poison, as described in the previous note, does not come across as dignified but as a vindictive homicide and a self-

indulgent suicide. The noble warrior traditionally took his own life by falling on his sword. Cf. *Philotas* or *Die Hermannsschlacht.*

21 Cf. ADAM.   Zu seiner Zeit, Ihr wißts, schwieg auch der große
                Demosthenes. Folgt hierin seinem Muster.
                Und bin ich König nicht von Mazedonien,
                Kann ich auf meine Art doch dankbar sein.
      LICHT.   Geht mir mit Eurem Argwohn, sag ich Euch.
                Hab ich jemals – ?
      ADAM.   Seht, ich, ich, für mein Teil,
                Dem großen Griechen folg ich auch. Es ließe
                Von Depositionen sich und Zinsen
                Zuletzt auch eine Rede ausarbeiten:
                Wer wollte solche Perioden drehn?
      LICHT.   Nun, also!

(Kleist, *Sämtliche Werke*, 142–152). See also my discussion of this dialogue in *Pursuit of Power*, 12–13. Klesel's downfall may also be attributed in part to incriminating documents confiscated by his enemies: he pleads with Seyfried, "Laßt mich zu Hause ordnen noch Papiere, / Man hat so Viel was nicht für Jeden taugt" (2683–4).

22 Machiavelli relates in *Il Principe* how Caesar Borgia adopted the same tactic: he invited all his main opponents to a dinner to settle their differences and then had them strangled (Machiavelli, *The Ruler* [a translation of *Il Principe*], 51). Leonhard will use this same approach to assure his appointment as "Kassierer." He gets his rival for the position drunk.

23 Effi Briest's seducer Crampas, as his name implies, has several ironically diabolical features and Fontane's novel consistently associates him with gambling and cards.

24 Luise announces in III/4, "Ferdinand! dich zu verlieren! – Doch! man verliert ja nur, was man besessen hat, und dein Herz gehört deinem Stande – Mein Anspruch war Kirchenraub, und schauernd geb ich ihn auf" (s809).

25 In the first scene of the same act (III/1), describing the ignominious fate he foresees for the Miller family, Wurm suggests that the parents "erkennen [es] noch zuletzt für Erbarmung, wenn[er] der Tochter durch [seine] Hand ihre Reputation wieder[gibt]" (s802).

26 German drama would have to wait until Büchner's *Dantons Tod* to present both stances as manifestations of the same pleasure principle: "Jeder handelt seiner Natur gemäß d.h. er thut, was ihm wohl thut" (*Sämtliche Werke und Briefe*, 1:27).

27 Goethe, *Faust I*, 3211–16.

28 Ibid., p. 46.

29 One of Faust's curses pointing out the arrogance of the intellect comes
   to mind: "Verflucht voraus die hohe Meinung, / Womit der Geist sich
   selbst umfängt!" (1591–2).

30 Seidlin, "Schillers 'Trügerische Zeichen,'" 257. Seidlin sees in the letters
   not only a plot expedient but a metaphor for the tragedy's main message: "Nirgends sonst in Schillers Werk, kaum irgendwo sonst in der
   gesamten dramatischen Literatur wird der brutale Bruch zwischen
   Wahrheit und sichbarem Zeichen so überwältigende Wirklichkeit wie
   in Luises Briefszene. Hier schreibt jemand vor unseren sehenden
   Augen, aber jedes Wort, das dem Papier anvertraut wird, ist ein Stück
   monumentaler Lüge. Wieder sind es ein Brief und die Umstände, unter
   denen ein Brief verfaßt wird, die in symbolischer Verkürzung eine
   metaphorische Summe menschlicher Existenz ziehen, jene Summe, die
   das Werk als Ganzes darbietet" (256).

31 When Luise renounces her hope of union with Ferdinand and refuses
   to flee with him (III/4), he immediately jumps to the false conclusion:
   "Ein Liebhaber fesselt dich, und Weh über dich und ihn, wenn mein
   Verdacht sich bestätigt" (s810).

32 Luise, in her dying words, obviously sees Wurm only as an agent of
   the Präsident, not as the one really responsible: "Dieser Brief ... Meine
   Hand schrieb, was mein Herz verdammte – dein Vater hat ihn dik-
   tiert" (s855). However, I would agree with Seidlin's assessment: "Nicht
   nur zufällig heißt *der wahre Feind* Wurm, einer, der von innen her die
   Fäulnis verbreitet, und nicht Walter, die Figur, die über die äußere
   Organisation der Welt zu präsidieren hat" ("Schillers 'Trügerische
   Zeichen,'" 259).

33 Cf. "Hinsichtlich der Situation und der Personengruppierung ist die
   äußere Ähnlichkeit mit dem von Schiller gelobten, erfolgreichen Schau-
   spiel Frhr. O. v. Gemmingens: *Der deutsche Hausvater* (1780) auffallend"
   (Fricke and Göpfert, ed., Schiller, *Sämtliche Werke*, 1:953–4).

34 Under a section entitled "Literarische Einfluüsse," Schafarschik writes,
   "An erster Stelle muß aus dem Sturm und Drang ... Heinrich Leopold
   Wagner mit seinem Drama *Die Reue nach der Tat* (1775) genannt werden
   ... Die Handlung läuft in *Kabale und Liebe* ganz ähnlich ab wie in *Die
   Reue nach der Tat*" (*Erläuterungen*, 67).

35 Since the noble son (Karl) gave his word to marry the pregnant *Bürgermädchen* (Lottchen), the Hausvater insists that his son fulfil his word to
   her but live in the country out of sight of conventional society: "Du
   [Karl] sollst meine Güter in Besitz nehmen; es ist mir ohnedem lieb, daß
   ein Beispiel wie dieses aus den Augen der Welt komme: es ist doch
   immer Zerrüttung bürgerlicher Ordnung, und, solange das Vorurteil
   dauert, gefährlich, wenn es zur Nachahmung reizt" (Gemmingen, *Der
   deutsche Hausvater*, 83).

36 Gemmingen, *Der deutsche Hausvater*, 15.

37 Ibid., 39.

38 Ibid., 41.

39 Ibid., 41.

40 Ibid., 41.

41 Wagner, *Die Reue nach der Tat*, 529.

42 Ibid., 513.

43 Ibid., 469.

44 Ibid., 520.

45 Grillparzer, *Sämtliche Werke*, 4:254.

46 Fricke, "Anmerkungen zu *Kabale und Liebe*. In Schiller, *Sämtliche Werke*, 1:954.

47 Ibid., 1:953.

48 Kunz, "Anmerkungen des Herausgebers," 5:478–9.

49 Quoted in Kunz, "Anmerkungen des Herausgebers," 5:479.

50 Bachmaier provides a useful chronology of the "Entstehung" of *Ein Bruderzwist*, (753–4).

51 Kunz, "Anmerkungen des Herausgebers," 5:480.

52 Ibid., 5:481.

53 Ibid., 5:486.

54 Ibid., 5:483.

55 Goethe, *Die natürliche Tochter*. In *Werke*, 5:3–5. All subsequent references to this drama will be drawn from this edition and verse numbers preceded by G will be included in the text.

56 Kunz, "Anmerkungen des Herausgebers," 5:491.

57 Klesel himself provides a sarcastic rationalization for such involvement: "Will Einer erst die Herrschaft Gott verschaffen, / Sieht er in sich gar leicht des Herren Werkzeug / Und strebt zu herrschen, damit Jener herrsche" (2528–30).

58 Goethe, *Faust I*, 2738–43.

59 This subtle distinction is important. For example, in the original version of Büchner's revolutionary pamphlet, "Der hessische Landbote," he referred to the exploiters as "die Reichen." Pastor Weidig, unwilling to alienate the liberal bourgeoisie, amended Büchner's text to read "die Vornehmen."

60 Kautsky, "Funktionen," 10.

61 A subsequent scene (II/5) demonstrates convincingly that Eugenie did not turn to the one person, the "Freundin [ihres] Herzens, / An Mutter Statt Geliebte" (G903–4) whom she would normally be expected to confide in. When the Hofmeisterin announces the meaning of the "Schmück der Fürstentochter" (G1012), the following dialogue ensues: "EUGENIE. Wie kannst du das vermuten? / HOFMEISTERIN. Weiß ich's doch! / Geheimnisse der Großen sind belauscht" (G1014–15).

62 "Macht" is Klesel's leitmotif and he is feared, to use Rudolf's apt characterization, as "jener list'ge Priester" (1403).

63 Hobbes, *Leviathan*, 48.

64 Kleist places his court secretary into the same ethos in *Der zerbrochne Krug*.

65 Cf. "Hebbel knew the environment of *Maria Magdalena* from experience as he knew no other in his dramas" (Purdie, *Friedrich Hebbel*, 125).

66 Cf. "Hebbel's poetic powers were increasing with incredible rapidity; his resentment at the menial conditions of his life grew proportionately, and he withdrew himself more and more from the circle of his friends" (Purdie, *Friedrich Hebbel*, 10).

67 Hebbel, *Werke*, 5:159

68 Hebbel, *Werke*, 1:366. All subsequent references to *Maria Magdalene* will be drawn from this edition and page numbers preceded by H included in the text.

69 Ibid., 4:114.

70 Economic and religious diction informs both *Kabale und Liebe* and *Maria Magdalene*. With reference to the former play, see Guthke, "*Kabale und Liebe* – eine Tragödie der Säkularisation."

71 In a conversation with the actor/director Heinrich Anschütz, Hebbel himself juxtaposed *Kabale und Liebe* and *Maria Magdalene* in an attempt to defend his tragedy against the charge of immorality: "'Ich [Anschütz] glaube nicht, daß Ihr Trauerspiel von der Zensur zugelassen wird.' / 'Warum nicht? Man gibt ja *Kabale und Liebe*'" (Bornstein, *Friedrich Hebbels Persönlichkeit*, 1:193).

72 Hebbel, *Werke*, 4:605. Pörnbacher proposes Hebbel himself as a model for Leonhard: "Hebbel verwendet für die Charakterisierung dieser Figur selbstporträthafte Züge, vor allem sein Verhältnis zu Elise Lensing" (*Erläuterungen*, 14). Hebbel did get Elise Lensing pregnant (twice!) only to abandon her ultimately for a better match (Christine Enghaus).

73 Similarly Klesel knows how to exploit Ferdinand's religious bias in the second act.

74 Cf. "Ein Verlöbnis, das nach alter Rechtsauffassung die Festsetzung des Ehevertrags bedeutete, konnte als solches Vertragsverhältnis nur in beiderseitigem Einvernehmen gelöst werden. Das Schweigen Klaras auf Leonhards Brief bedeutete ein Einverständnis damit, so daß Leonhard frei war" (Pörnbacher, *Erläuterungen*, 25).

75 Goethe, *Faust I*, 335.

76 Cf. "MEPHISTOPHELES. Sie ist die Erste nicht," p.137. Cf. also: "He grasps the opportunity of her high-strung response to refuse her plea, in words that are a variation on the Mephistophelian theme" (Purdie, 117).

77 Goethe, *Faust I*, 1651–3. While Goethe's dramatic poem served as one of the models for *Maria Magdalene*, it, in turn, inspired Johann Nestroy's

farce *Der Unbedeutende* (1846). "Als Name für die weibliche Hauptrolle wählt er Klara … Um seiner Karriere zu nützen, ruiniert der skrupellose Sekretär Puffmann bedenkenlos durch Verleumdung Klaras Ruf und rät dem Vater ihres Verlobten, sie einfach sitzen zu lassen" (Pörnbacher, *Erläuterungen*, 64).

78 Hebbel's own description of his relationship to Beppi Schwarz noted earlier points to this conclusion. Pörnbacher, however, argues, "Zur Charakterisierung [des Sekretärs] verwendet Hebbel Erinnerungen an seinen Freund, den Juristen Emil Rousseau (1816–38), mit dem er seit seinem Heidelberger Aufenthalt eng befreundet war" (*Erläuterungen*, 14).

CHAPTER EIGHT

1 Fontane, *Irrungen, Wirrungen*, 3:126.
2 Ibid., 3:125–6.

Works Cited

Bachmaier, Helmut (ed.). *Franz Grillparzer Werke*. 6 vols. Frankfurt a.M.: Deutscher Klassiker Verlag 1987.

Baumann, Gerhart. "Grillparzer. *Ein Bruderzwist in Habsburg,*" In *Das deutsche Drama von Barock bis zur Gegenwart*, ed. Benno von Wiese, 1:422–50. Düsseldorf: August Bagel 1968.

Baumann, Gerhart. *Zu Franz Grillparzer*. Heidelberg: Lothar Stiehm 1969.

Bible, The Holy, King James Version, London: Eyre and Spottiswoode, no date.

Bornstein, Paul (ed.), *Friedrich Hebbels Persönlichkeit. Gespräche, Urteile, Erinnerungen.* 2 vols. Berlin: Propylaeein 1924.

Büchner, Georg. *Sämtliche Werke und Briefe*, ed. Werner R. Lehmann. Munich: Hanser 1979.

David, Claude. "Grillparzers *Bruderzwist in Habsburg.*" In *Ordung des Kunstwerks. Aufsätze zur deutschsprachigen Literatur zwischen Goethe und Kafka*, 77–98. Göttingen: Vandenhoeck and Ruprecht 1983.

Duckworth, George E. *The Nature of Roman Comedy. A Study in Popular Entertainment*. Princeton: Princeton University Press 1971.

Eibl, Karl. "Ordnung und Ideologie im Spätwerk Grillparzers am Beispiel des argumentum emblematicum und der *Jüdin von Toledo.*" *Deutsche Vierteljahresschrift* 53 (1979): 74–95.

Fontane, Theodor. *Sämtliche Werke*, ed. Edgar Groß. Munich: Nymphenburger Verlagshandlung 1959.

Fricke, Gerhard. *Studien und Interpretationen. Ausgewählte Schriften zur deutschen Dichtung*. Frankfurt a.M.: Hans F. Menck 1956.

Fülleborn, Ulrich. "Geschichtsdrama und geschichtliche Begebenheit. Ein Beitrag zum Thema 'Grillparzer und die Geschichte.'" In *Geschichtsdrama*, ed. Elfriede Neubuhr, 189–207. Darmstadt: Wissenschaftliche Buchgesellschaft 1980.

Gemmingen, Otto Heinrich, Freiherr von. *Der deutsche Hausvater*, In *Deutsche National-Litteratur*, ed. Joseph Kürschner. Vol. 139. Stuttgart: Union Deutsche Verlagsgesellschaft no date.

Goethe, Johann Wolfgang von. *Goethes Werke*, ed. Erich Trunz, Josef Kunz et al. 14 vols. Hamburg: Christian Wegner 1962.

Gomme, Arnold W. *Essays in Greek History and Literature*. Oxford: Basil Blackwell 1937.

Gregolin, Jürgen. "Habsburg ohne Zwist. 'Ist beßer ruhn als nutzlos thätig seyn.' *Ein Bruderzwist in Habsburg*." In *Gerettete Ordnung: Grillparzers Dramen*, ed. Bernhard Budde and Ulrich Schmidt. 255–78. Frankfurt: Lang 1987.

Griesmayer, Norbert. *Das Bild des Partners in Grillparzers Dramen*. Vienna; Stuttgart: Wilhelm Braumüller 1972.

Grillparzer, Franz. *Sämtliche Werke*, ed. Peter Frank and Karl Pörnbacher. Vol. 4. Munich: Hanser 1965.

– *Werke*, ed. Helmut Bachmaier. 6 vols. Frankfurt a.M.: Deutscher Klassiker Verlag 1987.

Guthke, Karl. "*Kabale und Liebe* – eine Tragödie der Sekularisation." In *Schillers Dramen. Neue Interpretationen*, ed. W. Hinderer, 58–86. Stuttgart: Reclam 1979.

Hebbel, Friedrich, *Werke*, ed. Gerhard Fricke, Werner Keller, Karl Pörnbacher. 6 vols. Munich: Hanser 1963.

Hegel, Georg Wilhelm Friedrich. *Phänomenologie des Geistes*. In *Sämtliche Werke*, vol. 2. Stuttgart: Fr. Fromann 1951.

Hering, Gerhard F. "Zum Thema 'Bruderzwist.'" *Grillparzer Forum Forchtenstein*, 37–42. Vienna; Munich: Österreichischer Bundesverlag 1965.

Hobbes, Thomas. *Leviathan*. Menston: The Scolar Press 1969.

Horowitz, Asher and Horowitz, Gad. *"Everywhere They Are in Chains." Political Theory from Rousseau to Marx*. Scarborough: Nelson 1988.

Kautsky, John H. "Funktionen und Werte des Adels," In *Legitimationskrisen des deutschen Adels 1200–1900*, ed. Uwe Hohendahl and Paul Michael Lützeler, 1–16. Stuttgart: Metzler 1979.

Kelly, George Armstrong. "Notes on Hegel's 'Lordship and Bondage.'" *Review of Metaphysics* 19 (1965–66): 780–802.

Kleinstück, Johannes. "Don Cäsar und die Ordnung. Zu Grillparzers *Ein Bruderzwist in Habsburg*." *Literaturwissenschaftliches Jahrbuch der Görresgesellschaft*, N.F. 6 (1965): 207–26.

Kleist, Heinrich von. *Sämtliche Werke und Briefe*, ed. Helmut Sembdner. 2 vols. Munich: Carl Hanser 1961.

Kommerell, Max. "Bertrachtungen über die Commedia dell' arte." In *Dichterische Welterfahrung: Essays*, ed. Hans-Georg Gadamer, 159–73. Frankfurt am Main: Klostermann 1952.

Kunz, Josef, "Anmerkungen des Herausgebers zu *Die natürliche Tochter*." In *Goethes Werke*, 5:477–504. Hamburg: Christian Wegner 1962.

Langvik-Johannessen, Kåre. *"Ein Bruderzwist in Habsburg*-Versuch einer Offenlegung der inneren Handlung." *Grillparzer Forum Forchtenstein* 34–42. Vienna, Munich: Österreichischer Bundesverlag 1967.

La Rochefoucauld, François, duc de. *Maximes.* Paris: Garnier 1967.

Lessing, Gotthold Ephraim. *Werke,* ed. Jost Perfahl. Vol 1. Munich: Winkler 1969.

Ludovici, Anthony M. *A Defence of Aristocracy.* London: Constable 1915.

Machiavelli, Niccolò. *The Ruler (Il Principe).* Trans. by Peter Rodd. London: The Bodley Head 1954.

Martin-Kruckenberg, Rolf. "Über die Darstellung des 'Bösen.'" *Theater der Zeit* 20 (1965) H.7. 13f.

Mason, Eve. "A New Look at Grillparzer's *Bruderzwist.*" *German Life and Letters* 25 (1971–72): 102–15.

Müller, Gernot. "Grillparzer, Rudolf II und die Rhetorik." *Studia Neophilologica* 53 (1981): 127–47.

Nadler, Josef. *Franz Grillparzer.* Vaduz: Liechtenstein 1948.

Naumann, Walter. "Grillparzers Drama *Ein Bruderzwist in Habsburg.*" *Euphorian* F.3, 48 (1954): 412–34.

– *Franz Grillparzer. Das dichterische Werk.* Stuttgart, Berlin, Cologne, Mainz: W. Kohlhammer 1967

Nietzsche, Friedrich. *Werke in zwei Bänden.* Munich: Carl Hanser 1967.

Norman, Richard. *Hegel's Phenomenology. A Philosophical Introduction.* London: Sussex University Press 1976.

Petronius, Arbiter. *Satiricon,* ed. Franciscus Buechler. Berlin: Weidmann 1882.

Politzer, Heinz. "Grillparzers Bruderzwist – ein Vater-Sohn-Konflikt in Habsburg." In *Festschrift für Bernhard Blume,* ed. Egon Schwarz, Hunter G. Hannum, Edgar Lohner, 173–94. Göttingen: Vandenhoeck und Ruprecht 1967.

– "Götterdämmerung der Geschichte: *Ein Bruderzwist in Habsburg.*" In *Franz Grillparzer oder Das abgründige Biedermeier,* 351–72. Vienna, Munich, Zürich: Fritz Molden 1972.

Pörnbacher, Karl (ed). *Erläuterungen und Dokumente. Friedrich Hebbel. Maria Magdalena.* Stuttgart: Reclam 1985.

Purdie, Edna. *Friedrich Hebbel. A Study of his Life and Works.* Oxford: Oxford University Press 1969.

Reeve, William C. *In Pursuit of Power: Heinrich von Kleist's Machiavellian Protagonists.* Toronto: University of Toronto Press 1987.

Rousseau, Jean-Jacques. *Œuvres complètes.* Editions Gallimard 1964.

Schäble, Günter. *Franz Grillparzer.* Velber bei Hannover: Friedrich 1967.

Schafarschik, Walter. *Erläuterungen und Dokumente. Friedrich Schiller. Kabale und Liebe.* Stuttgart: Reclam 1980.

Schiller, Friedrich. *Sämtliche Werke,* ed. Gerhard Fricke and Herbert G. Göpfer. Vol. 1. Munich: Carl Hanser 1984.

Scott-Prelorentzos, Alison. *The Servant in German Enlightenment Comedy.* Edmonton: The University of Alberta Press 1982.

Seidlin, Oskar. "Schillers 'trügerische Zeichen': die Funktion der Briefe in seinen frühen Dramen." In *Jahrbuch der deutschen Schillergesellschaft*, ed. Fritz Martini, Walter Müller-Seidel, and Bernhard Zeller, 247–69. Stuttgart: Alfred Kröner 1960.

Sengle, Friedrich. *Das historische Drama in Deutschland. Geschichte eines literarischen Mythos.* Stuttgart: Metzler 1969.

Shklar, Judith N. *Freedom and Independence: A Study of the Political Ideas of Hegel's Phenomenology of Mind.* Cambridge, New York: Cambridge University Press 1976.

Sternberger, Dolf. "Politische Figuren und Maximen Grillparzers." *Merkur* 17 (1963): 1142–53.

Stockum, Theodorus Cornelis van. "Grillparzers *Ein Bruderzwist in Habsburg.* Ein Versuch." *Neophilologus* 35 (1951): 24–9.

Thompson, Bruce. "An Off-stage Decision. An Examination of an Incident in Grillparzer's *Ein Bruderzwist in Habsburg.*" *Forum for Modern Language Studies* 12 (1976): 137–48.

– "Grillparzer's Political Villains." In *Grillparzer und die europäische Tradition,* ed. Robert Pichl et al., 101–12. Vienna: Hora 1987.

Wagner, Heinrich Leopold. *Die Reue nach der Tat.* In *Sturm und Drang. Dramatische Schriften,* ed. Erich Loewenthal and Lambert Schneider. Vol. 2. Heidelberg: Lambert Schneider no date.

Wassermann, Felix M. "Kaiser Rudolf und seine Umwelt in Grillparzers *Bruderzwist*: die Tragödie des Herrschers zwischen Weisheit und Tat." *Monatshefte* 43 (1951): 271–84.

Wells, George Albert. "The Problem of Right Conduct in Grillparzer's *Ein Bruderzwist in Habsburg.*" *German Life and Letters* 11 (1957/8): 161–72.

– *The Plays of Grillparzer.* London, New York: Pergamon Press 1969.

Wiese, Benno von. "Geschichte und Gottes-Ordnung in Grillparzers Altersdramen." In *Die deutsche Tragödie von Lessing bis Hebbel,* 1 Teil, Tragödie und Theodizee, 434–54. Hamburg: Hoffmann und Campe 1967.

Yates, W.E. *Grillparzer. A Critical Introduction.* Cambridge: Cambridge University Press 1972.

Index